G000146278

GREATER ANTILLES

BERMUDA, BAHAMAS

HAMPSHIRE COUNTY LIBRARY
917.29
1852652563
6002627218
WITHDRAWN

First Edition
1991

TABLE OF CONTENTS

FEATURES

GUIDELINES

Tallahassee
Jacksonville
USA
Daytona Beach
ATLANTIC
OCEAN
Orlando
Tampa
St. Petersburg
FLORIDA
Lake Okeechobee
GULF
OF
MEXICO
West Palm Beach
GRAND BAHAMA
Boca Raton
Freeport
Marsh Harbour
GREAT ABACO
The Everglades
Ft. Lauderdale
Hialeah
Hollywood
Miami
BIMINI IS.
BAHAMAS
ELEUTHERA
Nassau
Exuma
Florida Bay
Rock Sound
NEW PROVIDENCE
Andros Town
Key West
FLORIDA KEYS
CAT ISLAND
Straits of Florida
ANDROS ISLAND
BAHAMAS
Sound
Rolleville
GREAT EXUMA
LA HABANA
(HAVANA)
Matanzas
Old Bahama Channel
Cárdenas
Deadman's Cay
LONG ISLAND
Güines
WEST
RAGGED ISLAND RANGE
Pinar del Rio
Cienfuegos
Guane
G. de Batabanó
Santa Clara
Sancti-Spiritus
ISLA DE LA JUVENTUD
Ciego de Avila
CUBA
Camagüey
Victoria de las Tunas
CUBA
Holguin
G. de Guacanayabo
Manzanillo
Bayamo
Guantanamo
Palma Soriano
GREATER
CAYMAN IS.
(U.K.)
Georgetown
Montego Bay
Spanish Town
Kingston
JAMAICA
JAMAICA
HONDURAS
Trujillo
CARIBBEAN
GREATER ANTILLES
0 200 km
0 100 miles

LIST OF MAPS

AN SALVADOR
Colonel Hill
MAYAGUANA
ACKLINS I.
Caicos Passage
TURKS AND
CAICOS ISLANDS
(U.K.)
CAICOS IS.
Grand Turk
TURKS IS.
GREAT INAGUA
Matthew Town
I N D I E S
ÎLE DE LA TORTUE
Monte Cristi
Puerto Plata
DOMINICAN
REP.
Cap Haïtien
Santiago
G. de la Gonâve
HISPANIOLA
ÎLE DE LA GONÂVE
Port-au-Prince
San Pedro de Macoris
La Romana
Santo Domingo
Barahona
HAITI
Puerto Rico Trench
PUERTO RICO
(U.S.)
San Juan
Bayamon
Carolina
Mayagüez
Ponce
Canal de la Mona
(U.K.)
Charlotte Amalie
Road Town
VIRGIN ISLANDS
(U.S.)
ANGUILLA
The Valley
ST. MARTIN
A N T I L L E S
SEA

PANADERIA
LOPEZ

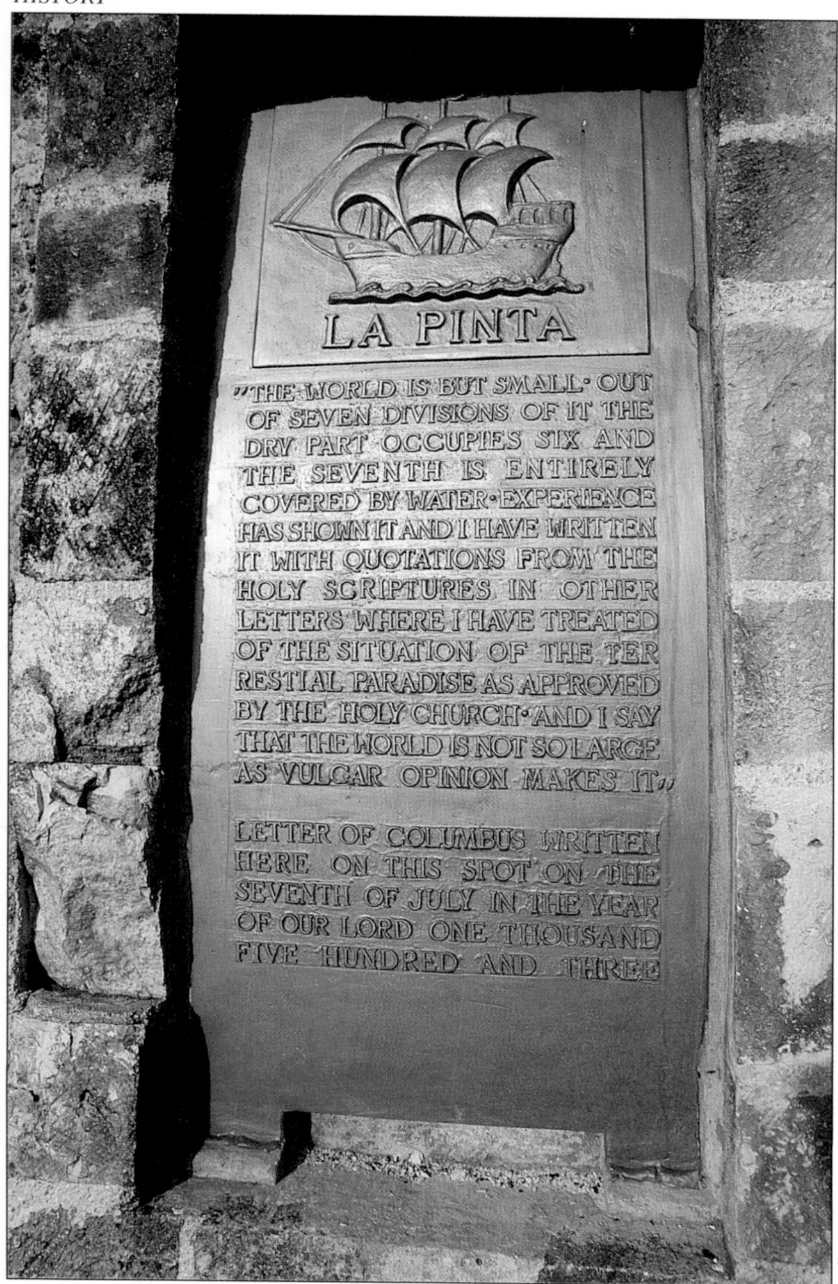
LA PINTA
"THE WORLD IS BUT SMALL · OUT
OF SEVEN DIVISIONS OF IT THE
DRY PART OCCUPIES SIX AND
THE SEVENTH IS ENTIRELY
COVERED BY WATER · EXPERIENCE
HAS SHOWN IT AND I HAVE WRITTEN
IT WITH QUOTATIONS FROM THE
HOLY SCRIPTURES IN OTHER
LETTERS WHERE I HAVE TREATED
OF THE SITUATION OF THE TER
RESTIAL PARADISE AS APPROVED
BY THE HOLY CHURCH · AND I SAY
THAT THE WORLD IS NOT SO LARGE
AS VULGAR OPINION MAKES IT"
LETTER OF COLUMBUS WRITTEN
HERE ON THIS SPOT ON THE
SEVENTH OF JULY IN THE YEAR
OF OUR LORD ONE THOUSAND
FIVE HUNDRED AND THREE

HISTORY OF THE GREATER ANTILLES

Although it has been 500 years since Christopher Columbus claimed the New World for Spain in 1492, the story of the Caribbean Sea and its necklace of islands begins much earlier. Eons before that, oceans and volcanoes and coral reefs conspired to become the incredible Caribbean that tourists now see and celebrate. Earth plates shifted and collided, forcing up mountains as high as 1,800-3,000 m (6,000-10,000 ft) in Cuba, Hispaniola and Jamaica, and splitting into ocean trenches as deep as 6,000-12,000 m (20,000-39,000 ft). Pico Trujillo, in the Dominican Republic, is almost 3,200 m (10,500 ft) high, a veritable Alp.

Caves turn some islands into Swiss cheese, creating beguiling tourist attractions such as the Crystal Caves in Bermuda, or the Green Grotto Caves in Jamaica. Hot springs continue to bore into the mountains at Cuomo, Puerto Rico, and rheumatics flock to the Milk River Spa in Clarendon on Jamaica's south coast, to bathe in the most radioactive mineral waters in the world, which supposedly have healing powers. Another spot in Jamaica, a tarry, lifeless geographical purgatory on the island's south coast, is appropriately named Hell.

It is clear that the geologic forces that shaped the West Indies were powerful ones, and their work is by no means finished. Such jolts and folding, squeezing and rending created a mighty canal in the ocean through which the powerful Gulf Stream speeds northward as fast as six knots, bathing Bermuda and other Atlantic islands as far away as the Azores in warm waters spawned in the south.

Preceding pages: The endless Caribbean beaches; Bermudan portrait; Puerto Plata; street scene; flame tree. Left: Columbus was here.

Bermuda, sticking up in the middle of the Atlantic like a Brobdingnagian fish trap, is probably the tip of what, a few hundred million years ago, was a volcano. Long before anyone claimed the island, it was considered a sort of devil's trap, lying in wait for unlucky seamen.

Even today, the Devil's Triangle, also called the Bermuda Triangle, is alleged to have mysterious powers to confound sailors and pilots. There are sound scientific explanations for the Triangle's famous disasters, disappearing ships and lost pilots. Almost every accident and disappearance could have occurred anywhere. Still, the legends remain part of the lore – and of the fun – of vacationing here. Vendors tap into a motherlode of perpetual income as tourists continually snap up T-shirts that proclaim, "I survived the Bermuda Triangle."

The Bahamas and Caymans lie so low that they barely kept their heads above water during the massive upheaval that split two continents. Other islands, such as Cuba and Hispaniola, rise far above the sea, lush with forests and fertile soil. It is this mixture of abundance and dearth, highs and lows, deserts and rain forests, baking beaches and cool mountain glades, that give the Greater Antilles such variety for visitors.

However strange it may seem, the history of the islands consists of segments tied together with the thread of one island product, rum. Starting with rum and sugarcane, through the yo-ho-ho-and-a-bottle-of-rum pirate years and the era of the rumrunners during America's Prohibition, it flowed ceaselessly into the "rum and Coca Cola" merriment that marks today's tourism boom.

Days of Discovery

After discovering the Bahamas, Cuba, and Hispaniola, Columbus lost his flag-

ship *Santa Maria* on the coast of what is now the Dominican Republic. Dismantling the ship, he used the lumber to build shelters for a community that he called *Navidad,* and left behind a small group while he returned to Spain. But Indians killed the hapless settlers, burned the village, and left nothing but sad remnants to greet Columbus when he returned with a larger force.

Another settlement was established near present-day Puerto Plata, in 1494, and priests said a mass for the crew – which now included the captured Indian chief who had destroyed the first settlement. It was the first mass said in the New World. Whether the Indian was converted to Catholicism and forgiven or executed for burning *Navidad,* is lost in the mists of history. Columbus's subsequent voyages took him to the Lesser Antilles, Jamaica, Dominica and Guadeloupe, and finally on to Trinidad and the north coast of South America, so almost every island boasts some beach or harbor where Columbus is claimed to have set foot.

Above: The arrival of Columbus in San Juan sanitized on a relief. Right: An original Carib face.

Throughout his explorations, the ever-hopeful, though misguided Columbus sent scouting parties with a letter of introduction to the Khan, still hoping he had found what he had set out to discover, a trading route to the Orient. To this day, thanks to Columbus and his confounded sense of direction, the islands he thought were India are known as the West Indies, and aborigines throughout the New World are called Indians.

Another of Columbus's legacies is the wild goat population found roaming many of the islands, descendants of pairs of goats that he put ashore here and there, planning to collect their progeny on future voyages, for provisions. Goats are still a major source of meat, leather, and milk in the islands.

On his fourth voyage, Columbus reached Central America. During that period a Spaniard named Bermudez dis-

covered the island subsequently named Bermuda. Columbus returned to Spain and died in disgrace and despair. He is thought to be buried in the Cathedral of Santa Maria La Menor, in Santo Domingo, on the island that had won his heart, although several other locales also claim to be the explorer's final resting place. "When you see Hispaniola, you won't want to leave it," he had written in his log in 1492, and although this wish may in fact have been fulfilled, verification of whose bones reside in Columbus's crypt is impossible at this late date. The islands he had discovered would forever carry the name of the Indies, which he never reached, and to this day they lie in a sea named, not for him, but for the Carib people he found here.

Arawaks and Caribs

Columbus encountered two different groups of Indians on his arrival 500 years ago. They were the Arawaks, a farming folk called by various other names including Tainos, Lucayans, Iguayos, or Caiquetios, and the fierce Caribs, who had swarmed north out of Paraguay conquering any tribes that stood in their way.

A pugnacious people who preferred warfare to fishing or hunting, the Carib warriors continually raided Arawak settlements, killing the men and stealing the women. It is likely they practiced a sort of ritual cannibalism in which they ceremonially consumed the ashes of their deceased. This custom gave flight to the Spanish imagination and soon the legend of Carib man-eaters made the rounds. The real reason behind the legend, however, was that it legitimized Spanish treatment of Indians. Even the brave Caribs were no match for the guns and guile of their European adversaries, who either killed them off or enslaved them. The Arawak, who had welcomed Columbus and his crew to the island, lived long enough to regret their friendly stance.

Few Indians, warriors or pacifists alike, survived battle, slavery, deportation, and the Conquistadores' version of

religious conversion, which usually meant dying a slow and agonizing death.

The dreaded Inquisition settled in the Americas with the Spanish, who tortured and killed not just heathen Indians but any French or English Protestants they got their hands on, as well as any of their own countrymen whose faith seemed to be slipshod. The autodafé was very much a part of everyday New World life under the Spanish. Indians by the hundreds of thousands succumbed to this and other unwanted European contributions such as smallpox, measles, and the common cold. Many of these people, by some reports thousands, were unable to accept the Spanish yoke. They committed suicide by eating raw *cassava* – the starchy root that was, ironically, also their staff of life. Freshly harvested, the root is poisonous; squeezed of its poison and baked into bread, it was the Indians' most important food. On Jamaica alone, 60,000 Arawaks disappeared between 1509, when the Spanish arrived, and the onset of British rule in 1655. All the Lucayan Indians of the Bahamas, believed to number about 40,000 when Columbus landed, had disappeared by the time Ponce de Leon arrived in 1513.

Above and right: Ancient agricultural means still survive in Matanzas province, Cuba.

Amazingly, pockets of Caribs survive today in remote areas of the Lesser Antilles, primarily in the mountains of Dominica and St. Vincent. It is unlikely that any are purebred, but, like many of their ancestors throughout the Americas, they pass power and wealth through the female line. The Indians on a reservation in Dominica still have a tribal queen.

Today, the best place for experiencing Indian life as it was before Columbus, is rarely included in Caribbean guidebooks even though it is technically in the Caribbean Sea. The Locono Indians living along the Caribbean coastline of Venezuela and Guiana probably sprang from the same ancestors as the Arawaks. They are farmers and seafarers, still

living in huts made of sticks and thatch, sleeping in hammocks, and paddling canoes much like those described by the early Spanish explorers. The words tobacco, canoe, barbecue, hammock and hurricane are among the Amerindian contributions to our present language.

Archaeology is still in its infancy in the Greater Antilles. Indian villages were generally small and scattered, and the zeal of the Spanish in destroying what they considered "pagan" cultures was unequaled. Still, almost every island has at least some Amerindian artifacts in museums, and finds continue to be made. In 1988, a cave on Long Island in the Bahamas yielded three carved figures dating to the Arawak period, and Arawak drawings can be found in caves on Cat Island, as well as in numerous cave sites in Jamaica where spelunking is an increasingly popular diversion for both serious researchers into Caribbean history and an increasing number of tourists.

The stone and pottery display at the Musee du Peuple Haitien, in Port-au-Prince is one place to get glimpses of pre-Columbian life. So is the Museo del Hombre Dominicano in Santo Domingo. Probably the best excavation is the one near Utuado, in Puerto Rico, where a 700-year-old Taino ceremonial ball field, complete with roads and plazas, has been unearthed. To the fun-loving Arawaks, just as among their cousins the Maya, a fast-moving ball game was an important rite as well as a serious game. It was played with a ball of rubber, a substance that was readily available to the Mayans but became more prized the farther the Indians roamed from the mainland where rubber was grown. Unlike the Mayans, the Arawaks did not murder the captain of the losing team. As James Michener pointed out in *Caribbean*, they concluded that it would be pretty stupid to kill the second best ball player in the tribe.

Pirates and the Sea

The Spanish were interested in only one thing: gold. When another Spanish

explorer, Cortez, discovered that gold was far more plentiful on the mainland – and could be easily taken from the weaponless Indians, Queen Isabella's attentions turned there, while pirates took over the Caribbean.

A pirate by any other name was still a pirate, freebooter, or buccaneer, but there was a certain moral distinction to be made. Privateers, who were known as pirates only to their enemies, were privately employed seafarers who were supplied with ships and arms by some sponsor – Queen Elizabeth I and Cardinal Richelieu were among the participants – and were sent forth to prey on enemy shipping interests.

Since the English, French, Dutch, and Spanish were almost always at war with one another at some time, there was never any lack of excuses to loot, pillage, rape and burn as a legal act of defense.

Above and right: Two important items in the privateer's dubious trade, symbols of the Caribbeans violent, moved past.

The wages of sin may be death, but for successful privateers they were riches, power, and a chance to be lionized by their countrymen. For their success in attacking enemy ships and bringing home the fortunes of war, British knighthoods, or the French version of the same, were given to half a dozen famous pirates including Sir Henry Morgan, Sir Francis Drake, Pierre Balain D'Esnambuc, and Urban de Roissey. The most famous of Holland's privateers, Peyt Hein, was made an admiral in the Dutch navy. Henry Morgan, perhaps the most bloodthirsty of all, was made lieutenant governor of Jamaica. In the great moral dung heap that was the Caribbean of the seventeenth century, only the privateer, who sailed against the enemies of his homeland and under the auspices of his queen or his investors, could go to his prayers with a clear conscience.

The Spanish rounded up gold and silver on the mainland, then had to run a gauntlet of reefs, storms and pirates to get it back to Seville. Much of the swag ended up in the hands of English, French, Dutch and stateless freebooters. And much ended up in caves and pits and at the bottom of the sea – where occasional finds continue to be made by treasure hunters and their latest high-tech equipment. These uncounted millions in gold and silver are the stuff of which legends are made – legends that tell of treasure chests buried on almost every island you will visit in the West Indies.

Visitors to the British Virgin Islands are invited to snorkel in a cave said to be the setting for Robert Louis Stevenson's *Treasure Island*, and the burial site of a fabled treasure. There are few cays where you will not be told of some still-to-be-found buried treasure left by Captain Kidd, Anne Bonney, Henry Morgan, Jean LaFitte, or some other unlucky swashbuckler who had been forced by stormy seas or certain capture to jettison the spoils of war.

The old adage, "Set a thief to catch a thief" ultimately prevailed. The age of piracy ended dramatically when Captain Woodes Rogers, who had earned his stripes and lost impressive portions of his anatomy as a privateer in the War of Spanish Succession, was sent to the Bahamas as its first royal governor. He snared pirates by the dozen, hanged at least eight, and sent others to England for trial. It was not long before remaining pirates fled elsewhere to ply their trade, or joined Rogers in creating a peaceful, law-abiding Bahamas. Nassau became a Gibraltar against all comers – French, Spanish, and pirates alike, and the plantation era took center stage.

The European Connection

From the time of the first European footstep, the history of the Greater Antilles has been tied to European wars, alliances, ambitions, economies, and religions. Spain discovered that sugarcane, which grew in the Canary Islands, also thrived here. Low-lying islands were natural salt pans, where fortunes in precious salt could be easily obtained by evaporating seawater. Before refrigeration, salt was the only preservative and worth its weight, literally at times, in gold. Fortunes were founded on salt and sugar as well as cocoa, tobacco, pineapple, cotton, lumber, spices such as nutmeg, bananas, coffee, and all the other consumables that could be grown where soil, slaves, sun and rainfall were plentiful. And these agricultural treasures had to be protected from all other jealous contenders.

British islands built defenses against the Spanish, the Spanish had to build forts against the Dutch, the French feared the English, and so forth, all depending on which European powers were currently embroiled in warfare. On many islands, the only points of historical interest today are the forts, and what forts they are! Built by slave labor, they sprawl over countless acres, climb to dizzying heights, and are so impregnable that many were never taken in battle. Even to

the tourist who comes to the Caribbean for shopping, sunning, skin diving or beachcombing, and has no interest in history, the forts are a must because they are always situated on the best viewpoints, their cannons aimed at the prettiest and most photogenic harbors.

Along with forts galore come some of the world's most impressive palaces. The 22-room Alcazar on Hispaniola was built by Diego Columbus in 1514. Its limestone walls are more than 2.75m (3 ft) thick. The massive fortress of San Felipe, at Puerto Plata, was built in 1540. The 18th century Palace of the Spanish General is now a museum in Havana. Nassau's massive Fort Charlotte bristled with 42 cannons, not to mention miles of tunnels and dungeons. Sans Souci Palace and the Citadelle, both in Haiti, built by the slave-King Henri Christophe to defend against the French, was finished in 1817. Fully a tenth of the 200,000 slaves who built it lost their lives during the project and are thought to be entombed in its walls. The 42-m (140-ft) walls, up to 12m (40 ft) thick at their bases, rise from a 900-m (3,000-ft) mountain. It is one of the most dazzling architectural sights in the Antilles. Henri's excesses, however, caught up with him. His own guards turned against him and in a final act of arrogance he shot himself with a golden bullet.

Above and right: Might made right in the Caribbean, El Morro in San Juan and Puerto Plata, Dominican Republic.

Great forts throughout the West Indies, from Bermuda's Fort St. Catherine to Puerto Rico's impregnable El Morro, still stand silent sentinel, reminders of a time when each island stood alone against a hostile world.

As peace treaties were signed overseas, islands were bartered back and forth like box lunches. In 1695, the Duchy of Brandenburg got Tortola and St. Thomas; from 1642 to 1654 Tobago belonged to Courland, then passed to the Dutch, the French and finally the British. The 1697 Treaty of Rijswick gave Haiti to France and the Dominican Republic to Spain.

The English seized Jamaica in 1655 and it remained British until its independence in 1962. The Treaty of Versailles in 1783 gave islands including the Bahamas and Grenada to Britain. In 1784, Sweden walked off with St. Barts.

After it became an independent nation in 1776, the United States waded into the fray too. For one brief period they raised the Stars and Stripes over Nassau, but the winds of war blew both ways. Thousands of Americans who wanted to remain loyal to the crown fled the rebelling states and settled in the northern Bahamas. To this day, Abaconians are blond and blue-eyed in contrast to the rest of the black Bahamas, and their speech has the words and accents of their Carolinian forebears. America, and Cubans living in America, were responsible for the ousting of Spain from Cuba at the start of the 20th century in the Spanish-American War, and the long arm of Uncle Sam, in the guise of President Ronald Reagan, reached out only recently to "rescue" tiny Grenada from alleged Communist take-over.

Meanwhile, the French Revolution had fanned flames of freedom among the New World's slaves too. An uprising in Haiti was so effective that planters were forced to give slaves their freedom, at least for a while. Julien Fedon, a black planter in Grenada, led a violent uprising against the British in 1795. After a bloody night on St. Croix, slaves took control of the island for six months.

The first black republic in the Caribbean, and probably in the world, was formed in Haiti, in 1804, when slaves rose up against the planters. They had been freed once, by the Spanish in 1793, but double-cross had followed assassination had followed betrayal. The seeds of hatred and turmoil, planted centuries ago, continue to thrive in this politically and socially troubled nation to this very day.

At Port-au-Prince, in Haiti, a statue honors the *Marron Inconnu,* which translates as the Unknown Runaway Slave.

The word maroon, by the way, came into English as marron, meaning stranded in some out-of-the-way spot.

Despite its distance from the other islands, Bermuda too kept busy during these turbulent times. Some of the arms supplied to George Washington during the Revolutionary War were smuggled through British Bermuda. The Waterlot Inn, where some of the scheming for the project is said to have been done, is now a landmark restaurant catering to the tourist trade. The raid on Washington, D.C., during the war of 1812, in which the White House was burned, was launched from the British stronghold of Bermuda. A multi-projector slide show tells the whole, exciting story in an air-conditioned theater in Somerset, Sandys Parish, Bermuda. The theater in the Old Cooperage is open daily.

Meanwhile back in Europe, another shake-up and trade-off occurred after the Napoleonic Wars. The treaties of Paris gave Cuba, Puerto Rico and what is now the Dominican Republic to Spain. France

retained control of Martinique and Guadeloupe, the Dutch and Danes got bits and pieces, and Britain happily pocketed just about everything else.

For a century, the Caymans belonged to Jamaica. In a strange twist of fate years later, the Caymans voted to remain true to the Queen while Jamaica took the road of rebellion and independence. Today, the Caymans, rivaled only by Bermuda, are the wealthiest nation in the Caribbean; Jamaicans, still struggling with the growing pains of a new nation after 30 years of self-rule, make up the servant class there, and tellingly, more Jamaicans now live outside the country than in it.

Columbus's favorite island, Hispaniola, was split centuries ago, and it may never be reunited. French pirates seized the western end of the island from the Spanish and, a few years later in the 1697 Treaty of Rijswick, France legally acquired the title to the lands. Soon France was in control of the entire island, until slaves revolted and created the separate nation of Haiti. Aided by Britain, Dominicans restored Spanish rule, then revolted again and left themselves open for a takeover from Haiti. The Dominican Republic itself was born in 1844 in the throes of yet another revolution. During the century that followed no less than 56 revolutions shook the Dominican half of the island, while a countless succession of leaders rose to power and fell from grace in neighboring Haiti.

Above: Reminder of colonial past – the French Cloister on Paradise Island . Right: Recreated past in Altos de Chavon.

Toussaint L'Ouverture, still considered a national hero in Haiti, was elected governor in 1801. Toussaint gained the title L'Ouverture (the opening) because it was said that in battle he created holes in enemy forces everywhere. Betrayed by Napoleon, Toussaint died in a European dungeon in 1803. Nevertheless, France was finally finished in Haiti through the combined forces of enraged slaves and the yellow fever that swept through the French forces.

Haitians fought for and won their independence, which was then stolen from them by a series of somewhat demented despots. Dessalines proclaimed himself emperor. Henri Christophe declared himself king. Legend says that to show off his unimpeachable power to a British guest, he forced some members of his palace guard to jump to their deaths from the towering ramparts of his palace.

He was neither the first nor the last of Haiti's rulers to be despots with a tendency toward megalomania. In 1915 American forces moved in to prevent an alleged takeover by Germany, and by 1916 they had spread into the restless Dominican Republic. The US forces remained on the island until the end of World War One. They were re-called into service against the Dominican Republic by President Johnson in 1965 to quash what the State Department regarded as a subversive rebellion.

Portugal, Sweden, and other minor players retired early from the Caribbean sweepstakes. It was not until the Spanish-American War in 1898 that Spain was conclusively ousted from the Americas. Denmark sold her interests in the Virgin Islands to the United States for hard cash in 1917. Only Britain, Holland and France remained.

Today, Britain remains a significant presence in the Greater Antilles, with major interests including Bermuda and the Bahamas. Many of her former colonies are independent but remain part of the Commonwealth. Until now, Caymans, British Virgins, Bermuda, Montserrat and the Turks and Caicos are still British Crown Colonies.

While Europeans battled over the Antilles, freebooters and privateers moved in and stole the show, as well as millions and millions of dollars in booty. Some were independent operators with loyalties to no government. Others were subsidized, covertly if not openly, by European royalty, merchants, or conglomerates. Usually, the common folk were caught in the middle. At times, everyone had to unite against the pirates and,

during slave uprisings, whites, Orientals and free blacks joined forces against rampaging slaves.

The history of the Greater Antilles has been a violent, ugly, and sometimes comical free-for-all.

The persecuted fled here for protection. Greedy carpetbaggers rushed here in the hopes of getting rich quickly and easily. The industrious trooped here in search of opportunity. Soldiers of fortune came to offer their swords to the highest bidder. And all of them needed slaves, who were imported from Africa in such vast and heartless numbers that it was the black Afro-West Indians who eventually inherited the earth of the Caribbean.

The customs and beliefs they brought with them lived on and today form the very essence of the islands' flair.

Above: A traditional business on the islands, or boys will be boys? Right: Fishing still provides a livelihood for many, sometimes using the simple, tried and true means of one's ancestors.

The Slave Era

Slavery was not new, let alone shocking, to the world of the 16th century. Long before Columbus, it was common practice in the New World for Indians to make slaves of the peoples they conquered. Arawaks had long been the prey of the Caribs; the Caribs were enslaved by the Spanish. Africa, where tribal wars supplied a never-ending reservoir of losers, was a bounteous hunting ground for slave traders who put into any of three or four dozen slave markets along the western African Gold Coast to load their ships with hapless humans sold by African warlords or rounded up by the Europeans, mostly Dutch and English, who operated the slave camps.

Later, from Europe, came white indentured servants, debtors, and political and religious refugees, all of them hardly more than slaves either. It took only a century after Columbus landed for plantations, and the slaves operating them, to become a multi-national business. The slave trade alone brought in about $7 million a year, with the strongest and best trading for as much as eighteen pounds sterling a head. It is estimated that as many as 75,000 souls per year were being shipped to the sugar-cane fields by the start of the 18th century.

At the zenith of the slave years, a planter could spend hundreds of dollars on a strong, well-trained field slave with good bloodlines, and as much as two thousand dollars for a highly trained house slave. So lucrative was the slave trade that some planters turned to breeding slaves as a cash crop. It was cheaper than sending ships to Europe, and it bypassed the slave-trader middlemen. And selective breeding could assure quality control, emphasizing a stronger, smarter, more saleable product.

This inhumane industry started collapsing in the wake of the Enlightenment at the end of the 18th century, at the same time when Americans were revolting against England, and French peasants were rising up against the monarchy. Egalitarianism, combined with a growing sense of moral outrage that human beings were being bought and sold, became an unstoppable tide of opinion.

A happy postscript to the slave era lives on in Samana, in the Dominican Republic. In 1824 a ship filled with escaped slaves who had found freedom via the Quakers' "underground railroad" was forced ashore here. The marooned Blacks formed a community, lived in peace with the local islanders who were still holding on in the name of Spain. Today many Samanans still speak some of the Elizabethan English of their ancestors.

Slave trading was outlawed in Jamaica as early as 1807, and by 1834, slaves were freed throughout the British colonies. Owners of plantations were given a compensation of 40 pounds sterling per slave, but they nevertheless bitterly complained that it was too little to substitute for the cheap labor they had had at their disposal. But history marched on. Within the next few decades, the rest of the hemisphere followed suit.

When slave-holding Southerners fled from North America to the Bahamas after realizing their Confederate cause was lost, they brought slaves with them but were forced to free them with no compensation at all. Blacks in the Bahamas and throughout the British islands had been freed 30 years before those in America. So passionate was the anti-slavery sentiment in the British islands that even before emancipation, an English planter on Tortola was hanged for killing a slave who had disobeyed an order. After emancipation, slave ships en route to America were intercepted at sea, and their human cargo set free.

The slave era was finished, and with it a way of life. Plantations were abandoned; great houses by the hundreds fell into disrepair; jungle reclaimed hard-won fields. Only on a few islands were former slaves put to work in the cane fields. Today, the sugar industry, which once

thrived due to slave labor, plays only a lesser role in the Caribbean economies.

Freedmen, left to their own devices, eked out a living by fishing, small-scale farming, collecting sponges, harvesting salt, making and selling charcoal or hiring themselves out as laborers at wages that sometimes were indistinguishable from slavery. When the Duke of Windsor, who was governor of the Bahamas during World War II, funded a massive drain-and-fill project on New Providence, he paid workmen a dollar a week. At the same time, the duchess was busily refurnishing Government House in lavish style. Historic gaps between rich and poor throughout the West Indies have left a legacy of social tension and political inequalities that have, in turn, lead to violent reactions especially during the time when Caribbean islands were achieving independence.

Above: Breaking the chains of slavery. Right: Sugarcane, both a symbol of economic progress and slavery.

Bermuda and the Bahamas

Because these islands are in the Atlantic, and are not technically part of the Caribbean, and because Bermuda is particularly isolated, their histories took a few extra and interesting twists. Although the name of Christopher Columbus pops up with wearying regularity in Antilles guidebooks, it is the Bahamas where he actually made his first landfall in the New World. The best guess, now commonly accepted as historical fact, is that he first went ashore at San Salvador. Known to the Indians as *Guanahani*, the island was first called Watling's Island, after a pirate who settled there and built a mightly castle.

Columbus, dismayed by the miles of reefs and shoals threaded through by only a few, hard-to-find deep-water passages, called the land *bajamar*, or shallow sea. The word became Bahama. Except for rounding up and carting off the islands' Indians when his supply of slaves in Hispaniola ran low, Columbus did not spend

a lot of time in the Bahamas. Most of the islands were small and sere, lacking in fresh water or rich soil. Everybody in the Caribbean – the Spanish, English, and French – claimed the Bahamas but nobody wanted to live there, not even Ponce de Leon, whose search for the Fountain of Youth took him to Bimini.

Bermuda was settled by accident in 1609 when a ship en route from England to the Virginias fetched ashore here. The island chain had been charted by the Spanish mariner Juan de Bermudez, whose chief goal was to give them a wide berth. Hundreds of ships struck the reefs here before, during and even after the Spanish mapping.

In those days navigation methods were primitive. Besides, nobody sailing this part of the vast and apparently bottomless sea expected that a 35km (22mi) snag of rocky cays, only two miles wide at its broadest point, would suddenly rise up out of the ocean and maul them. The islands were particularly fearsome to the Elizabethan world. The "Bermoothes", as they were known, are thought to have been the inspiration for Shakespeare's *The Tempest*.

Sir George Somers, whose *Sea Venture* was wrecked on Bermuda in 1609, cobbled together a couple of new ships and went on to Virginia, but a few sailors jumped ship, and stayed. By 1612, another group of settlers had arrived from Virginia and by 1640 they were at such odds with each other that one splinter group moved to the Bahamas.

Bermuda, like the rest of the West Indies, thrived during the slave era, using some Africans but also importing a great number of white, indentured servants from England. As a result, Bermuda is not as overwhelmingly black today as most of the other Indies. It is also the most British of islands, having been a Crown Colony since 1684. Even its language is different – more British- American than West Indian – and it is comparatively rich. There is no unemployment, no homelessness, no hunger – just a proud, warm-hearted people.

The same religious wars that sent the Pilgrims scuttling from Britain to Massachusetts, resulted in the settlement of the Bahamas. Captain William Sayle, who had been governor of Bermuda, and a group called the Eleutherian (Greek for freedom) Adventurers cast off in l647 for the Bahamas, but were shipwrecked off the islands then called *Cigatoo* by the Arawaks, now known as Eleuthera. The spot where the set up shop at the time is now a lonely beach marked only by a sign. After looking around for the best places to settle, they founded a community at what are now Spanish Wells and Harbour Island. Nassau too was gaining settlers thanks to its excellent harbor, fine fishing and the easy prey provided by passing Spanish galleons. The first settlers came in l656 and named the island New Providence. The "old" Providence had already been settled, in Rhode Island.

Above: Real life in the Dominican Republic. Right: Cock fighting, a form of gambling for everyman.

The islands were put under British rule but remained lawless for generations. Nassau was burned, invaded and plundered until, by the beginning of the 18th century, it was completely in the control of pirates. Hundreds of buccaneers also dwelled in Port Royal, Jamaica, a notorious pest-hole where gold, rum, and life itself were cheap. In 1692, in the aftermath of a violent earthquake, most of the town broke away and sank into the sea.

Pirates who survived migrated to Nassau, swelling the power of piracy there. The Bahamas were undergoing a population explosion. Planters poured in from England, eager to reap profits from sugarcane. Runaway slaves from America made their way to the Bahamas where, even before emancipation, pockets of escaped slaves formed their own communities in the bush. Blacks dumped off slave ships if any sort of contagious disease broke out, waded ashore on uninhabited islands, where they multiplied, thrived, and were eventually granted

property rights. By 1718, more than 1,000 buccaneers were said to call Nassau their home port, and the Crown had had enough. The hero of the new era was Captain Woodes Rogers who had already cut a wide swath through the South Pacific – acquiring an impressive collection of scars and disfigurements on the way. So impressed were the pirates by Governor Rogers's toughness that most of them turned in their skull-and-crossbones flags, joined the new governor, and went to work building forts to defend New Providence.

Today, the Bahamas have a predominantly black population, are independent members of the Commonwealth, and maintain an identity and culture that has remained distinct from both the West Indies and from the United States, which is no farther than 80 km (50 mi) away.

The Lean Years

For the next two centuries, most of the Caribbean slumbered. Farming had always been a hazardous affair in the Greater Antilles, and the end of slavery spelled the end of the plantation era. Those planters who remained were wiped out when various blights hit pineapples or cotton, or when the price of sisal, sponges or aloe fell, or when European beet sugar became cheaper than cane sugar.

A wealth of hardwood forests had been hacked down never to recover, ending both the lumber and boat-building industries in Jamaica, Great Abaco and the Caymans. Islands that had supported dozens of plantations and thousands of lives became ghost towns. Many remain so to this day.

Only wrecking, the salvaging of goods from shipwrecks, supplied some material support to the hard-pressed islanders. Almost every island has its stories of how false lights were set out to lure ships onto the reefs, where they could be easily picked clean of their valuable cargoes by marauding and scavenging pirates. Entire fortunes in the Bahamas, Florida, and as

far east as Barbados, were founded on such treachery. It was not until the mid-18th century that seafaring in the West Indies became safe from piracy, thanks to better charts and navigation methods, coupled with an increasingly dense network of lighthouses. One notable exception to the wreckers' greed was the heroism of Caymanians, who worked so selflessly to save victims of the *Wreck of the Ten Sails,* for which they were relieved of paying taxes in perpetuity by King George III.

The Americas Civil War provided for a vigorous economic boom, especially in the Bahamas. The British gleefully sided with the Confederacy, for it had been, after all, only a half century since the Yanks had defeated Britain in the war of 1812. The Bahamas were the ideal place to run the Yankee blockade. Once through the Bahamas, ships had only to make the quick dash across the Gulf Stream to Florida, Charleston or New Orleans. Officially, the Bahamas were neutral, but Union ships were turned away while Confederate captains got the red carpet treatment. Mother England was glad to sell arms to the rebels, and was equally happy to get silky Sea Island cotton in return.

Above: Dominican coffee drying the natural way. Right: Havana cigars, forbidden fruit for Americans since the early Sixties.

Prohibition provided for another era of prosperity on the islands. From 1919 to 1933, liquor could not be made or sold legally in the United States. It was a bonanza for the rum distilleries of the Caribbean and the ships that ran the illegal cargo – some of it whisky from as far away as Scotland and wines from distant France – through Bermuda and the Bahamas and into American speakeasies.

Repeal on the other hand, which occurred at the height of a worldwide depression, was devastating for the islands. It was not until World War II that people had work again, building landing fields and defenses. There was war work for everyone, from Bermuda to the oil refineries of the Lesser Antilles. Bermuda, because of its aloof and strategic location, was one of the war's hot spots. It was here that mail and ships were intercepted and stripped of contraband, messages were decoded, and ships and planes refueled. Even today, old-timers at the Hamilton Princess might share with you memories of the days when the hotel's underground vaults housed one of the war's most expert code-busting teams.

Bermuda's remoteness, not to mention its superb golf courses, has also made it a popular location for conferences among political leaders. Visitors have included Franklin Delano Roosevelt, Harold Macmillan, Edward Heath and American presidents Eisenhower, Kennedy and Nixon. Even Winston Churchill came here during the war, despite the risks. But in recent years, it is business conferences, rather than politics, that have supplied a tide of dollars to local economies. Luxury

hotels throughout the Caribbean spill over, not just with fun seekers, but with free- spending conventioneers combining work and pleasure.

Roots of Tourism

As the plantation era ended, Antilleans realized that they still had a highly marketable commodity – warm winters, salt breezes to bring balmy air to the lungs, and an unhurried pace to soothe the jangled nerves of an increasingly technical world. The problem was that access to the islands was difficult, and those who survived the treacherous sea voyage could not always find suitable accommodation. By 1851, tourism-hungry Bahamas were offering 1,000 pounds sterling to any company willing to run a vessel from New York to Nassau. The reward hardly attracted many captains and crews so the ante was raised in 1859 to 3,000 pounds. That caught the attention of a Canadian entrepreneur named Samuel Cunard, who started a regular New York-Nassau service with a paddle-wheel steamer named *Karnak*.

In 1872, a steamer service started from New York to Bermuda. By 1873, the Bahamas were attracting some of the fashionable tourists who had by then already discovered the sunny benifits of Florida. Henry Flagler leased the Royal Victoria Hotel and rented rooms to the carriage trade – finally displacing the blockade runners, deserters, adventurers and riffraff who had been the Bahamas' chief tourists since the American Civil War. By 1925, the Royal Mail Line was bringing tourists into the Bahamas from Canada, Britain, and the United States. Pan Am flying boats started a daily service into Nassau and Havana from Miami and Key West in the 1920s and the silver bird has been the Caribbean's economic salvation ever since.

By the end of the World War II, the islands were ready to reap a tourism boom. Almost every island bigger than a pea patch had an air strip built by the Allies. Flying boats were still in use, and as

STOL aircraft came on the scene, even the smallest islands could expect fly-in tourists. Thousands of winter-weary northerners longed for beaches and sun, and thousands of soldiers and sailors, who had fallen in love with the Caribbean during the war, were eager to return with their wives.

Just as tourists had poured into the islands during Prohibition for relief from the rigid, abstinent spell at home, today they might skip over to Freeport or Paradise Island for casino gambling, which is not legal in most of the United States. During the 1920s and into the 1950s, Cuba was Florida's playground – a paradise of sunshine, dance, feasting and fishing very much at the expense of the local population. Carpetbagging by US-led companies has often led to dissatisfaction in the Caribbean and elsewhere, but in Cuba the exploitation provided the perfect ground for an easy Communist takeover. 30 years later, however, even tough Castro is making concessions to the tourist trade in search of hard currency, the island's very special history is fast making it one of the Caribbean's very special destinations.

Today tourism is the Greater Antilles' chief cash crop and, on some islands, the only one. The course has not been a steady one. Most of the stories of hooliganism have been blown out of proportion, and drug-connected violence in the islands has been mild compared to the drug-related mayhem of the South American continent or the mainland cities of the United States. One suspects that bad publicity springs as much from lingering, thinly-veiled racism directed at the predominantly black Caribbean as from political and economic realities faced by these emerging Third World nations.

Neverless, the West Indies have had their share of strikes, sit-downs, skirmishes, scandals and horrendous public relations debacles such as the election-inspired street riots in Jamaica and the torching of a San Juan tourist hotel filled with Christmas vacationers during a bitter labor dispute.

Haiti, perhaps more than other Caribbean nation, seethes with a vast reservoir of historic hatreds that still boil over from time to time, while the pitiably poor Haitian people roam the seas, taking refuge where they can find it. Haiti's tourist industry, despite its magnificent potential, is on very thin ice. Some guidebooks give lengthy descriptions of its sites and delights, but warn tourists to be very cautious about going there. Others do not list the nation at all.

A happier story is that of the Turks and Caicos Islands, a group that does not find its way into all Caribbean guidebooks but maintains a growing and loyal guest list nonetheless. Geographically they are part of the Bahamas. Politically they are a British Crown Colony. Tourism-wise, they remain in a pleasant yesteryear, instilling a real sense of discovery among the lucky pioneers who seek them out.

Most island governments realize that tourism provides clean, easy money without smokestacks, and they encourage their people to make hospitality a proud and profitable business. Some settlements, such as the entire, space-age community of Freeport and the extensive La Romana resort area in the Dominican Republic, were built from the ground up for the sole purpose of providing touristic pleasures. Nevertheless, travelers still find the occasional cool welcome, the mysterious price hike, surly waiter or rude taxi driver. And words like rush and deadline do not occur in the down-island vocabulary. Consider it a continuation of the roistering, unpredictable hills and valleys of West Indian history which deserves every bit of respect a foreigner can muster. To visit here will always be high adventure.

Right: Some gifts from the sea are a good deal larger than others.

CULTURE OF THE GREATER ANTILLES

Although this area stretches from Bermuda to the Caymans and includes societies as diverse as Cuba and Haiti, there are fascinating commonalities to the cultures. Language, politics and prosperity may be very different, but people of this region share the same heritage of sun and sea in all guises of benevolence and fury. Residents know all too well how suddenly serene breezes can turn into devastating hurricanes. Political turmoil and negative publicity belie a typically island-bred racial harmony, developed as a survival skill and mingled with centuries of intermarriage. All Caribbean inhabitants, except for the few remaining Indians, came from elsewhere, and most maintain proud loyalty to the home island, no matter how small or poor. Jamaica's motto, "One people out of many", could apply to almost every society in the Antilles.

Meet the People

The best way to meet local folk is to visit their homes, churches, work places and clubs. Among those island groups that offer person-to-person programs are Jamaica, Puerto Rico, and the Bahamas. Contacts are made through the various tourist boards of each country. In general, advance planning is needed to match you with a family of similar ages and interests, although at well-run programs, such as Jamaica's, arrangements can sometimes be made a day or so in advance. If you want to be certain, write or phone before your visit, with specific dates, times and special interests.

Left: The Tropicana show in Havana, Cuba, a concession to mass tourism.

Music and Dance

Nassau's changing of the guard ceremony, held on alternate Saturday mornings at Government House, has the pomp of some centuries-old British rite. But one only has to see the Royal Bahamas Police Force Band on parade to appreciate the unique blend of Africa, Britain, American jazz, Spanish flamenco and homegrown *calypso* that make up West Indian music and dance.

Most of today's rhythms and forms have their origins in Spain, France and England, with a strong African component and a few remnants of the stately dances performed by Arawak slaves for their Spanish masters. Each century and each new wave of immigration have added a new layer of sound, rhythm and spirit. Baked together by an indefatigable sun, it resulted in a new art form combining drama, dance and, especially, music. The rich heritage of Spanish music came to the Antilles with the first explorers and mingled with the songs and instruments of the Indians, who had primitive percussion instruments and flutes, but no stringed instruments. Strings came from Spain, with instruments that were forerunners of today's guitars and *cuatros*. The resulting mix flourishes in many forms from salsa to pop. Opera star Plaçido Domingo recently recorded an entire album of songs by Ernest Lecuona, a popular, romantic Cuban composer of the 1930s and 1940s. What you will hear most on West Indian radio stations, however, is the melodic calypso, that is when it is not being supplanted by the relatively recent upstart, the syncopated, bottom-heavy sound of reggae.

Out of Spain and through Cuba came the bolero. The plena is purely Puerto Rican, blending the spontaneity of calypso with the rhumba rhythms of Africa. In Haiti, where people take to the street in joyous *bambouches*, one can see remnants of ancient quadrilles danced by

plantation owners in their lace jabots. Regular folk performances are given at Port-au-Prince at the outdoor Theatre de Verdure. Even in prim Bermuda, festival days inspire people to explode into *gombey*, while in the Bahamas, the local version of the same dancing festival is called *goombay*. Tourists can never seem to quite get the hang of the sensuous merengue, which varies from island to island, but is popular throughout the region. It all happens in the hips, in muscles and joints that outsiders did not know they had. Liquid motion it might be called.

Reggae, which originated in the slums of Kingston, has spread through the Caribbean, and across the seas to America and Europe. It derived from a progression of musical styles, developing from a form called *ska,* which was a descendant of rock steady, blues and *mento,* harkening back to plantation days.

Above: Taking a break from the festivities. Right: Carnival is always a particularly colorful occasion.

Today, *Sunsplash,* a multi-day festival showcasing the best reggae performers, is probably the largest annual event in Montego Bay, if not Jamaica. It is usually held in mid-summer. Attendance is heavy, so make your bookings months ahead. For reggae groupies, a pilgrimage to the Bob Marley Museum in Kingston is a must. The complex includes his home and the studio where he made his last recordings.

Turning to a lighter issue than the frequently political reggae, limbo dancing has been turned into a sort of cheap burlesque appearing in every cliché Caribbean show in every tourist trap night club, but it originally came from Africa. Performed by lithe West Indians, it can be a pleasure to watch. Attempted by tourists who have had too much to drink, it usually looks pretty silly.

Calypso lyrics, although seemingly harmless rhymes, often contain biting satire. Improvised calypso is more than just a delightful show for tourists; it is a powerful cultural force throughout the islands. Many a politician has sunk without

a trace, all because he or she was skewered by a clever calypso rhyme that stuck in the public's mind.

Today the most omnipresent music throughout the Antilles is that of the steel bands. It is the Caribbean's own music, born in oil drums left over from World War II. Said to have originated in Antigua, *pan* music spread to Trinidad and throughout the rhythm-loving world. In fact, in most major U.S. cities where street-performing is allowed you are likely to hear steel band music bouncing off the highrises, often played by genuine islanders who can make more money from handouts than from any other job an island upbringing may have qualified them for.

Every major city in the Greater Antilles has at least one good center for the performing arts. Consult current local information for programs. Many of the performances are by visiting groups or artists from Europe or the Americas. Locals may be starved for Shakespeare or Bach, but you, the tourist, have access to such classics at home. So, if it is local culture you are after, you are more likely to see one of the national dance groups, or an authentic folk group, during a simple street festival, or at the docks welcoming cruise ships.

Local newspapers, which are often flimsy and overpriced, are invaluable sources of current information, as are the posters in shop windows and on telephone poles. Often, small neighborhood events are advertised no other way. Local radio stations are also a good source of news about the festivals and fund raisers, street dances and bake sales, that are so important to social life throughout the Caribbean.

It may not be folk music, but the *Casals Festival*, held annually in Puerto Rico in June, is nevertheless a classical music event of world-wide importance. Housed in the Fine Arts Center in San Juan, it features big-name artists, conductors, choirs and orchestras performing classical music from Bach to Shostakovich.

Arts and Crafts

The best and most authentic handicrafts are those made from native materials. These include seashells, plaiting and weaving done from palm or sweetgrass, batik, wood carving and jewelry. In the Caymans, where turtles are raised commercially, beautiful tortoiseshell items are sold. It may not, however, be legal to take them home with you to countries that consider tortoises an endangered species. So you should check customs regulations before buying.

Amber, which is fossilized sap, is harvested in the Dominican Republic and turned into gift items. Most desirable are those pieces that have trapped some ancient insect. Black coral is no longer harvested legally in most of this region, but jewellers work with imported coral. A word of caution: Some people will try to sell imitation black coral. In general,the Caymans are especially well known for their talented designers of jewelry in sterling and coral.

Above: Woodworking in Jamaica. Right: Naive painting, an art form throughout much of the region.

Haiti is famous for its wood carvings, using gleaming dark woods, and its gay and radiant paintings. See the best examples in the Musee d'Art Haitien and the Centre d'Art, in Port-au-Prince, then take to the streets. Quaint examples of local art, some good and some execrable, are for sale on every street corner and at the Mahogany Market. Some Haitian art also finds its way onto street stalls throughout the rest of the Antilles.

Cuba, long the inspiration of fine artists, has provided the world with a wealth of beautiful exuberant, colorful paintings. One of the largest collections of pre-Castro art in the world is in the Museum of Arts and Sciences in, of all places, Daytona Beach, Florida.

A museum of folk art has been opened in Santiago de los Caballeros, in the Dominican Republic; works of local artists are displayed in the Museo del

Hombre Dominicano in Santo Domingo.

The Gallery of West Indian Art, in Montego Bay, Jamaica, features the brilliantly colored cedar work of a laundress and self-taught artist named Hyacinth. In Kingston, the National Gallery displays a wealth of native paintings including an especially fine 19th century collection depicting life on the plantations.

Bermudans have long made a specialty of fashioning their native cedar wood into sculptures and furniture. A blight killed the cedar trees in the 1950s, but they are coming back and it is now legal to use the wood again. Cedar carvings, candles, caning, pottery, artwork and doll house furniture made by local craftsmen are sold at the Craft Market at the Royal Naval Dockyard and The Cooperage in Somerset. Hand-blown glass is sold at the artists' studio at Bailey's Bay.

Affluent, art-loving Bermuda has a number of good art galleries and native artists. In the Princess Hotel at Southampton, a gallery showing the bronzes of Desmond Fountain is open daily, and more life-size Fountain sculptures are placed haphazardly around the hotel's pool and grounds. Another one stands on the marketplace at the wharf downtown. His statue of Sir George Somers at Ordnance Island, St. George's, was unveiled by Princess Margaret in 1984.

Local arts and crafts are sold at the Briege House in St. George's, and in the St. George's Historical Society Museum. Carole Holding's studio there served once as the slave quarters of an 18th century home.

The Bermudiana Collection of art is on display at the Masterworks Foundation, above the Britannia Gift Shop in Hamilton. The originals, some of them done by Bermuda visitors 150 years ago, are available as copies in poster, print, or postcard form. The present pieces are just the start of what everyone hopes will become an extensive chronicle of paintings from throughout Bermuda's history.

Galleries in Nassau include the Nassau Art Gallery, which sells originals and prints by Bahamians Elyse and Wayde Taylor. Works of Abaco artist Albert Lowe are sold in a museum and gallery at Green Turtle Cay, and the village also has a fine sculpture garden displaying figures from Bahamian history.

The famous sculptor Randolph Johnston settled at Little Harbour, Abaco, in the 1950s. His bronze honoring the Afro-Bahamian Woman is on display on the waterfront in Nassau. Works by Johnston, his ceramist wife and his sculptor son and daughter-in-law are for sale at Little Harbour and at galleries in Nantucket and Palm Beach. His book, *Artist on His Island*, offers a peek into pioneer life on a remote island in this century. Unlike other sculptors, whose work is cast at foundries, Johnston studied metallurgy and smelting, and completed all stages of his own works, from concept to casting, under the most primitive conditions.

The Crafts Market in Kingston is filled with little stalls and colorful local goods.

If you reach an impasse in the bargaining process (give in early: bargaining is not the blood sport in the English islands that it is in most Spanish and French islands), ask for a *brawda*. That is a bonus, laid on as a final concession. Jamaican handiwork and antiques are also sold at Things Jamaican, at Devon House, which is also located in the city of Kingston.

Jamaica's best artists can exhibit their wares in free space provided for by the Mutual Life Centre. Visitors are admitted as a courtesy – this is a working office – so dress appropriately. For works by the "Jamaican Chagall," Edna Manley, visit the Frame Centre Gallery. Both are in Kingston.

The Galeria Botello in Old San Juan conceals a great wealth of Latin American art. The building was the home of Angel Botella, one of Puerto Rico's best-known artists, who died in 1986. Botella's works are for sale, as are *santos*, the carved wooden saints that are a Puerto Rican craft passed on from father to son.

Above: A Carnival puppet on Trinidad. Right: The Church's velvet glove...

Other authentic Puerto Rican crafts including papier mâché masks are shown at Puerto Rican Arts and Crafts, at 204 Fortaleza, and at the lively La Plaolete del Puerto at Pier 3. Puerto Rico's Fine Arts Museum at 253 Cristo, houses the island's Institute of Culture collection. The building itself, a good example of colonial style, was restored in 1990.

The Dominican Republic has a complete arts community, Altos de Chavon, where artists and craftsmen live, study, work, and sell. For Dominican and Haitian paintings, shop at the Galeria de Arte Nader, in Santo Domingo. At the Galeria de Arte Moderno, displays of modern art by native artists are shown. Reproductions of Taino art are sold at Tu Espacio; Ambar Tres sells hand-made jewelry, including the famous Dominican amber.

Native themes are treated in hand-print cottons throughout the islands, and almost every island group has its own little batik factories and fabric shops. Some are available by the piece or yard; others are made into clothing. One of the most economical ways to add one of these prints to a wardrobe is to buy a simple *java wrap*, which may also be called a *pareu*, *sarong*, or *lava-lava*, depending on where you are.

Overall, one can safely say, the native arts are thriving in the sunny climes of the Caribbean, thanks no doubt in great part to the influx of hard currency from tourism. Governmental support also helps in Jamaica, to cite one example, where the Institute of Jamaica in Kingston draws students from throughout the Caribbean to study music, art, and dance.

Voodoo and other Religions

Rastafarianism, most conspicuous in Jamaica but extant throughout the Antilles, sprang from a Black Nationalist

movement, and a worship of Ethiopian Emperor Haile Selassie. Its adherents eat neither animal products or salt, wear their hair in huge, wild piles of uncut plaits – called dreadlocks – often held together by a pouch-like cap, and smoke marijuana, which they call *ganja*, as a religious ritual. You will see what appear to be Rastafarians, but it is unlikely you will encounter a genuine one unless you head for the hills. *Rastas* shun the materialistic world of "Babylon", so despite the banter about smoke and the locks peeking out beneath a colorful knit Tam O'Shanter, the cab driver or barman you deal with on your travels is not likely to be the real thing.

In Bermuda, you will also see Muslims in flowing robes. Although it is on the wane now, the American-based Muslim movement was once quite strong here.

Two African religions exist in pockets in the Antilles. In *Shango,* an African cult found in Trinidad, the god of thunder and lightning has twelve apostles. *Santeria* is another Afro-Indian cult, based in Cuba. Voodoo, which means deity, was brought from Dahomey in Africa. Although Voodoo and related black magic practices such as Obeah, in Jamaica, are usually associated with Haiti, they appear throughout the Caribbean rim, including the Caribbean shore of Central America. Voodoo practices often include mix with elements of Christianity, especially symbols used in Roman Catholic rituals.

Sanitized versions of Voodoo ceremonies are offered tourists at Haitian hotels, but it is again unlikely that you will observe an authentic ceremony unless you are sponsored by a local friend. Visitors were once welcome at a Voodoo temple at Mariani near Port-au-Prince, but like many of Haiti's tourism features, it is closed during periods of civil unrest, which have unfortunately been more frequent of late than outbreaks of peace.

Like Voodoo, Obeah is a sort of witchcraft that makes use of bad spirits to protect the good and punish the disobedient. Cat Island in the Bahamas is feared by other Bahamians because of its powerful

Obeah; Obeah is also practiced prominently in Jamaica as well as in the Bay Islands off Honduras, in the western Caribbean.

Rather than trying to infiltrate some of these exotic ceremonies, you will get an equally authentic and considerably more mainstream sample of island religious practice by simply showing up for services at any church or synagogue. In most communities the churches and temples are the center of social, religious, political and economic life. No matter what denomination the congregation, the service will undoubtedly be far different from the Lutheran or Baptist or Catholic service you may be familiar with at home. To sit in a crude, windowless, out-island church with dogs asleep under the benches, and sing unaccompanied hymns from a battered hymnal after hearing a thundering sermon by a preacher who works during the week as a common laborer, is to share a rare singular moment with people you will never look upon as strangers again.

Above: The far reaches of the faith in Samana. Right: Nature's small gems.

Going to local churches, dances, charity affairs and other gatherings is one way to get rare insights into local morals and attitudes. Another, strangely enough, is to go to the movies – any movie – and observe where people laugh, where they lose interest in a complicated plot, where they cheer the heros or villains, or where they draw their breath in fear. Observe, too, how they react to commercials, newsreels or patriotic gestures, such as the playing of *God Save the Queen* on British islands, and you will learn volumes about local attitudes. Just one example was a movie that missionaries showed on a small, backward out-island. The plot was about a girl who was led down the primrose path by a slick, handsome stranger. He seduced, then abandoned her. She was left pregnant, alone and disgraced. The islanders, whose views on bearing children out of wedlock are more liberal, were baffled by the girl's dismay. The more she cried and tore her hair, the harder they laughed.

Outsiders can never fully understand the passions of local mores, religions and loyalties because they may go back for centuries to nations and tribes long forgotten. In some countries it may be fun to attend political rallies, sporting events or concerts. Even if you never understand the rules of cricket, you will be intrigued by the powerful emotions this placid game generates in its fans. Go to a soccer match in Jamaica, or watch *el beisbol* in the Dominican Republic. Such journeys offer a glimpse into the depths of passion inherent in those cultures.

The Nature of Things

The sweet, spicy perfume of uninhabited islands floats miles out to sea and promises the traveler a bouquet. A landing may reveal anything from a lush rain forest or a desert-like, featureless scrubland. Part of this diversity results from the soil or lack of it. Another factor is weather, which can be very diverse in this part of the world. Some islands or parts of islands remain desert-dry, the rain clouds always passing them by. On others, tall mountain peaks rarely shed a veil of moist clouds. The name given to Jamaica by the Arawaks, Xaymaca, meant *well watered*. Yet bone-dry Nassau has to import much of its water from nearby Andros. While tourists are sweltering at the sea- shore on Hispaniola or Puerto Rico, people in the cooler uplands only scant miles away are reaching for their sweaters. In Cuba, you can drive from hot to cool in less than an hour. In the higher islands nighttime temperatures can fall as low as 5° C (40° F).

A number of plants are native to the Greater Antilles. Such names as *cassava* and *guava* are in fact Arawak. Long before Columbus came, pineapple was grown by the Caribs, who made their young men run through its knife-life

leaves as a rite of puberty. Only later was pineapple introduced to Hawaii. Still, most of the fruits and flowers we think of as native today actually arrived as shoots and seeds with various waves of settlers. The Spanish brought oranges and sugar cane. Breadfruit, now so important to the West Indian diet, first arrived in Jamaica with Captain Bligh of the famous *Bounty*.

The English had less luck with their native seeds in this hot, often arid country, but they learned to adapt – even if it meant pollinating squash by hand because of the lack of bees. In the Abacos, this is still known today as "marrying the pumpkins".

Most tropical species flourish in the heat and humidity, so all the inhabited islands are a tumble of flashy bougainvillaea, hibiscus, oleander, and poinciana. In the bush, you can find flowering cactus, sweet bay and thousands of other native and naturalized species. In Puerto Rico alone, 3,000 plant species have been identified, including twenty native orchids and 500 ferns. The medicinal bene-

fits of many of these plants – some of them forgotten, some still to be discovered, and many still used in the hinterlands by knowledgeable, but increasingly harder to find, bush doctors – will keep scientists busy for years.

Ships carried rats and cats, while humans brought along boars and donkeys. Descendants of these creatures still live in the bush – sometimes in large herds. Horses, hogs, chickens, goats and cattle were brought to the islands and survived. Many island homes have series of pipes laid across their driveways or entry paths, to keep roving animals out. Humans can step across and cars drive over, but hooves fall through, effectively keeping stray donkeys and cattle away from the house. These same wandering animals also play havoc with drivers' reflexes when they suddenly appear in headlights at the end of a blind curve on a narrow Caribbean road. Mongooses, brought in to control rats and mice, now run wild on many islands. Bats are common, and some islands even boast snakes (such as the fer-de-lance, a kind of rattlesnake), iguanas and scorpions.

Above: El Alcazar in Santo Domingo, an example of Spanish colonial architecture. Right: Clapboard for the poorer folk.

Of course, the most intrusive problem for tourists will likely be insects – mosquitoes, no-see-ums and the occasional flying cockroach in your room. Do not check out of the hotel in a huff. Plan ahead: If you are staying on a boat or in a self-catering unit, add roach powder to your provisions list. One interesting creature, the hutia, an endemic rodent once thought to be extinct, has been rediscovered, to the joy of scientists, still existing on Atwood Cay, in the Bahamas and on Hispaniola. The rabbit-like zaguti can be found occasionally in the wild in the Caymans and Dominican Republic.

Iguanas and nocturnal barking geckos are everywhere, harmless to humans, indeed even welcome because they eat bugs. Singing tree frogs will lull you to sleep in certain parts of Jamaica.

Vast colonies of flamingoes still live at Inagua, and the Bahama parrot is sometimes seen in the wild. And there really is an almost ever-present yellow-bird, immortalized in a calypso song and story.

Architecture

Necessity is not only the mother of invention, but the godmother of Antillean architecture. Early settlers had to build with whatever materials were available and to suit the prevailing climate. In Bermuda and the Bahamas, where winters can be chilly, homes had to be cozy enough during winter winds, yet as breezy as possible to endure the summer sun. In areas where rainfall is scant, inventive systems had to be found to channel and collect every drop of rain that fell on every roof.

Bermuda, blessed with a subsoil layer of sandstone that hardens after it is exposed to the elements, has quarried tons of this stone to build neat and nearly hurricane-proof stone homes and shops. Note the clever design of the water-catching roofs. They are a special Bermuda trademark, and have to be re-limed every five years or less by law. Another familiar Bermuda feature is the *moon gate*, said to be a symbol of good luck for lovers. The perfectly round arches are ideal in design to suit the stones quarried here. Stone mansions and windmills have for centuries been symbolic of St. Croix. After hurricane *Hugo* in 1989, the worst in island history, the circular stone structures remained undamaged while other, more modern buildings were reduced to rubble. Although thatched roofs are disappearing in the Antilles, except on beach shelters, they are works of art. A closer examination of these apparently simple coverings reveals the amount of work and poetry woven into them.

Many fine wooden homes are still found in some areas. They are built of the more durable heart pine, mahogany, lignum vitae and other native, termite and rot resistant woods, many of them depleted long ago.

The Greater Antilles, home of some of the most simple and practical architecture, also contains some of the largest and most spectacular structures in the West Indies. The Renaissance Cathedral of Santa Maria La Menor, for example, was built in Santo Domingo in the 16th century. The Alcazar, close by, built in 1514 and furnished now as it was then, is a splendid sample of old Spanish architecture. Other samples and fragments of old Spanish and Spanish-Moorish design are situated in Old San Juan, in the familiar minaret-clad forts of Puerto Rico and in Old Havana. It is fun to wander entire blocks of old streets that have been turned into tourist shopping areas, noting little architectural details such as the lancet doorways in Charlotte Amalie and the colonnaded walkways in Chistiansted.

Beyond the neon, flashy window displays and tacky T-shirts, an eloquent historical and social tale unfolds in tiny alleyways, unique doorways, wrought-iron gates and tortuous old cobblestone or brick streets. By observing types of architecture in your Antillean travels, you will see how they reflect every wave or whim that came from European homelands, from the Gothic-style cathedrals of Cuba and Hispaniola to massive, 16th and 17th century stone forts with their then state-of-the-art defenses, to pompous Victorian, to comfortable Georgian, to utilitarian Bauhaus.

Above: A hospitable gesture in the Dominican Republic. Right: A show on Cuba – you sip rum, he takes in petrol and spits fire.

Tourist Taboos

Although most of the Caribbean is highly advanced and its people well accustomed to overseas visitors, your stay will be more pleasant for you, for locals and for the next visitors if certain courtesies are observed. In general, West Indians are modest in their dress, and they are offended by miniature shorts and bra tops, or even bare midriffs, in town. Except in the more Americanized resort areas, local women rarely wear slacks and almost never wear shorts. Topless bathing is common in a few areas, but it is offensive on many islands and even illegal on some. Bermuda's dress code is particularly strait-laced. Get advice from your innkeeper before venturing out in tiny shorts or a sleeveless T-shirt. Do not wear hair curlers in public, ride a scooter or bike without a shirt, or wear Bermuda shorts to a formal affair unless you wear knee socks with them (Just remember how the movies depict the British military in the colonies).

You should be sensitive about pointing the camera. Bahamians in the out-islands love to have their photos taken but they want to be pictured in their Sunday best. Like most of us, they may not appreciate being photographed in their work clothes. Haitians, Turks and Caicos Islanders and St. Lucians are among those who hide from the camera, but you could encounter such feelings almost anywhere. Even on modern, sophisticated St. Croix, fishermen at the Fredricksted docks dislike having their pictures taken. Everywhere people ask for payment to have their photo taken. If you take an instant camera and give persons photos of themselves or their family, they are usually more agreeable about letting you take the next shots the camera of your choice. Be forewarned, though, that lines may form when you start giving away Polaroid shots. To make your film go a long way, group families together. A good place to get such photos is at a church after Sunday services.

The word *boy* may be insulting to certain black West Indians, who could associate the name with a time when colonial masters used the term. Americans, whose speech is sprinkled with the innocent *Oh, boy*, or *Boy, it's hot*, might offend without intending to. To call a person a *native* may also be taken as an insult. A few other language differences apply. In Puerto Rico, a *motel* is a place

where lovers meet secretly. Do not ask for a motel unless you are willing to pay by the hour. A discothèque is a nightclub, which may or may not be a disco.

As for the prolific numbers of small business persons throughout the islands, straw market matrons have become strident and rude in many areas, and they tend to become increasingly miffed if you linger without buying. It is best not to touch an item unless you are a serious shopper, and do not bargain too hard if you do not intend to buy. Haggling, by the way, is bad form in Bermuda, permitted up to a point in the British islands, and a national sport in most others.

Souvenir markets are for tourists, but it may be unbecoming to get in the way at those markets that are run by and for local people. Keep in mind that many of these islanders have carried a hard-earned crop or catch some distance to town, with the hope of selling it quickly to local housewives. To you, it may be quaint and colorful but to these people it is a serious livelihood.

Drugs

Officially, drugs are illegal throughout the Greater Antilles, so do not be misled by the fairly easy availability of locally grown marijuana, as well as an increasing array of imported substances in some areas. It is one thing to get busted in your homeland, and another to be arrested in a foreign country. At best, an arrest will be expensive, will ruin your holiday, and can delay your trip home. At worst, it can land you in a very unpleasant prison, administered under local law and well out of reach of any constitutional guarantees that apply in your home country. So, if sunshine is not enough to raise your spirits, just stick to local rum – it is good and legal! If you take prescription drugs, carry them in their original drugstore container showing the RX number, and bring a written prescription as a precaution. You may have to produce it for customs authorities or local law enforcement personnel. Firearms are also strictly taboo in most of the West Indies, and to bring so much as a spear gun, a bullet, or a part of a gun into Bermuda is illegal.

Above: Drugs, a dangerous form of hospitality. Right: No idle boast in Negril, Jamaica.

Fairy Tales and Legends

One of the largest land masses in the Bahamas is the swampy, sparsely inhabited island of Andros. It is here that the mischievous chickcharnies lurk, causing trouble for the unwary. They have three toes, red eyes, three fingers, and a body like a bird. If something goes inexplicably awry, as it so often seems to do in the easy-going tropics, you know you have seen chickcharnies at work.

They are pussycats, however, compared to the terrors of Voodoo. Naughty children can be kept in line by the threat of the *loup-garou*, the werewolf, who can leave his body at night and suck the blood of humans. And he likes children's blood best of all.

One of the world's great horror stories is that of the Bermuda Triangle. When one starts delving into it, it proves elusive. Almost everyone imagines that it includes Bermuda, the Bahamas and unspecified chunks of the Caribbean, but when sensationalist writers start cataloguing all the disasters caused by the curse of the region, they stretch the boundaries to include every ship wreck, murder and hangnail in the western hemisphere. Some believe the story has been put straight in *The Bermuda Triangle Mystery Solved,* by Lawrence D. Kausche, New York, in 1975.

Carnival!

A yearly festival of some sort is an integral part of Greater Antillean culture, but do not expect every island to celebrate in the same way, or even at the same time. What they have in common is that they are riotous street parties, elaborately

costumed, loud as a cannon shot, and as easy to slip into as an old shoe. Strip off your inhibitions and wade right in is the order of the day.

In many islands, especially those with a strong Catholic heritage, the big street carnival is a Mardi Gras-type festival just before Lent. It is as frenzied as Lent is solemn, and in most islands it is held in every village, not just in the capital.

In the Bahamas, where it is called *Junkanoo*, and Bermuda, where it is called *Gombey*, carnival is at Christmas and New Year. Bermudans also have *Gombey* on Easter Monday. People take to the streets in colorful costumes and run happily amok for hours.

In San Juan, carnivals mark the *Feast of San Juan Bautista* in June, with ten days of street parties, parades and contests. The big event in the U.S. Virgin Islands is the *Crucian Christmas Fiesta,* featuring *Mocko Jumbi*, a 6-m (20-ft) stilt-walker.

Other folk events have been especially created for the tourist trade, but many of them have developed into important cultural contributions. On seeing that their songs or crafts or dances impress outsiders, islanders take renewed interest in their heritage. Such events as the *LeLoLai Festival* in Puerto Rico, based on the ancient *Jibaro* festival, and *Goombay Summer*, in the Bahamas, are well worth attending.

Libraries

Important libraries for students, or for those whose vacation would be incomplete without a browse among the bookshelves, include: The Archives and General Library, San Juan, housed in a constructure built as a prison in 1877. Collections include important books and documents from island history and works of Eugenio Maria de Hostos, one of Puerto Rico's great writers. Casa del Libro in San Juan is devoted to printing and bookmaking. Rare books include some from the 16th century. Luis Munoz Marin Archives, University of Puerto

Rico, in Rio Peidras, is devoted to the speeches, letters and papers of the island's famous journalist-statesman. The National Library of the Dominican Republic is located in the Plaza de la Cultura in Santo Domingo. The National Library of Jamaica in Kingston is tops for West Indian studies.

Hurricane Season

The Arawaks called the summer wind the *uracana*. Hurricanes, an annual threat but only rarely a reality in any given spot, are nevertheless a subtle and dreaded leitmotif that threads through Antilles life much as the death theme recurs in the opera *Carmen*. They are the warp and woof of island culture as you would expect of storms packing winds of 300 kmh (200 mph). Higher winds have been reported, although often the anemometer breaks before peak winds are reached, and few have ever ventured out to measure the wind in a drowning rain that may drop as much as 1-5 cm (3 in) in an hour, for hours on end. In a 1909 hurricane, Jamaica received 337 cm (135 in) of rain in a week, more than most islands get in a year.

An awesome loss of life and property results, when a hurricane also spawns tornadoes. Almost every island has been damaged at one time. Entire farms and villages have been wiped off the map forever, harbors filled in, and new sea routes opened. No one who has not seen a major hurricane can conceive of the unworldly fury they can unleash.

Here are just a few examples. In 1852, Rum Cay, in the Bahamas, had a thriving salt industry. It was destroyed by a hurricane in 1903 and any attempt at recovery was stopped by another hurricane in 1926. By 1970, only 70 people lived on an island that once had a population of 3,000.

Right: Security is a Havana cigar, even on a precarious ladder.

The little island of Cayman Brac was swept so clean of identifying buildings and trees in the 1932 hurricane that people who survived the storm could not even tell where their own homes and farms had been. A hurricane destroyed the sugar cane crop on St. John and the industry never recovered.

It was not until recent years that people throughout the Caribbean could count on reliable weather forecasts. In fact, many did not even understand the nature of hurricanes. People at the Brac did not know that a second storm, perhaps worse than the first, would occur after the eye of the hurricane passed. When calm came, they left the caves where they had taken shelter, just in time to confront the second wave. Many died.

Modern communications were slow to come to the remote Turks and Caicos Islands. One hurricane in this century caught most of the men fishing at sea. An entire generation of women and children were left alone. Bermuda owes its settlement to a severe storm. Records do not show whether it was a full-blown hurricane, but it was enough to shipwreck an expedition that was en route to Virginia.

Hurricane *Hugo* ravaged Montserrat and the Virgin Islands in 1989. Within nine months, a generation of so-called storm babies were being born there. Amid devastation and death, even the most modern young islanders admit that somehow they felt compelled to reaffirm life by adding a new one to their families. And these cataclysms are never referred to as, say, "the 1932 Hurricane" or "Hurricane David". It is always "The Storm". Decades later, a date will be stated as "I was married two years after 'The Storm'", or "After 'The Storm' I went to the States to pick apples". This reveals both the singular power and infrequency of hurricanes. The storm season comes and goes, but tourism remains a year-round pleasure. Go and enjoy, but keep an eye on the barometer.

UPER COLM
HAY PARA TODOS

ADO RUIZ
DISTRIBUIDOR
AGUA
Sultana
PURA, FRESCA, CONFIABLE.
"EL AGUA MACORISANA"

BERMUDA

Bermuda is one of those islands that rank pretty high on the paradise quotient. The beaches are pristine and pink, a by-product of the coral reef foundation of the island. The vegetation is tropically lush, with explosions of color variegating the green hills by day and sweet scents of hibiscus and frangipani filling the air at night. The sky always seems blue, with just enough puffy cloud formation to make it interesting, but not enough to block out the sunshine for long. There are no rainy seasons here; just periodic rain showers that move swiftly by. The tidy houses, or in some cases mansions, are painted in vibrant pastels and topped with sparkling white roofs cut in geometric slopes to catch whatever rain does fall. Due to careful upkeep, the streets are as clean as the beaches.

Apart from all the physical beauty, though, is the basic attitude of the place. As a British island, Bermuda exhibits the emphasis on proper behavior and manners that one might expect in the United Kingdom. The people are soft-spoken and unfailingly polite, although they might subtly raise an eyebrow as hordes of tourists disembark from the cruise ships that dock on Front Street in Hamilton – the main drag in the main town – but they would not dream of ever saying anything untoward. Besides, as they well know, without the tourists, Bermuda would not be the financial power that it has become.

Preceding pages: Life goes on; wild masks of Gombey dancers. Left: Rastafarians have spread even to Bermuda.

Because of these factors – a robust economy and high standard of living, one of the highest in the world, in fact – Bermuda officials are very discriminating about visitors to the country. They do not particularly want residents from other countries, notably their poorer neighbors farther down in the Caribbean, coming in, staying and taking Bermudan jobs, or coming here and then not getting jobs and becoming a drain on the economy. So they make sure that if you are coming in, you are also well-prepared for leaving. This is one of the few countries in the world where immigration officials demand to see your return ticket before they will stamp your passport, and if you cannot show it, you are not getting in. They will also keep track of you once they have let you in. In one recent case, whispered about by the locals, an American woman decided to stay on months after her designated departure date and was arrested and forcibly sent home. Sometimes, if they deem it necessary, Ber-

mudans waive their manners, it seems. Residents, however, do not see such actions as a lapse of manners; they see them as a special form of protection for their very special island. Visitors, many of whom have been here before, invariably agree.

Origins

The earliest known visitor to Bermuda swept by in 1503, but he did not stay around too long. The Spanish explorer Juan de Bermudez had other things on his mind – primarily leaving the sometimes stormy Atlantic Ocean and sailing to the placid Caribbean Sea – so he simply discovered the place and stayed the course. Another reason for his swift retreat was that he considered the reef-laden island inhospitable and called it the *Isle of the Devils*, believing it to be inhabited by evil spirits who lured ships to their demise.

Above: Detail on the Somerset Cricket Club.
Right: Need anymore be said?

Given the number of ships that actually met their sad ends here, he was not necessarily wrong in his pessimistic view.

Forty years later, someone with the initials T.F. carved them on a rock and disappeared without ever revealing the rest of his identity. Fifty years after that, a British captain named Henry May was ship-wrecked here. He described his adventures in great detail when he finally returned to England.

The line of shipwrecks continued into the 1600s – with important results. One large vessel, the *Sea Venture*, setting sail from England in 1609 and bound for the Jamestown settlement in the colony of Virginia, ran into a hurricane and smashed against a reef on the eastern end of Bermuda. All 150 passengers survived and were transferred to the island where they lived for a year while two other boats were built. In May 1610 the passengers boarded the new vessels to continue their journey to Virginia.

Two men, however, elected to stay behind, but as it turned out, not for long.

When the original party reached Jamestown several weeks later and found the population starving, they quickly hightailed it back to balmy Bermuda. The admiral, Sir George Somers, died of exhaustion shortly afterward, however. His nephew, Matthew Somers, brought the body back to England for burial. In what could be seen as macabre, but was meant to be a sentimental tribute, Sir George's heart was buried separately in Bermuda, near where he had landed. He was thus able, at least in death, to defy the laws of physics by being in two places at once.

While Matthew was in England, burying the bulk of Uncle George, he recounted his experiences on the island. Suddenly, this ever so distant spot became all the rage. Two years later, another batch of Britains arrived, this time intentionally, at the eastern end of the island and founded the town of St. George, named after Sir George Somers and Saint George, the patron saint of England. It remained the capital for 203 years.

They also set about carving the island up. By 1616, the 57-sq km (22-sq mi) collection of islands was divided into eight parishes, each named after a member of the company that had funded the expedition. These names remain: Sandys, Southampton, Warwick, Paget, Pembroke, Devonshire, Smith's and Hamilton were the original parishes; St. George's was added later.

In 1620, having built bridges, churches and government buildings, the Bermudans convened their first Parliament in St. Peter's Church. Within 30 years, the obviously restless residents started branching out to other islands. In 1649, a group of Bermudans colonized the Bahamian island of Eleuthera. In 1668, others formed a colony on Turks Island, in the Turks and Caicos Islands, south of the Bahamas.

In 1684, Bermuda solidified its identity as a British Colony with the right to

self-government and concentrated its efforts on the economy. Shipbuilding became a major industry as did trading. Piracy, however, seemed to be their strongest suit with a continuous supply of ships beaching on reefs, and providing a steady source of income. Because of this emphasis, however, they let another priority slip, namely agriculture. Lacking their own food sources, they were forced into dependency on their American neighbors for imports – a relationship that was to deepen as time went on. During the American Revolutionary War, that relationship caused immense dissension in many families as islanders split between colonial solidarity and loyalty to Mother England. Food was more important than bloodlines, however, and the Bermudans in several dramatic ways threw their support behind the colonists. In one case, after George Washington wrote to the island's citizens asking for gunpowder in exchange for continuation of friendly relations, several citizens slipped bags of the stuff onto two Ameri-

can warships anchored outside St. George's harbor. The governor was not exactly pleased by the action but as a result, Bermuda's food supply went as uninterrupted for the duration of the war. The balance evened out during the next American conflict. In the War of 1812, Bermuda toed the British line, serving as a Royal Navy base and storage port for captured American ships.

During the American Civil War, the islanders once again took sides. Perhaps due more to location or economic opportunity than anything else, Bermudans sided with the Southern Confederacy and became a transfer point for Southern trade. By running blockades, they provided the South with guns in exchange for Southern cotton, which was delivered to desperate European consumers. As a result, the island's economy flourished temporarily, but by the end of the war, with unsold goods stuck in warehouses, the islanders were deeply in debt.

Above: The British face of Bermuda. Right: One of the Moon Gates in Hamilton, a bit of modern design.

Twenty years later, the economic climate improved with the birth of tourism as a serious business. Today it is still the island's paramount industry. One of the earliest tourists was Princess Louise, daughter of Queen Victoria and wife of Canada's governor-general. She came down in the winter of 1883 to escape Canada's ferocious weather and started a burgeoning trend.

Until trade and travel restrictions wrought by World War II curtailed civilian travel, Bermuda was a fashionable winter haven for members of high society who would venture down with steamer trunks and compliant servants to play endless games of croquet on the acres of lush, green lawns.

During World War II, everyone, including the islanders, had more serious things on their minds. Once again, Bermudans found themselves playing a part in a war. This time, though, the role was more cloak and dagger, as a base for

code-breaking and spycatching between the United States and Europe. Numerous coded messages and stolen masterpieces were stopped and their carriers captured. To thank the interceptors, Winston Churchill visited the island in 1942 and was so impressed by it that he recommended it as a location for summits of world leaders. To date, it has served that function five times, involving American presidents from Eisenhower to Bush, as well as states persons from all around the globe.

Tourism also returned after the end of the war, but its tone diminished somewhat from its erstwhile lofty heights. Cruise ships began bringing passengers other than society swells, and the season expanded – no longer did visitors come only in the winter with their servants; they came on their own year-round. Now, visitors clog the island in summer. Winter is less busy and may be a good time to visit, especially because lower prices make this otherwise expensive island more attractive.

Touring Bermuda

The first information that any prospective visitor to Bermuda needs to know is where, exactly, the island is located. A surprisingly large number of people have no idea. Most assume it is deep in the Caribbean, another one of the rum and sunshine islands, perhaps an offshoot of Puerto Rico or Jamaica.

In truth, the group of 150 islands, linked together by bridges, that form what is known as Bermuda, is not even in the Caribbean at all. It is north of it, in the Atlantic Ocean, about 812 km (508 mi) east of Cape Hatteras, North Carolina. As a result, traveling from the U.S. is easy. It is only about an hour-and-a-half flight from the major cities of the East Coast. Flying from Europe is a bit trickier, since the British tend to control the routes, requiring connections through Britain. But the evidence is that with 1992 and the gala commemorating the 500th anniversary of Columbus' discovery of the New World, other European routes will open

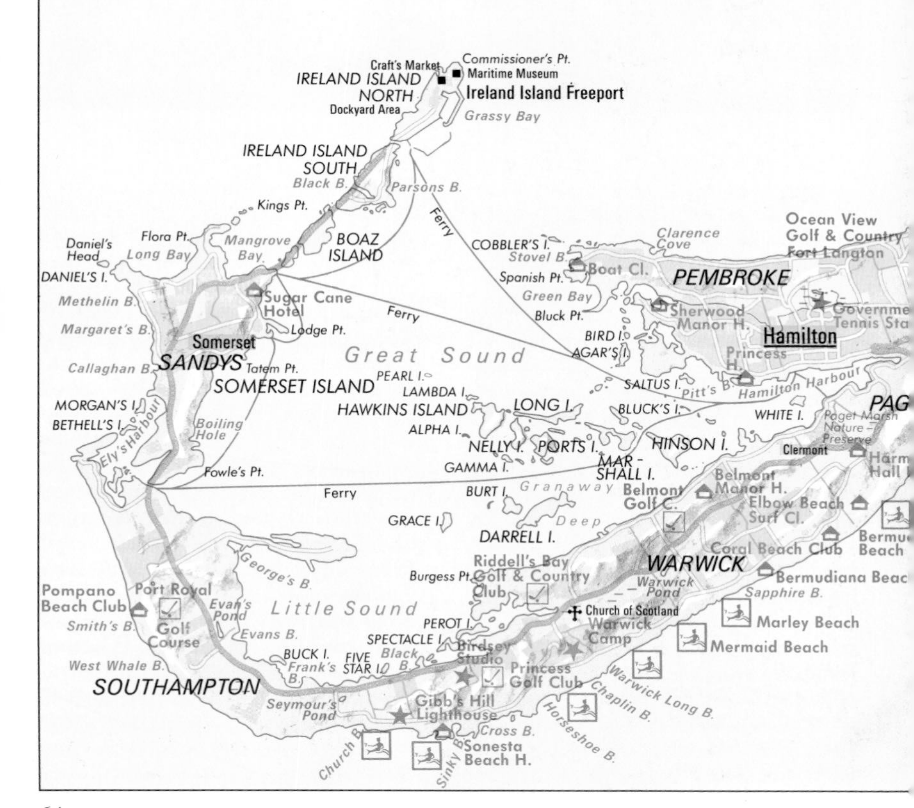
NORTH
ATLANTIC OCEAN
Craft's Market
Commissioner's Pt.
Maritime Museum
IRELAND ISLAND NORTH
Ireland Island Freeport
Dockyard Area
Grassy Bay
IRELAND ISLAND SOUTH
Black B.
Parsons B.
Kings Pt.
Ferry
Daniel's Head
Flora Pt.
Long Bay
Mangrove Bay
BOAZ ISLAND
COBBLER'S I.
Stovel B.
Clarence Cove
Ocean View Golf & Country
Fort Langton
DANIEL'S I.
Boat Cl.
Spanish Pt.
PEMBROKE
Methelin B.
Sugar Cane Hotel
Ferry
Green Bay
Bluck Pt.
Sherwood Manor H.
Margaret's B.
Lodge Pt.
Somerset
BIRD I.
AGAR'S I.
Hamilton
Princess H.
SANDYS
Callaghan B.
Tatem Pt.
Great Sound
SOMERSET ISLAND
PEARL I.
LAMBDA I.
SALTUS I.
Pitt's B.
Hamilton Harbour
MORGAN'S I.
BETHELL'S I.
HAWKINS ISLAND
LONG I.
BLUCK'S I.
WHITE I.
Paget Marsh Nature Preserve
Boiling Hole
ALPHA I.
Ely's Harbour
NELLY I.
PORTS I.
HINSON I.
Clermont
Fowle's Pt.
GAMMA I.
MARSHALL I.
Belmont Manor H.
Ferry
BURT I.
Granaway Deep
Belmont Golf C.
Elbow Beach Surf Cl.
GRACE I.
DARRELL I.
Riddell's Bay Golf & Country Club
Coral Beach Club
George's B.
Burgess Pt.
WARWICK
Bermudiana Beac
Pompano Beach Club
Port Royal
Warwick Pond
Sapphire B.
Evan's Pond
Little Sound
Church of Scotland
Smith's B.
Golf Course
Evans B.
PEROT I.
Warwick Camp
Marley Beach
SPECTACLE I.
Mermaid Beach
BUCK I.
FIVE STAR I.
Black B.
Birdsey Studio
West Whale B.
Frank's B.
Princess Golf Club
Warwick Long B.
SOUTHAMPTON
Chaplin B.
Seymour's Pond
Gibb's Hill Lighthouse
Horseshoe B.
Cross B.
Church B.
Sinky B.
Sonesta Beach H.

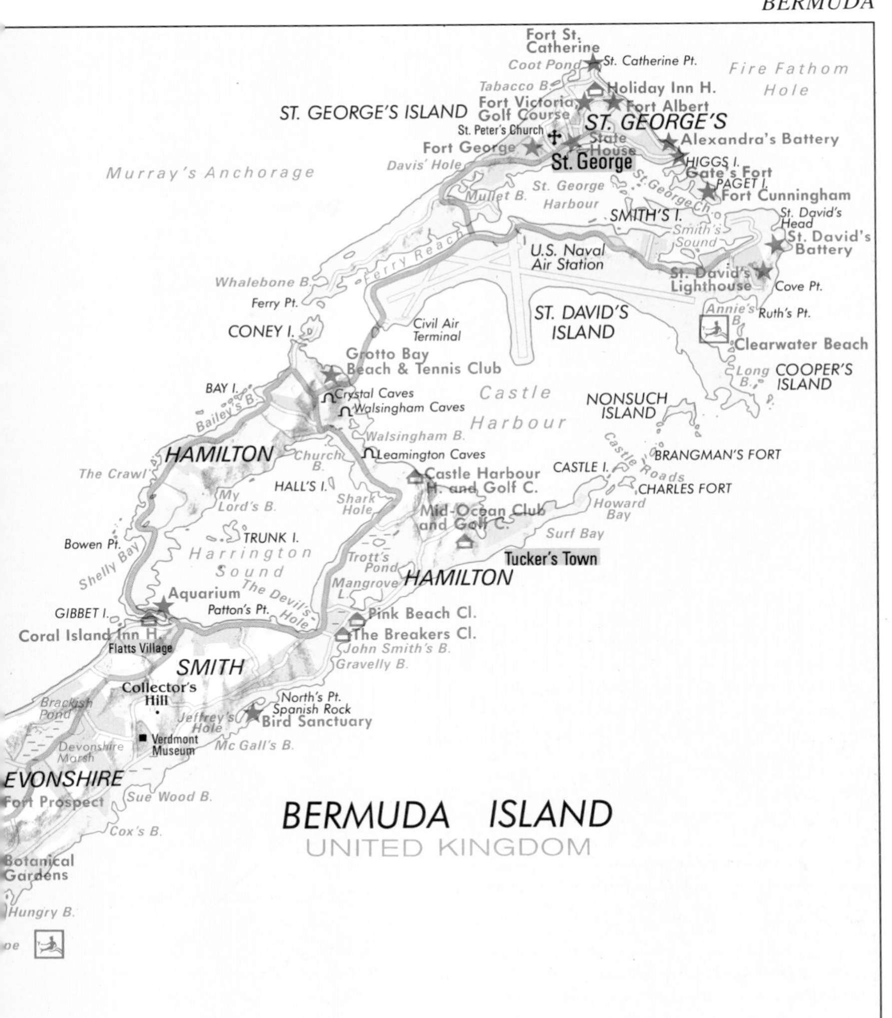
Fort St. Catherine
Coot Pond
St. Catherine Pt.
Fire Fathom Hole
Tabacco B.
Holiday Inn H.
Fort Victoria
Golf Course
Fort Albert
ST. GEORGE'S ISLAND
ST. GEORGE'S
St. Peter's Church
State House
Alexandra's Battery
Fort George
St. George
Davis' Hole
HIGGS I.
Gate's Fort
PAGET I.
Fort Cunningham
Murray's Anchorage
Mullet B.
St. George Harbour
St. George Ch.
SMITH'S I.
St. David's Head
Smith's Sound
St. David's Battery
Ferry Reach
U.S. Naval Air Station
St. David's Lighthouse
Cove Pt.
Whalebone B.
Ferry Pt.
Annie's B.
Ruth's Pt.
ST. DAVID'S ISLAND
CONEY I.
Civil Air Terminal
Clearwater Beach
Grotto Bay Beach & Tennis Club
Long B.
COOPER'S ISLAND
BAY I.
Crystal Caves
Castle Harbour
NONSUCH ISLAND
Bailey's B.
Walsingham Caves
Walsingham B.
BRANGMAN'S FORT
HAMILTON
Church B.
Leamington Caves
Castle Roads
The Crawl
CASTLE I.
Castle Harbour H. and Golf C.
HALL'S I.
CHARLES FORT
My Lord's B.
Shark Hole
Howard Bay
Mid-Ocean Club and Golf C.
Surf Bay
TRUNK I.
Bowen Pt.
Harrington Sound
Tucker's Town
Shelly Bay
Trott's Pond
Mangrove L.
HAMILTON
Aquarium
The Devil's Hole
GIBBET I.
Patton's Pt.
Pink Beach Cl.
Coral Island Inn H.
The Breakers Cl.
Flatts Village
John Smith's B.
SMITH
Gravelly B.
Collector's Hill
North's Pt.
Spanish Rock
Bird Sanctuary
Brackish Pond
Jeffrey's Hole
Verdmont Museum
Devonshire Marsh
Mc Gall's B.
EVONSHIRE
Fort Prospect
Sue Wood B.
BERMUDA ISLAND
UNITED KINGDOM
Cox's B.
Botanical Gardens
Hungry B.
BERMUDA ISLAND
0 3 km
0 2 miles

up to satisfy the increasing supply of celebratory travelers.

Traveling around Bermuda is also, at the moment, restricted, and there is no evidence that it will open up at all. Because of the small land mass of the island, the number of cars is kept to a minimum – one to a family, none for visitors to rent. What visitors usually do is rent mopeds – a fun but sometimes dangerous mode of transit. Every season brings a number of incidents of unaccustomed tourists getting into scrapes on these bikes. But there are several options to doing it yourself. One quaint, if expensive alternative, is a horse-drawn carriage called the Bermuda buggy ride. The carriages cluster near the cruise-ship dock on Front Street in Hamilton and are a fun way to do a bit of leisurely old-fashioned sightseeing. As for public transit, buses cover the major routes and are priced according to the number of zones traveled. A typical fare is only $1 or $2. The buses conveniently serve as sightseeing vehicles as well as transportation.

Above: Where sloops once foundered. Right: An archaic remain in St. George.

Taxis are metered and fares are somewhat expensive given the relatively short distances traveled. But drivers tend to be courteous and very enlightening on island information. Beware, however, of gypsy cabs – drivers turning their regular cars into cabs. It is illegal to do this and the trips are invariably more expensive than in metered cabs.

Ferries are another option. The best transportation around the island has got to be the ferries – they are worth taking even if you do not particularly need to go where they are going. Inexpensive – the longest haul, from Somerset to Hamilton costs $2 – and scenic, they are the most relaxing method of exploring the island. And, best of all, there is never any nerve-wracking traffic to get stuck in.

Sandys Parish on the west side of the island, was named after one of the large shareholders of the original Bermuda Company, but is more frequently referred to as **Somerset**, after its main town. Things are usually pretty quiet out here, but lately the development of the **Dockyard Area** has been bringing tourists west from the main towns of Hamilton and St. George. The area is instantly recognizable by the commanding stone walls. A fortress was built here by convicts over a century ago, when Bermuda was aiding the British in the war of 1812. The burning of Washington, D.C. was launched from the island; the residents obviously wanted necessary protection from angered Americans.

Over the years, though, the dockyard fell out of use and into disrepair. Finally, in 1975, the buildings were restored and redesignated as the **Maritime Museum**. It is a museum that really feels like a seagoing vessel due to its authentic contents, among them salvaged artifacts from the *Sea Venture*, the ship that carried the first settlers to Bermuda.

Southampton Parish is located just south of Sandys. It is a long, thin stretch of land with a great landscape – views of both the north and south shores, exhibiting choice coastal scenery: rolling surf, craggy rocks, softly multicolored sands. This is definitely beach territory, with **Horseshoe Bay** parading the most beautiful and famous specimens. Snorkeling is a prime activity in this area because of the clear water and wide assortment of coral. A good spot to try is **Church Bay**.

Warwick Parish was named after another major shareholder in the original Bermuda Company and seems to have everything – beautiful beaches, hotels, golf courses, even the oldest Church of Scotland outside of Scotland. The parish is also home to **Warwick Camp**, the barracks of the British army during the two world wars and currently bivouacked here for the voluntary Bermuda army. This accounts for the incongruous sounds of gunfire in the peaceful air.

Paget Parish has its share of charming beaches and more than its share of historic homes, as well as homes in general, due to its proximity to the main town of Hamilton. Natural wonders abound as well in the large **Botanical Gardens** and **Paget Marsh Nature Preserve.** Perhaps Paget's greatest contribution is in the world of tennis, however. The first tennis court on the island was built in 1873 in this very parish, on the grounds of the historic house of Clermont, by a tennis-loving family, the Grays. A guest of the house named Mary Outerbridge, played there and was so taken with the game that she brought a rule book and tennis gear back to New York, where the game was officially introduced in 1874.

Pembroke Parish: The centerpiece of this parish is undoubtedly **Hamilton**, the capital of the island and one of the most photogenic cities around. Pastel-colored shops line the main street, known as **Front Street**. Other charming touches include the birdcage, a wire traffic cage in which a policeman wearing the famed Bermuda shorts directs traffic, and the horse-drawn carriages parked near the overhanging trees. One spot that is both practical and historic is the **Perot Post Office** on Queen Street. This pretty white building was part of an estate built by the father of William Bennett Perot, Hamilton's first postmaster. Perot invented the postage stamp here at a friend's suggestion, because residents would come to the post office after hours and leave letters to be mailed without the proper fees.

Near the post office are the government buildings: **City Hall**, on Church Street, complete with its weathervane in the shape of the *Sea Venture*, the ship that brought the first settlers to Bermuda; the pink **Sessions House**, where the Assembly meets, and the limestone **Cabinet Building**, on Parliament Street; and finally the former **Town Hall** on Front Street, now home of the Supreme Court. Because of the concentration of shops and restaurants on Front Street, visitors could be excused for not making it all the way down to the Court building. But they should give it a try; the Chief Justice and barristers wear the traditional British wig and black robes and there is space in the galleries for visitors. Anyone who has not seen an English court in session would definitely find it enlightening.

Towards the other end of Front Street, near the Visitor's Service Bureau and the dock for local ferries, is the **Royal Bermuda Yacht Club**, an organization begun in 1844 by sailing buffs, that still attracts avid sailors. It sponsors the Newport to Bermuda yacht race that takes place with great fanfare every other year.

Farther down the road is a pink palace, the **Princess Hotel**, the first luxury hotel on the island, and **Pitt's Bay**, a protected anchorage for small boats and a residential section of historic, postcard-perfect homes.

At the end of the parish is **Spanish Point**, a rocky, isolated stretch where a group from the *Sea Venture* discovered evidence that Spanish explorers had been to the island before them.

Devonshire Parish: Travelers have often compared this part of Bermuda to England – the rocky cliffs look the same, so does the countryside, all lush, green and hilly. There is not a great deal of development in this section, merely an 18th century church, a cottage colony and a few housekeeping apartments. Notable are the marshlands, including **Devonshire Marsh**, an area usually referred to as Brackish Pond by the locals. In fact, the whole area was once known as Brackish Pond. It is prettier, though, than that unfortunate name would suggest.

Smith's Parish boasts a few points of particular interest to the sightseer. **Flatts Village** is charming – a small, old-fashioned village with views of Harrington Sound – but the old Flatts would have been the one to see. In the 17th and 18th centuries, this was a hangout for smugglers; ships would pull in in the dead of night to stash their goods before heading on to the customs inspectors at St. George's.

Along **South Shore Road**, past **John Smith's Bay**, is another point of interest, **Spanish Rock**. The real rock is not there anymore. What is there is a metal cast of it, but the controversy that it inspired lives on. Early settlers found the inscription "T.F." and the date 1543, an inscription some feel was made by the Spanish explorer Theodore Fernando Camelo. Others believe the inscription was left by Portuguese explorers.

Farther down South Shore Road is one of the treasures of the National Trust, **Verdmont**, a 17th century Bermuda mansion. Built by Captain William Sayle, a colorful local character and three times governor of the island, it is a handsome house filled with Bermudan and English antiques. Take special note of a china coffee service in the upstairs parlor; it was reportedly a gift from Napoleon to George Washington that never made it to the colonies because the ship transporting it was seized and brought here. The

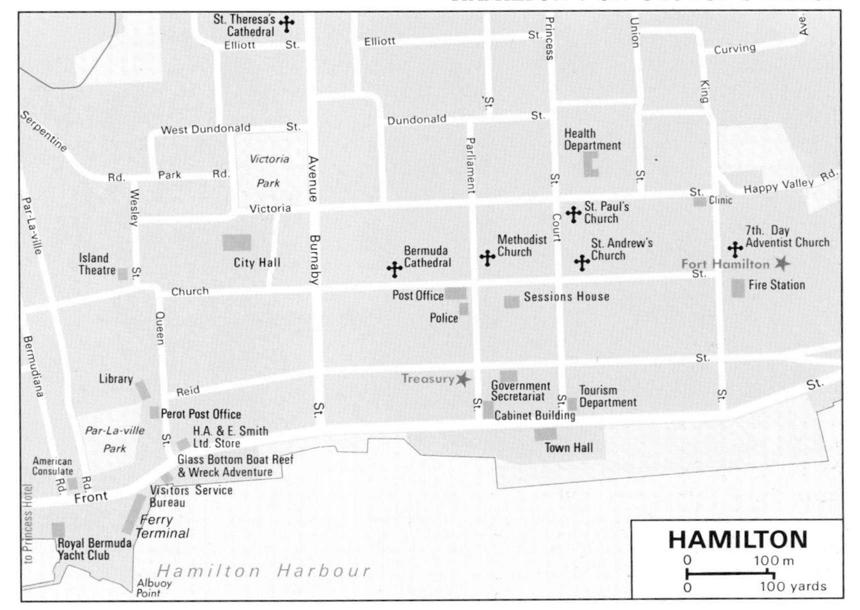

coffee service was later sold at an auction and then donated to this museum by the descendants of the original buyer.

In **Hamilton Parish**, the natural attractions take center stage. Between **Bailey's Bay** and **Castle Harbour** are a proliferation of caves. **Leamington Cave** and **Crystal Cave** are open to the public, with footbridges crossing the subterranean lakes and spotlights on the stalagmites and stalactites. Two more caves, **Cathedral Cave** and **Prospero's Cave** are located in the grounds of the Grotto Bay Beach and Tennis Club. One has to explore on hands and knees in the former, whereas the latter has been transformed into an underground nightclub.

St. George's Parish is the home of the old capital of the island. It is still the most charming town with a pretty town square, the old **State House**, the oldest building, (circa 1620) in Bermuda, narrow, winding streets, historic houses and **St. Peter's Church**, the oldest continually used Protestant church in the western hemisphere. The town square, **King's Square**, is the focal point and the residents do lay it on a bit thickly here for the tourists. A town crier in traditional garb distributes business cards that say "Town Crier", locks miscreants in the stocks and pillory and dunks the truly wicked. It sounds kitschy, but most visitors seem to love the good-humored intention.

There is also great shopping in St. George's, with many branches of Hamilton stores and homegrown stores carrying many exclusive imported goods from around the world.

Sports

Because of its climate – officially subtropical with extremely hot summers and temperate winters that can still be decidedly cool and damp on certain days – Bermuda has sports for all seasons. In the fall and winter, when swimming really is out of the question, sportive types head for the links – the golfing is excellent here. The island's most famous course, the **Mid-Ocean Club**, in the posh

Tucker's Town section of Hamilton Parish, may be the toughest course. It is also a private one, but an introduction by a member is possible. Ask at your hotel, or phone 293-0330. Also worth trying if you can get an introduction is the private **Riddell's Bay Golf & Country Club**, in Southampton Parish. Phone 238-1060 for information.

Public courses much beloved by golfers include the **Castle Harbour Golf Club**, also in Tucker's Town, Hamilton Parish. Phone 293-8161 for information. The **Belmont Hotel Golf and Country Club**, in Warwick, has quite a good reputation amongst aficionados. Phone 236-1301 for information. The **Ocean View Golf & Country Club**, in Devonshire, has a loyal following. Phone 236-6758. And the **Port Royal Golf Course**, in Southampton, 234-0974; the **Princess Golf Club**, also in Southampton, 238-0446; as well as the **St. George's Golf Club**, in St. George's Parish, 297-8067, are all highly esteemed by golfers from all over the world.

Above: Golfing attracts many visitors to Bermuda. Right: Another way of shouldering the heavy load.

Tennis is also popular on those cooler days of the year. Most of the larger hotels have courts or access to them. Another option is to reserve a court at the **Government Tennis Stadium**, off Cedar Avenue, in Pembroke. There are eight courts altogether, three of them lighted for evening play. Phone 292-0105. **Port Royal**, in Southampton, has four public courts. Phone 234-0974.

If the weather is warm and sunny, though, watersports invariably prevail. Scuba diving and snorkeling are sensational, given the abundance of coral reef vistas and submerged shipwrecks. Two diving organizations are **Blue Water Divers**, which leaves from Somerset, and **Fantasea Diving**, leaving from downtown Hamilton. Phone 295-3052.

A slightly more bizarre experience is **Hartley's Undersea Walk**, wherein one walks the ocean floor wearing a giant, brass old-fashioned, diver's helmet on one's head. For information contact the company at Flatts Village, Tel. 292-4434.

Cruising is also popular on these waters and there are charters all over the island to take you for a spin or furnish you with the means to take yourself. A few to consider are: the Glass Bottom Boat Reef & Wreck Adventure, leaving from Hamilton's Front Street, phone 295-3727; Salt Kettle Yacht Charters and Boat Rentals in Paget, phone 236-4863; Ocean Yacht Charters, Southampton, phone 238-0825.

Fishing, similarly, is a big deal here with seventeen local varieties available as the catch, although bonefish, the fiercest fighting fish in the sea, are the usual goal. Deep-sea charters include the Sea Wolfe, a 13-m (43-ft) sports-fisher, phone 234-1832. Reef fishing is offered on the 8. 5m (28 ft) Ellen B., phone 234-2963. Island-wide recommendations can be made by the Bermuda Charter Fishing Boat Association, which can be reached locally by phoning 292-6246.

Swimming is also a big favorite here, given the heat of the summer days and the beauty of the beaches. Among the best beaches are: Tobacco Bay, North Shore, St. George's; Shelly Bay, North Shore, Hamilton Parish; John Smith's Bay, South Shore, Smith's Parish; Elbow Beach, South Shore, Paget; Horseshoe Bay, South Shore, Southampton; and Church Bay, South Shore, Southampton.

Shopping

Shopping is widely regarded as one of the major Bermuda vacation activities – along with swimming and sailing. The stores are known for their fine selection of British and European goods and for their comparatively low prices. Their civility is also a trademark; shoppers do not have to waste time comparison-shopping for prices because the prices will all

be the same. When one store owner decides to reduce, or raise prices, he or she calls the others and they do the same.

For the quintessential Bermuda shopping experience, all one has to do is stroll along Hamilton's Front Street. There you will find **H. A. & E. Smith Ltd.**, at 35 Front St., phone 295-2288. A distinguished department store, it has been in business since 1889. It is but one place to go for fine china and crystal, gold jewelry and English clothing for men, women and children. **Trimingham's**, next door at 37 Front Street, phone 295-1183, is another huge department store also selling china, crystal, jewelry and clothing. This one also has a food department with home label specialties. **A. S. Cooper & Sons Ltd.**, a few doors down at 59 Front St., phone 295-3961, is Bermuda's oldest and largest china and glassware store. **Crisson's**, 71 Front St., phone 295-2351, offers fine jewelry, watches and gold, and has six other locations throughout Bermuda. **Bluck's**, 4 Front St., phone 295-5367, has specialized in china, crystal

and antiques for 140 years. **Irish Linen Shop**, 31 Front St., phone 295-4089, offers pure Irish linen mainly, but other countries' products are also represented, such as soft French provincial *Soleiado* cotton and delicate Belgian lace. **Archie Brown & Son Ltd.**, also on Front Street, 295-2928, offers a huge selection of British, especially Scottish woolens. Brown's carries Pringle of Scotland cashmeres exclusively.

Most major stores have branches in St. George's, and the Irish Linen Shop has an outpost in Somerset, but the former capital also has stores of its own. One good one is Taylor's, 30 Water St., 297- 1626, for a good supply of British woolens.

Outings

To get a sense of underground Bermuda, it is interesting to descend into the depths of the land itself – into Crystal and Leamington Caves in **Bailey Bay**. Unlike others which have to be explored on hands and knees, you can walk upright in these, on prepared paths and even bridges when the going gets rough.

The **Dockyard** was an outpost of the British Royal Navy until the 1950s. Now it is a combination museum-crafts center. The **Maritime Museum** is housed in several restored buildings of the fortress and highlights Bermuda's historic link with the sea. The nearby **Craft's Market** displays local crafts such as paintings, pottery and carved Bermuda cedar. **Verdmont** is a perfectly restored 17th century house and a national treasure on Collector's Hill, in Smith's Parish. **Gibb's Hill Lighthouse** is a 143-year old lighthouse and one of the few in the world made of cast iron. It is an English import and provides a superlative perch for an overall view of the island (on Lighthouse Road, between South Shore and Middle Roads, Southampton).

Birdsey Studio: A visit to 78-year-old Alfred Birdsey's studio is not just an opportunity to admire and buy his watercolor scenes of Bermuda, it is an oral history of Bermuda. Birdsey is an irreverent character who knows everything and everyone and does not mind sharing the information with visitors (Stowe Hill, Paget).

Nightlife

Bermuda is not exactly a wild place compared to the cities its visitors might call home, but it does have some activity after dark. Most of the larger hotels offer entertainment. But the more adventurous will want to explore. Some options: **Place's**, on Dundonald Street in Hamilton, where the locals congregate for reggae; **Scandal**, 119 Front Street, Hamilton, a slick spot for dancing to all types of music; and **Loquats**, 95 Front Street, a more subdued place with a pianist or saxophonist performing; **Prospero's**, the cave disco at the Grotto Bay Hotel.

Above: Keeping a watchful eye out for exotic tourists.

Access & Local Transportation

Travelers arrive either by jet, landing at the modern airport at the eastern end of the island or by cruise ship, docking in either Hamilton or St. George's. Taxis are always available for transport at any of those points. For information, tourists should contact the Department of Tourism, Global House, 43 Church Street, Hamilton HM 12, Bermuda.

Formalities

U.S. and Canadian citizens do not need visas or passports for stays up to three weeks, provided they can produce a return ticket, as well as proof of accommodations on the island. Other citizens will need a passport and possibly a visa. Contact local authorities for specific requirements. There is a departure tax of $15 at the airport, $30 per cruise ship passenger.

Currency

The Bermuda dollar is on a par with the U.S. dollar. Traveler's checks are routinely accepted, but credit cards may not be. Check first with individual businesses.

Tourist Information

For information, tourists should contact the Department of Tourism, Global House, 43 Church Street, Hamilton HM 12, Bermuda, or 310 Madison Ave. Suite 201, New York, NY 10017, 1-212/818-9800, or 1200 Bay St. Suite 1004, Toronto, Ont., Canada M5R 2A5, 1-416/923-9600.

Accommodation

LUXURY: **Marriott's Castle Harbour**, historic multi-facility resort overlooking Harrington Sound in Tucker's Town. Box HM 841, Hamilton HM-CX-293-2040. **The Princess Hotel**, Bermuda's first luxury hotel, just a few minutes walk down Front Street in Hamilton. Box HM 837, Hamilton HM-CX, 295-3008. **Sonesta Beach** is a huge modern hotel with one of the island's best locations – directly on the South Shore beach in Southampton – and the island's only spa. Box HM 1070, Hamilton HM-EX, 238-8122. **Southampton Princess**, a mammoth modern hotel high on a hill with views of the whole island. Box HM 1379, Hamilton HM-FX, 238-8000. **Lantana Colony Club**, elegant cottages on twenty lushly land- scaped acres. Box SB90, Sandys SB-BX, 234-0141. **Elbow Beach Hotel**, large, active resort. Box HM 455, Hamilton HM-BX, 236-3535. **Grotto Bay Beach**, a large hotel with sea views and caves at 11 Blue Hole Hill, Hamilton CR-04, 293-8333. **Cambridge Beaches** is the oldest cottage colony. Elegant, at 30 King's Point, Sandys MA-02,236-6517. **Pink Beach**, once the top cottage colony, still good. Private South Shore beach. Box HM 1017, Hamilton HM-DX, 293-1666.

MODERATE TO INEXPENSIVE: **Newstead**, a small hotel, once a mansion, overlooks Hamilton harbor. Box PG 196 Paget PG- BX, 236-6060. **Glencoe**, sailor's paradise, a small hotel on Salt Kettle Bay surrounded by water, former sea captain's eighteenth century mansion. Box PG 297 Paget PG-BX, 236-5274. **Reefs**, elegant cabana colony in the midst of greenery on a cliff over the sea. 56 South Road, Southampton SN-02; 238-0222. **Palmetto Bay Club**, guest houses on the water. Box FL 54, Flatt's FX-BX, phone 293-2323. **Waterloo House**, elegant, small hotel, gardens and patio on Hamilton's waterfront. Box HM 333, Hamilton HM-BX, 295-4480. **Rosedon** is a Colonial house with gardens. Staying here is like being a house guest of a prominent Bermuda family. Box HM 290 Hamilton HM-AX, phone 295-1640.

Restaurants

Fourways Inn, elegant, expensive, continental. Middle Road, Paget, 236-6517. **Tom Moore's Tavern**, expensive, elegant, in historic building. Bailey's Bay, Hamilton Parish, 293-8020. **Once Upon a Table**, cozy, romantic, with sophisticated local dishes. Serpentine Road, 295-8585. **Newport Room**, Southampton Princess. Sophisticated, French-inspired, phone 238- 8167. **Waterlot Inn**, better for drinks or brunch than for dinner, though historic – dating from 1670 – as is the list of past patrons, among them Eleanor Roosevelt and Eugene O'Neill. Waterfront setting but inconsistent food. Middle Road, Southampton, 238-0510.

Plantation is a friendly, plant-filled restaurant specializing in local fish. You really know you are on an island. Bailey's Bay, Hamilton, 293-1188. **Tavern on the Green** is a romantic restaurant inside the Botanical Gardens. Italian specialties, local ingredients, 295-7731. **Lobster Pot**, fresh seafood is the name of the game here; so is a long wait, especially at lunch when businessmen from Hamilton clog all the tables. But it is worth it. Bermudiana Road, Hamilton, 292-6898. **Swizzle Inn** is more of a hangout than a restaurant, a casual place for a burger and the island's insidious rum swizzles, near the airport in Hamilton Parish, 293-0091. **Dennis' Hideaway** is a favorite with the locals for its informality and fresh seafood. Cashew City Road on St. David's Island. No phone. **Carriage House**, english specialties for lunch and dinner. One of the few places on the island (the other is **Port O'Call**, on Front Street, in Hamilton) to get a proper English afternoon tea. Somers Wharf, St. George's, 297-1270.

NASSAU
BAHAMAS
BAHAMAS
BAHAMAS
BAHAMAS

NASSAU
BAHAMAS

NASSAU
BAHAMAS

NASSAU

BAHAMAS

BAHAMAS

The Bahamas are so close to the Florida coast that Miamians with fast boats can pop over to Bimini for lunch. Yet in crossing the Gulf Stream, the visitor glides into a shimmering land held together by a sunlit sea.

The language and pace of the chain of 700 islands are distinctly West Indian. Islanders, especially in the Abacos, drop their "h"s, Cockney style. They often transpose "v"s and "w"s, and have trouble pronouncing such words as *ask* (axe), *children* (chirrun) and *anything* with a "th" (thing becomes t'ing). Often the accent is on the last syllable, and a sentence may end with a Canadian "hay". The result is a lilting singsong that will continue to echo in your ears long after you have left the Caribbean.

To arrive is to reach; to have arrived is to done reached. To talk to is to hail; to suffer or lack is to punish ("we was punishin' for water"); to take is to carry, as in, "I carried my mother to town."

Objective and nominative cases are interchanged, and verbs mangled. (Him do; she done.) To have intended is to have "lotted", to "swallow the grunt" is what Americans call to eat crow. To give a blessing is to scold. And to do something alone is to do it, "me one."

Preceding pages: Nothing more need be said – the name Bahamas alone conjures sun, sand, sea and fun for the visitors.

If your landlord is providing a furnished cottage, he "finds" the linens and tableware, an archaic verb usage we use today in saying that a boat is "fully found". A favorite story among the yachting community is that of a sailor who hired a native guide to "read bottom" as they picked their way through a briar patch of shoals. From the bow, the guide kept singing, "Tin, mon, tin." Interpreting this to mean that the water was ten feet deep, the skipper steered a steady course, right into a reef. What the guide had been saying was, "Thin, mon, thin."

Although the Bahamas is independent, its government is still modeled after Britain's, with a prime minister and parliament. Justice is swift and the jails unpleasant, so tourists are advised to observe Bahamian laws, including those against illegal drugs.

The climate, unlike the trade wind belt to the south, can be chilly and unpredictable in winter and steamy and stagnant in summer. But the waters, as bright as turquoise neon and as clear as a Martini, are the most beautiful in all the world. Nowhere else can you find so many deserted beaches, or so many reef gardens to snorkel and scuba within a few feet of shore.

Two things make Bahamas waters unique. One is that most of the land floats on very shallow water. The other is that there are no rivers to carry silt into surrounding seas. Even in water 6 and 9 m (20, 30 ft) deep, you can see clearly as a manta ray performs a ballet far below the surface. A quick look at a topographical or marine chart tells you how low-lying these islands are, and how shallow their seas. The water is barely 180 cm (6 ft) deep over a surface of hundreds of square kilometers. The highest point in the Bahamas is only 206 feet above sea level on Cat island.

The Bahamas were the first islands discovered by Columbus, but because they had very little to offer except the Indians who were carted off into slavery, they were ignored by the Spanish for more than a century. Then, hearing that a fountain on Bimini could provide eternal youth, the Spanish king sent Ponce de Leon at the head of an exhibition to seek it out. The Fountain of Youth is, in Florida and the Bahamas, the equivalent of those cliché "Washington slept here" – inns in historic areas of the United States. Some oldtime Biminians say they did hear of a spring where people once came for healing, but the only sure thing about the Fountain of Youth is that it attracted a host of explorers to an area that for years had nothing else to offer – no soil, no fresh water, no resources, nothing except for beauty.

It was religious wranglings in Britain and Bermuda that finally brought settlers to the Bahamas, which had been claimed by England in 1629. It was a restless time, marked by the rising and splintering of Protestantism. In 1648, those who were fed up with the traditional Church were looking to the uninhabited Bahamas for a place to start a new, free life. Calling themselves the Eleutherian Adventurers, they settled the new land.

To many people, the Bahamas means Nassau on New Providence and Freeport on Grand Bahama, two cities that do not always represent the best of the islands or the islanders. Nassau, the capital, is the center of island culture, history, commerce and society. It is here that islanders themselves come to shop and party and to participate in the nitty-gritty of insular politics, to get higher education and to get in touch with their roots. The university is one of the finest in the West Indies, especially for hospitality training. A fun, insider thing to do is to make reservations for a meal here, prepared and served by students. Prices are modest and the food is first class.

Around New Providence and its most famous satellite cay, Paradise Island, are stunning beaches, resorts, villages and glittering casinos that leave an indelible impression. Nassau also has its share of important historic sites, a few tourist attractions, and a seedy colonial charm that recalls a dignified and regal past.

To many delighted tourists, Paradise Island is Nassau, the Bahamas, Monte Carlo and heaven, all rolled into one. Unending surf washes over miles of white sand shoreline. Hotels are modern and luxurious, casinos electric with excitement and restaurants world class.

In Nassau

Because it is here that most international visitors first arrive on the island of **New Providence** and its main city, Nassau, are good places to begin a tour. **Nassau** is a walker's city, compact and fairly safe to cover on foot – at least during the day. Stroll down Bay Street and peek into perfumeries and jewelry stores. Photograph the statue of Queen Victoria sternly surveying a realm that she would no longer recognize. Search out Randolph Johnston's landmark statue of a Bahamian woman with a child at Prince George Wharf. The sculpture was conceived and cast by one of the Bahamas' most preeminent artist families.

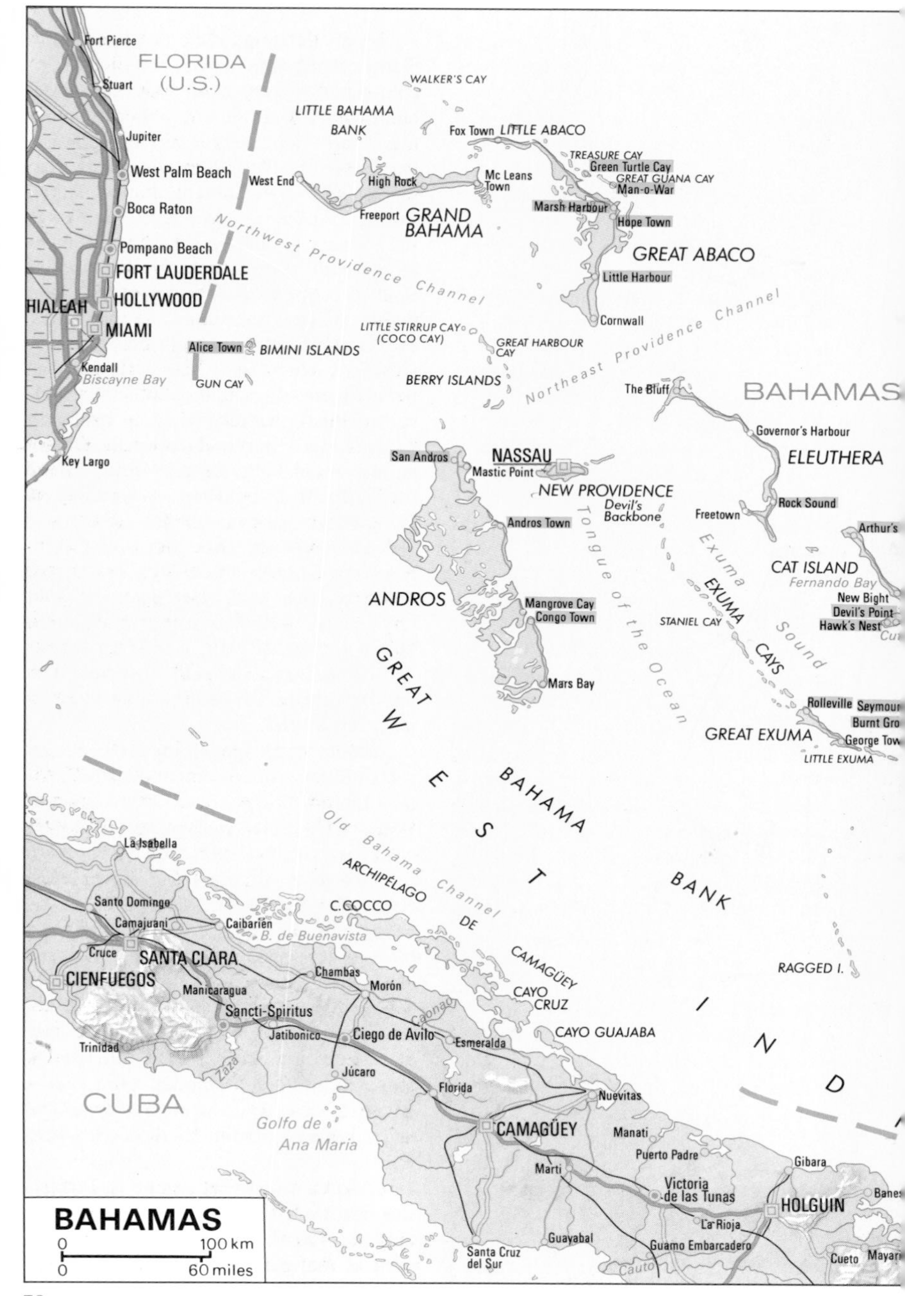

FLORIDA (U.S.)
Fort Pierce
Stuart
Jupiter
West Palm Beach
Boca Raton
Pompano Beach
FORT LAUDERDALE
HOLLYWOOD
HIALEAH
MIAMI
Kendall
Biscayne Bay
Key Largo
WALKER'S CAY
LITTLE BAHAMA BANK
Fox Town
LITTLE ABACO
TREASURE CAY
Green Turtle Cay
GREAT GUANA CAY
Man-o-War
West End
High Rock
Mc Leans Town
Freeport
GRAND BAHAMA
Marsh Harbour
Hope Town
GREAT ABACO
Little Harbour
Cornwall
Northwest Providence Channel
Northeast Providence Channel
LITTLE STIRRUP CAY (COCO CAY)
GREAT HARBOUR CAY
Alice Town
BIMINI ISLANDS
GUN CAY
BERRY ISLANDS
The Bluff
BAHAMAS
Governor's Harbour
ELEUTHERA
San Andros
NASSAU
Mastic Point
NEW PROVIDENCE
Devil's Backbone
Freetown
Rock Sound
Andros Town
Tongue of the Ocean
Exuma Sound
Arthur's
CAT ISLAND
Fernando Bay
New Bight
Devil's Point
Hawk's Nest
ANDROS
Mangrove Cay
Congo Town
STANIEL CAY
EXUMA CAYS
Mars Bay
GREAT WEST BAHAMA BANK
Rolleville
GREAT EXUMA
George Tow
LITTLE EXUMA
Old Bahama Channel
ARCHIPÉLAGO DE CAMAGÜEY
C.COCCO
CAYO CRUZ
CAYO GUAJABA
RAGGED I.
WEST INDIES
La Isabella
Santo Domingo
Camajuaní
Caibarién
B. de Buenavista
Cruce
SANTA CLARA
CIENFUEGOS
Manicaragua
Chambas
Morón
Sancti-Spíritus
Jatibonico
Ciego de Avilo
Esmeralda
Trinidad
Zaza
Júcaro
Florida
Nuevitas
CUBA
Golfo de Ana Maria
CAMAGÜEY
Manati
Puerto Padre
Gibara
Marti
Victoria de las Tunas
HOLGUIN
La Rioja
Guayabal
Guamo Embarcadero
Santa Cruz del Sur
Cauto
Cueto
Mayarí
Banes
BAHAMAS
0 100 km
0 60 miles

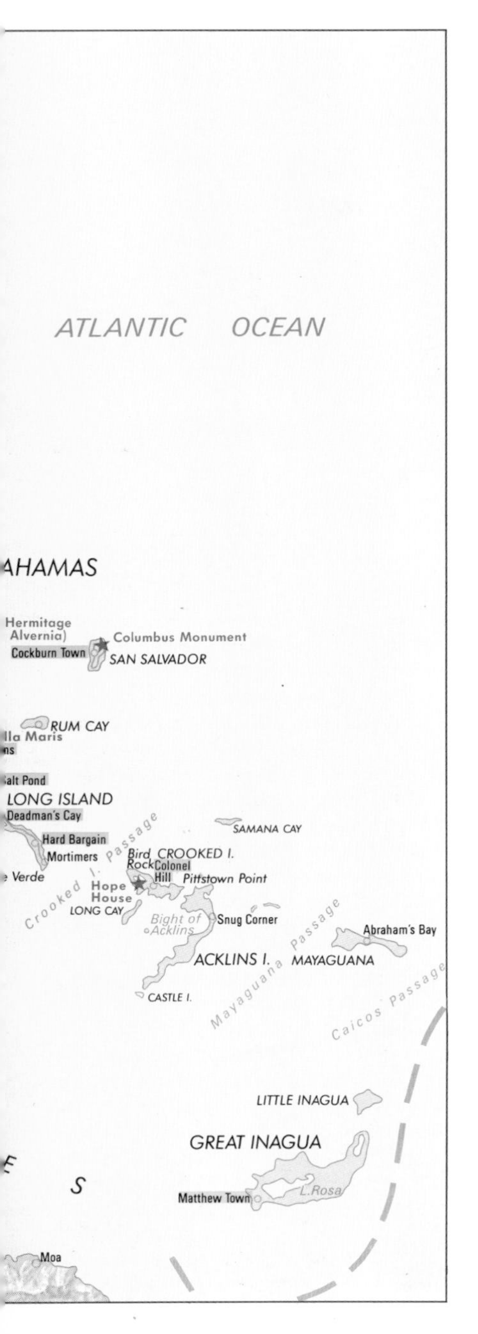

The old **straw market** burned down in 1974, but the new one is roomier, more colorful and more fun for shoppers. In the out-islands, children still gather the palm thatch and women still do the plaiting that is sent to Nassau in coils. It is then sewn, "often on ancient, hand-cranked sewing machines", into the hats and bags sold here at modest prices. Some of the bags are raffia-embellished to the point of absurdity, but straw work is an authentic native craft to take home. The bags make excellent purses or picnic baskets, and they last for years. You will see the people themselves using plaited work, albeit without the raffia kitsch, as lunch buckets, floor mats and work hats. Do not be shy about bargaining. Women of the market relish it, but they will go only so far. Some can become pushy and brash.

A new wrinkle throughout the Caribbean, the Bahamas included, is corn row plaiting. Young girls plait your hair into tiny braids, threaded with beads, for a dollar or two per plait. It is a fun way to "go native", and the plaits can be left in for days. Look for the braiding stalls in the straw market.

Another good spot to interact with locals is at the base of the landmark **Paradise Island Bridge**. In an area known as **Potter's Cay** fishermen come to sell their catch, and local women offer homegrown produce. The bridge itself is a good reference point, by the way. Built to allow the passage of tall ships, it is high enough to be seen for miles around. If you have a real sense of gustatory daring, buy a conch (pronounced *konk*) and ask the fisherman to prepare it for you to eat then and there. He will "scorch" (score) it, drench it in lime juice and perhaps add a splash of "old sour", and show you how to peel it away from the skin with your teeth.

Be forewarned that prices at Potter's Cay are high for everyone, not just for tourists. The Bahamas grow some food, such as mangoes, but most must be im-

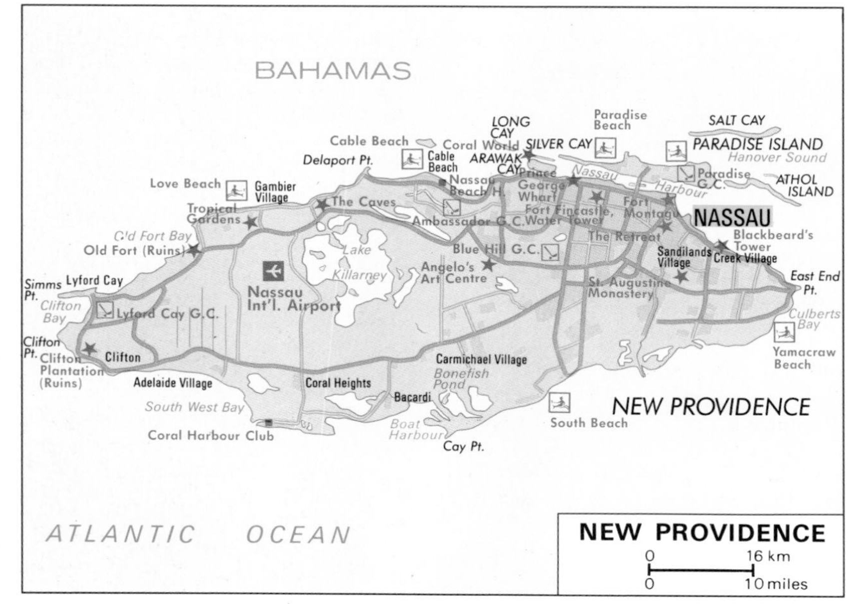

ported. The pineapple or bananas you could buy for a pittance in Haiti or Cuba are premium priced throughout the Bahamas, even if homegrown.

Bay Street, between downtown and the Paradise Island Bridge, is also the scene of the year's liveliest festivities. Where other islands celebrate carnival before Lent, here the big festival is *Junkanoo*, held on two nights during the Christmas season. Dressed in extravagant costumes they have worked on all year, revelers take to the streets in pre-dawn darkness and dance in complete abandon until dawn. Bonfires burn on street corners of goatskin drums throb. Whistles blow, horns blare, strangers grab strangers to dance or just laugh together. It is an indescribable cacophony, hypnotic in its rhythms and infectious in its frenzied fellowship.

East of the bridge on Bay Street, you will pass colorful marinas and bars, the hangouts of the many yachties who have made the place their headquarter. Moored at **Yacht Haven** in winter is the *Pied Piper*, featuring a unique reef diving adventure available only here and in Bermuda. It was invented by Bronson Hartley, and consists of a special helmet that lets you stroll on the sea bottom – without removing your glasses or contact lenses, or even getting your hair wet!

If you keep walking east from Yacht Haven you will come to **Fort Montague**, built to guard the eastern entrance to Nassau Harbor. It is a moldering ruin, with a good view of this end of the harbor.

Back downtown, you can stop at the **post office** to buy stamps in lieu of souvenirs. Bahamian stamps are among the world's most colorful, featuring tropical fish, seashells, and flowers. A philatelic bureau in the post office sells mint issues, first day covers, and collectible stamps.

If your trip does not include Nassau or Freeport, stamps can be purchased at any out-island post office too, and stopping at these rustic outposts is sometimes the

Right: If it ain't broke, don't fix it: British colonial style still survives.

highlight of a visit to a tiny village on a remote island. Kids and dogs cluster around at the sight of an outsider, and your visit will probably be the highlight of their day too. Buying a few stamps and sending a letter or postcard provides an ideal excuse for hanging around a bit and exchanging pleasantries.

Nassau's ancient, round, one-time **jail** is located at the center of the city. Although the library and museum now housed here are of very poor quality, the building itself is well worth a visit. The third-floor veranda where prisoners once exercised, offers a superb view of the downtown area. There are a few exhibits on the second floor and a friendly librarian will help you find material from island lore to recent editions of American, British and local periodicals.

Strolling through the heart of downtown Nassau you will pass the deserted **Royal Victoria Hotel**, built in 1861. During the American Civil War, it was headquarter for spies, rich Southern refugees, blockade runners and all the smart tradesmen who rushed in from England to take advantage of whatever opportunities were presented by the turmoil that was consuming North America. One disgruntled American skipper, sent to Nassau in 1862 to investigate the situation there, reported that "nearly the whole population is in open and notorious sympathy with the rebels".

In fact, guns were transported openly through the streets of Nassau and loaded onto Confederate ships, which where then provisioned and coaled and sent on their way. Any Yankee ships in the harbor found all sorts of delays and roadblocks in the way. Britain's slaves had been freed decades earlier, so the issue was not that the North was anti-slavery and Southerners were slave holders. The issue was profit. Well into the mid-20th century, the Royal Vic, as it is familiarly known, was the choice pied-à-terre of wealthy tourists and businessmen from

all over the world. Today it's a romantic ruin and, although there has been talk of restoration for years, the echoing relic remains untouched.

Nearby is the imposing **Government House**, where the Duke and Duchess of Windsor lived out the war years in luxury. After he abdicated the throne, the duke was appointed governor of the Bahamas. One of his accomplishments was to tame the swamps of Hog Island, now Paradise Island, with the digging of canals and a lake.

Travels on East Bay Street may also take you to the **Hotel Montague**, built in 1926, now another derelict edifice recalling an elusive past. Nassau's other hotel classic, the **British Colonial**, has been modernized and is part of the Best Western chain. It featured in the James Bond movie, *Never Say Never*.

A climb up the mossy Queen's Staircase of **Fort Fincastle**, rewards one with a view of the harbor. There is also a good view from the Water Tower, which has an elevator to take you to the top.

Chief among the city's forts, **Fort Charlotte** has recently been scoured and spiffed up for tourists. Guides lead you through the drawbridges and dungeons, and describe with almost ghoulish relish some of the bloodier aspects of Nassau's past, including its sacking in 1703 when the Spanish and French ganged up on the English garrison. This fort saw no fire at all, but the Spanish were scared off the island once by a fellow named Stephen Deveaux, who tricked the enemy into thinking he had a huge force. He dressed his handful of men in different costumes, and kept passing them through the Spaniards view as enemy forces seen from a distance. Thinking they were outnumbered, they retreated. In gratitude, the king gave Deveaux a large land grant on Cat Island. His descendants lived in the plantation mansion there until the 1950s. It has since become a ruin.

Around Nassau

West of the city, **Ardastra Gardens** consist of 11 ha (4 1/2 acres) of tropical splendor, rare Bahamian parrots, exotic small animals from around the world, and a famous regiment of marching flamingoes, performing three times a day. Admission is $7.50 for adults and $3.75 for children. The gardens are open daily, 9 am - 5 pm. Tel. 323-5806.

The **Nassau Botanic Gardens** are open Monday-Friday 8 am – 4:30 pm and weekends 9 am – 4 pm. Admission is $1 for adults and for children 50 cents. One of the world's largest collections of rare palms is in the gardens of **The Retreat**, a National Trust park on the east end of the island. Tours are conducted Tuesday through Thursday for only $2 per person. Call 393-1317.

Coral World offers a bright, real view of the world under the sea. A huge cylinder was simply lowered down over a real reef, allowing visitors to stand inside a dry tube and watch through windows as

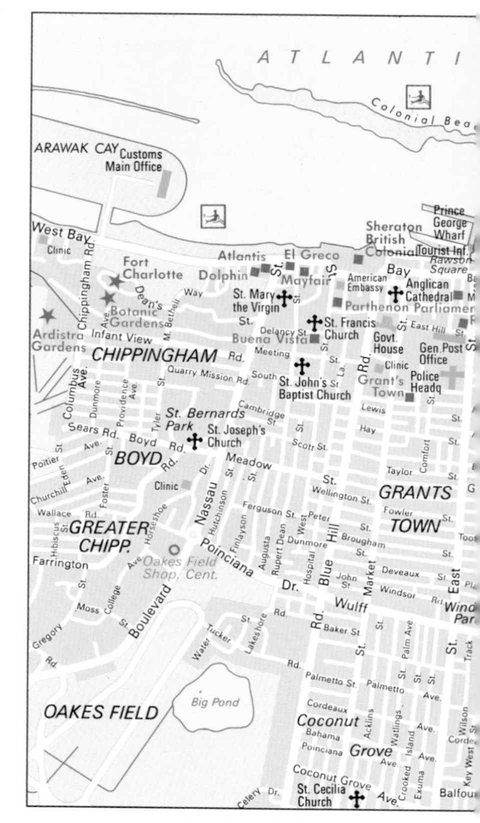

sea creatures swim about. It is open daily; hours vary seasonally.

There are few island pleasures more heady than splashing through the surf on horseback. Trail rides, including transportation to and from your hotel, are available from Happy Trails Stables, Tel. 362- 1820. If you prefer a quieter sport, a sanctioned club of the American Contract Bridge League holds duplicate bridge sessions every Tuesday. The fee is $5 per visitor. Call 327-7455 or 324-3043. The Paradise Island Bridge Club also welcomes visitors. Call 324-6565.

No trip to the Bahamas is complete without adventures in, on and under the water. All-day and dinner cruises aboard the *Calypso* are lubricated with unlimited

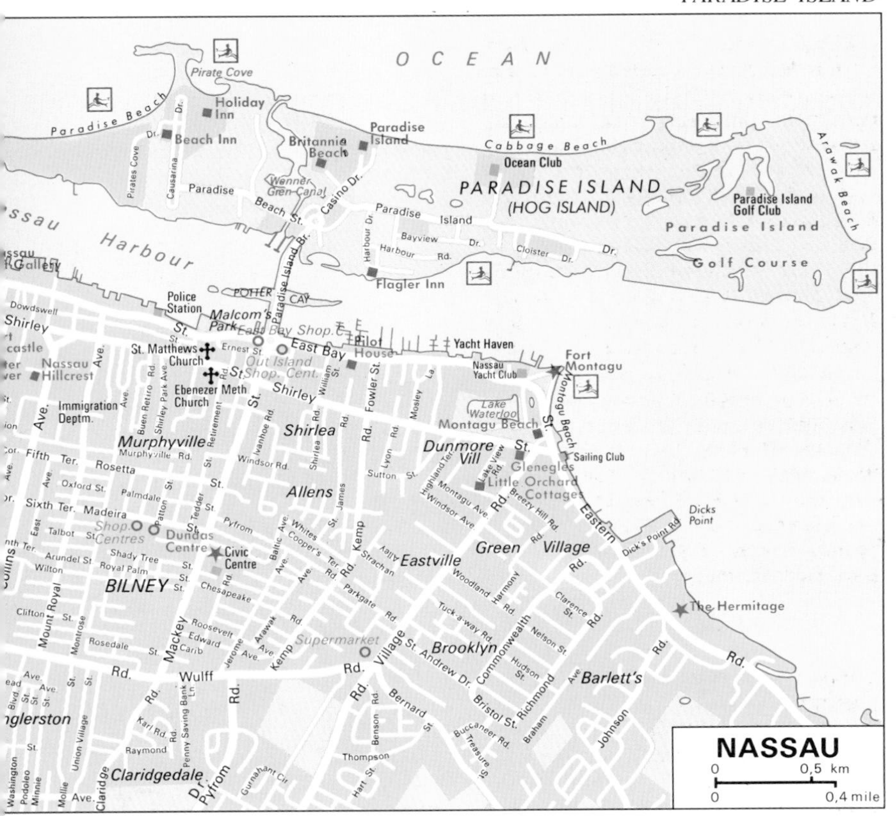

wine and rum punch. Book through your hotel or call 363-3577.

Deep-sea fishing boats and diving boats by the dozen ply the waters around New Providence, taking you to the brightest reefs or the sweetest honey holes. One of the largest diving operations on the island is at the Divi Bahamas Beach Resort, Tel. 326-439l. Your hotel can arrange for almost any kind of watersport, from fishing by the day or half day to waterskiing. Most beachfront hotels have boats, windsurfers, snorkel gear and other equipment for rent.

Big-time casino gambling is the golden fleece of tourist pleasures. If you are not sure of the fine points of craps, roulette, blackjack or baccarat, ask about lessons. They are given free, with complimentary cocktails, at Paradise Island and Cable Beach, now called the Bahamian Riviera.

Paradise Island

A toll bridge connects Nassau to **Paradise Island**, which was known as Hog Island until 1960. Its main trademarks are wide beaches, luxurious hotels and the oldest building in the Caribbean. The cloister of **Montrejau**, completed in France in the 13th century by Augustine monks, well before Columbus discovered the New World, was carried stone for stone over the ocean in 1962, and rebuilt on a hill in the midst of the splendid Versailles Gardens on Paradise Island.

Grand Bahama

Grand Bahama, the fourth-largest island of the Bahamas, lies only 55 miles from the Florida coast. Thanks to this proximity to the USA, its magnificent beaches and its exclusive hotel complexes, the island evolved into a major tourist outpost over the past 25 years. Both the industrial and touristic development of Grand Bahama began with the arrival of the American entrepreneur Wallace Groves, who founded the Abaco Lumber Company on Grand Bahama. W. Groves was pursuing a dream which ultimately came true with the founding of Freeport in 1956. Eight years later the beach area of Lucaya was expanded into a veritable tourist's paradise. An excursion around the twin city of **Freeport-Lucaya** suggests the modern wealth of the island metropolis, which finds no match anywhere in the Bahamas. The main sights, however, can be quickly enumerated: the International Bazaar, the newly constructed Port Lucaya Marketplace, with its panoply of shops and restaurants, the Straw Market, the Wallace Groves Library, the Underworld Explorers Society (UNEXSO) Museum (in the yacht habor of Bell Channel Bay/Lucaya) and finally, outside of Freeport, the Garden of Groves featuring the Grand Bahama Museum, the Hydroflora Gardens and the Rand Memorial Nature Center (a bird sanctuary).

Above: The fish market in Nassau is a place to go for local color.

Freeport/Lucaya is above all a paradise for swimmers, divers, golfers and tennis players. But everything really gets moving after sundown when the many restaurants, bars and discos come alive. The high point of night life on Grand Bahama is gambling. A far more peaceful atmosphere dominates the scene beyond the limits of the island's glittering capital. A seemingly endless pine forest sprawls in easterly direction, interrupted here and there by sleepy towns such as Freetown, **High Rock** and **MacLean's Town**. The southeastern coast is mainly a haven for sport fishers, but the **Lucaya National Park** also has something for the tourist: interesting caves, freshwater springs and one of the most beautiful beaches on Grand Bahama.

The **West End**, in the opposite direction, was once the largest settlement on the island, but it has suffered some dilapidation in the past years. This fishing town earned a reputation during the Prohibition as a point of departure for smugglers shipping much-coveted Grand Bahamian rum to the United States. In the immediate proximity is **Jack Tar Village**, which offers its guests a variety of activities from diving to golf.

THE FAMILY ISLANDS

The traveler visiting only Nassau or Freeport has still not seen the Bahamas. Likewise, the visitor who sees only the

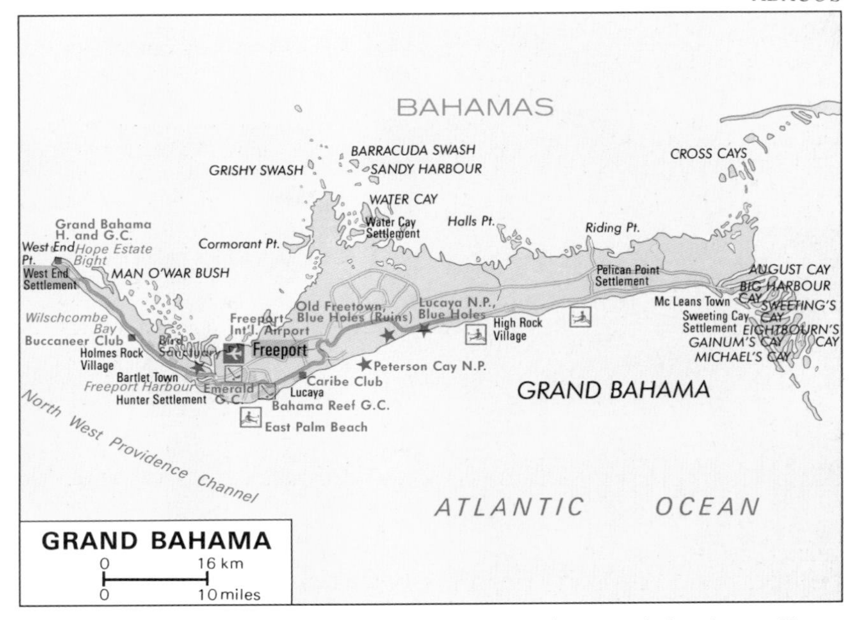

Exumas or only the Abacos misses much of the rich variety of a large and lovely island nation. A lifetime could be spent exploring, fishing, sailing, swimming and savoring these islands. A first, brief visit to the Bahamas themselves gives the impression that the Bahamas are the Bahamas. A longer and more profound visit reveals that the string of islands, running from Walker's Cay to Great Inagua, (called Family Islands or Out Islands) is really a series of island groups, each with its own particular charm and adventure.

The Abacos

While most Bahamians are black, descended from African slaves, the **Abacos** were originally white Americans who fled here during the Revolutionary War to remain under the British crown. A group of 600 Tories arrived in 1783 on the north end of **Treasure Cay**, and established a community. Although it is now just a lonely, wind-blown beach, an historic marker stands on the spot.

Abaconians are industrious, affluent, deeply religious and proudly Bahamian. Their homes are neat clapboard, painted white or a pastel shade surrounded by flowers, and generally look like prim New England houses. Cars are rare except on Great Abaco. Citizens are more likely to travel in electric golf carts, which are more practical for the steep, sidewalk-size streets.

Like other Bahamians, Abaconians suffered many setbacks before achieving the relative wealth they have today. Blight killed the pineapples one year, cotton another. Sisal, now seen growing wild, was once a major industry, but when the price fell to $1 per hundredweight during the 1930s, it no longer paid to harvest it. Collecting supported many Abaco families, but the industry was wiped out by a sponge blight in 1938.

The Abaco chain begins at **Walker's Cay**, which is chiefly a fishing resort frequented by Americans, and ends at the southern tip of **Great Abaco**, once a heavily forested island that supplied tim-

ber for building famous Abaco sloops and schooners. Entire homes were prefabricated here, and shipped to Key West at the turn of the century. Many of them, some even the size of mansions, can still be seen there.

Until recently, when a deep-water harbor was dredged off **Great Guana Cay** to accommodate cruise ships, the Abacos were sleepy hideaways off the beaten path. People came by yacht or private plane, but anyone else had to fly into Nassau, change planes for **Marsh Harbor**, then take a water taxi to Hope Town or Green Turtle Cay – a time-consuming trip. Now, however, these picturebook villages also host crowds of cruise ship passengers. Both Green Turtle and **Man-o-War** have quaint gift shops, colorful yacht harbors, evocative old cemeteries and other sights. Man-o-War is dry, but at Green Turtle stop at *Miss Emilie's Blue Bee Bar* to sample the *Goombay Smash*. It was invented here and has, in the meantime, grown into the national drink.

Above: A laid-back, romantic way to visit Nassau. Right: Flamingos stalking in the Ardastra Gardens.

Be forewarned, incidentally, that Bahamian drinks have the particularly vicious capacity of suddenly creeping up on you and knocking you down. Deceptively sweet and innocent, favorites such as the afore-mentionned *Goombay Smash*, *Bahama Mama* and *Yellow Bird* have the kick of a mule, especially in conjunction with the tropical heat.

Boat building is still practiced to some extent in the Abacos, but most of it is done in public view to show tourists how boats were built here for centuries using natural knees and native woods. *Albury's Sail Shop* used to provide canvas for Abaco boats. Now the shop's sewing machines turn out sturdy, colorful duffel bags. They are among the best and most durable souvenirs to be found in the islands. Native batiks and hand-printed fabrics can also be found in Abaco shops.

On **Green Turtle** there is a sculpture garden telling the history of the Bahamas,

and the **Albert Lowe Museum** containing the work of Alton Lowe plus historic items from the area. If you come by cruise ship, do not miss the chance to make these side trips.

The ships anchor off **Great Guana**, which has been turned into a big playground and renamed Treasure Island. Tenders shuttle between the ship and Great Guana, Man-o-War, Green Turtle, and Treasure Cay, which has golfing and shops but is thoroughly Americanized. The two native settlements, even though they can be a long ride away by tender, give you the best inside view of real Bahamian life.

The more boating you do while here, the better view you will have of this far-flung island group. Boats are rented at Marsh Harbor by the hour or day; sailboats are available by the week to qualified sailors. Once you are on the water, there are endless beaches and coves to discover, reefs to snorkel, fish to spear, and uninhabited islands to explore. If you can get to **Little Harbor**, you will find here the family of a modern Robinson Crusoe. Randolph Johnston, who taught art at Smith College in Massachusetts, brought his wife and children here in 1950. They lived in a cave and endured many hardships while building an island idyll devoted to their art. They now have a comfortable home, studio, shop, foundry and a little bar that is usually open evenings when yachties are in the harbor.

Randolph Johnston's bronzes are well known throughout the Bahamas; his wife Margot is a talented ceramist; their son Peter Johnston has a following of his own in galleries from Nantucket to Palm Beach. The island is a good place to hike. Among the important sights are the cave in which the Johnstons once lived, and the cliffs now protected under the National Trust.

Andros

Divers who have explored great reefs from Cairns to Belize single out the 224-km (140-mi) barrier reef off **Andros** as one of the best diving sites of the world. In size it is second only to Australia's Great Barrier Reef and, in beauty and variety, is to the Atlantic what Australia's reef is to Pacific corals, mollusks and colorful fish. For miles, the Andros reef shimmers just below the surface, host to an enormous aquarium of reef fish, gigantic predators, house-size sea fans, and cathedral-size "blue holes". At its edge is a sheer drop-off into nothingness, giving divers a chance to explore a vertical wall to the limit of their abilities.

To dive the Great Barrier Reef, visitors have to go far from shore by seaplane or diving boat. Here, as in most other parts of the Bahamas, brilliant sea gardens are found right off the beach. The best diving is only a quick sprint from shore, in a small boat. The island, the largest in the Bahamas, is only 32 km (20 mi) from New Providence at its closest point, but it has been barely touched by tourism because of its many swamps, its ferocious flies and its scarcity of resorts. Bahamians refer to it as **The Big Yard**. However, it is exactly this loneliness exclusivity that makes Andros a favorite with sportsmen, especially scuba divers and bonefishermen.

Andros, with its large lakes of sweet water, supplies much of New Providence with its water supply. Thanks to the large, freshwater lakes here, Andros is a stopover for birds migrating north from South and Central America. Nature lovers will spot a variety of birds and serious bird watchers come here time and again. There are also 40 or so varieties of orchid. So untouched has the island been that its old-timers still believe in chickcharnies, imaginary gremlins who look like birds and hide in pine trees to bring grief to any passerby who does not please them. Andros, like most of the Bahamas, was originally settled by Arawaks, but here and in Bimini they were probably also joined by Florida's Indians, forerunners of today's Seminoles.

Right: In the high season there can be almost more tourists than sand...

Airports are located at **Andros Town**, **Mangrove Cay**, **San Andros** and **Congo Town**, all reachable from Nassau or by charter out of Florida. Resorts in these settlements are small and rustic.

Bimini

You will sense you are in a border town if you visit the island that has long been a favorite among rum runners, wreckers, smugglers, dopers and blockade runners, not to mention a colorful New York politician, Adam Clayton Powell, who once lived here. He became a local hero by passing out big bills to expectant mothers. It is quite possible that your waiter's first name will be Adam, Clayton or Powell.

The Biminis are actually a sprinkling of islands, rimmed with brown sugar sands and surrounded by azure waters. There is **North Bimini**, with **Alice Town**, the chief settlement; **South Bimini** includes an airstrip, marina, and a twenty-room resort, plus a scattering of cays including **Gun Cay**, where divers explore a sunken concrete ship that once served as a rum runner's rendezvous. At **Cat Cay**, the rich and famous come to find blissful anonymity in an exclusive resort.

During the 1930s, Ernest Hemingway discovered the lush fishing of the Biminis as well as the cooling comfort of Alice Town's rustic bars. Today, Hemingway memorabilia are still on display at the **Compleat Angler**. Accommodation facilities have grown since his day, of course, but the fishing and drinking are as lavish and famed as ever.

Martin Luther King is only one of many who have raved about bonefishing in the shallow, translucent flats around the Biminis. The islands are also surrounded by reefs, including formations that some say are part of the lost conti-

nent of Atlantis. The same claim has also been made for reefs found off Andros. For fishermen, there are some reefs rich with grouper, the Gulf Stream is famous for its blue marlin, and all depths between. Sportsmen have an enormous choice of sportfishing for almost any species found in the tropics. Fishing captains can be found around the marinas and resorts in Alice Town.

The Berry Islands

A mere sprinkling of crumb-size dots on a shallow sea, the **Berry Islands** are an international center for sportfishing tournaments revolving around the aloof, exclusive **Chub Cay Club**. It is here and in **Great Harbour Cay**, that the only two telephones in the Berrys are located.

Although these islands and their surrounding waters are the favorites of yachtsmen, divers and fishermen, they have little accommodation to offer the traveler except for the small resort at Chub Cay. However, each year thousands of cruise ship tourists are introduced to **Little Stirrup Cay**, which has been renamed Coco Cay by the cruise lines that own it. A ship anchors off the uninhabited island and passengers are lightered ashore to enjoy a beach barbecue, two bars, island music, swimming and snorkeling on a choice of beaches, and shopping in a homespun straw market that is set up for the day by women from nearby islands. For those willing to make the hike, plantation ruins can be found deep inland.

Cat Island

It is one of the larger islands, and is the site of the highest point in the Bahamas, at 63 m (206 ft), yet Cat Island has been slow to get its share of the wealth that tourism brings to the Bahamas. Part of the problem is its distance from Nassau. Many other playgrounds are closer or easier to reach. The commercial airport is at **Arthur's Town**, which has no accommodation, so the ride to the resorts, which

are down-island at **Fernandez Bay**, **Cutlass Bay** and **Hawk's Nest**, can be long, bone-rattling, and very expensive.

Only the most persistent travelers will have time to seek out Cat Island, but it is one of the most primitive and fascinating of the Bahamas. People in the village of **Devil's Point** tell of a ship that wrecked off the point long ago. So afraid were the sailors of Cat Island's powerful *Obeah,* that they chose to die at sea rather than risk coming ashore here. Even today, the occasional *Obeah* charm will be set in farm fields to scare away thieves. Ruins of the old **Armbrister plantation** can still be seen at Fernandez Bay. When family members came back to the island on a flying boat in the 1930s, old family retainers greeted them as though they were the *ol' massah,* returning to take care of them. Sidney Poitier was born on Cat Island, and still lives on the island.

Above and right: Forms of fun – up in the skies and nature's beauty underwater.

The island's other claim to fame is **The Hermitage**, built atop the Bahamas' highest hill, called **Mount Alvernia**. It was built by Father Jerome, who was architect John Hawkes before he became a priest.

After building five churches on Long Island, he retired in seclusion to Cat Island where he spent the last years of his life lugging rocks up the hill on his back to build his retreat and chapel. His crude, but loving, seven Stations of the Cross were created in cement along the path. After his death in 1956, he was buried in a cave on the hilltop. It is a long, hot climb to this tiny, peaceful aerie, but well worth the effort. It is not until you reach it that you realize you have been the victim of a well-prepared optical illusion. What appeared to be a stately cathedral in the distance is actually a miniature, much closer than you thought. The hermitage is usually open to the public, unless a visiting cleric is in retreat here.

Eleuthera

When the definitive history of the Bahamas is written, this area will figure in prominence second only to lands discovered by Columbus because it was here that a group of English Puritans came from Bermuda to start a new colony in 1649. Led by Captain William Sayle, the Eleutherian Adventurers fended off hunger, disease, storms, Spaniards, pirates, agricultural pests and other ills to establish what was probably the first true democracy in the New World.

Extending for 144 km (90 mi) in length, **Eleuthera** includes several separate islands, among them **Spanish Wells** with its pale, inbred white residents. They are among the most famous fishermen of the islands.

Eleuthera's unusual pink beaches draw an international crowd. It is here, at the **Windermere Island Club**, that the British royal family sometimes spends its

holidays. The equally posh **Cotton Bay Club** has an eighteen-hole golf course designed by Robert Trent Jones. Room rates at both resorts start at over $300 nightly. The interior is dotted with farming communities still growing the incredibly sweet pineapples that were once a major crop in the Bahamas. **Rock Sound** is the island's major shopping center, although many resorts are found throughout the island.

The Exumas

Just as well-traveled divers point to Andros as one of the world's best diving sites, sailors who have circumnavigated the globe list the **Exumas** as one of the finest sailing areas in the world. Waters are an electric turquoise. Sand beaches stretch to the horizon, most of them with no footprints but your own. Villages are unspoiled, resorts unhurried, fishing and diving superb, and the sense of getaway and freedom is in a class by itself. The island group starts in a tangle of tiny cays known as the **Devil's Backbone**, and straggles south as almost 400 separate islands and cays, ending at Great Exuma. It is here that the *Family Islands Regatta* is held each April – a wet, wild, dead serious duel of smack boats that is one of the two best native events outsiders can attend. (The other is *Junkanoo*). Islanders are instinctive sailors; their boats are seaworthy, and their sailing is poetry.

The Exumas offer excellent hiking and exploring as well. At **Rolle Town**, on Great Exuma, you can see the gatepost that once marked the entrance to a plantation, and three 18th century graves. The entire string of islands is a National Trust Land and Sea Park. Except for lolling around villages and watching ice melt in your rum punch, there is not much to do in the Exumas other than beachcombing and watersports.

Great Inagua

Great Inagua is one of the largest Bahamian islands, but it has little to offer

the tourist except for its wildlife. The largest flock of West Indian flamingoes in the Caribbean flourishes here, and you might also spot a roseate spoonbill, rare reddish egret, or West Indian tree duck. The island is also roamed by feral cattle, donkeys and boar. It is all part of a national park. Write ahead to the National Trust, P.O. Box N-4105, Nassau, to arrange a ranger-guided tour. You can fly into **Matthew Town**, or take the scenic, snail's-pace route by mail boat. Accommodation is available at two guesthouses.

The largest industry on the island is the harvesting of salt, a million tons of it per year. It is one of the largest solar evaporation salt works in the world. **Morton Salt Company** operates a small guesthouse, and will arrange to see the salt ponds, but tourism is not their goal so it is not recommended that travelers overstay their welcome.

Above: Cleaning the fresh catch. Right: Typical modern residential architecture in the Bahamas.

Long Island

Long and skinny, running almost 96 km (60 mi) north to south but barely a stone's throw across, **Long Island** is strung on a main road that runs from **Seymour's** through **Burnt Ground**, **Simms**, **Deadman's Cay** and **Hard Bargain**, to the southern point, **Cape Verde**. Its first settlers were the Arawaks. In 1790 came American Loyalists who grew cotton, cattle and corn. You will still find Simm's descendants at the village bearing the same name, and they are willing to show you the ruins of the onetime family plantation.

Long Island offers a fine resort and marina, **Stella Maris**, where rooms and villas are available to house as many as 150 guests. Fishing is legendary, and the resort operates its own, 22-m (72- ft) diving boat.

Many visitors come by private plane or boat, but the paved strip here is also served by *Bahamasair* and *Stella Marisair*. Small guest houses are also found at Deadman's Cay, Salt Pond, and **Thompson's Bay**. This is a beautiful, end-of-the-world island dotted with plantation ruins, farms and native settlements with surprisingly fine churches – thanks to Father Jerome, the hermit architect who is buried on Cat Island.

San Salvador and Rum Cay

Because of the anniversary in 1992, marking 500 years since Columbus landed at San Salvador, the pace has picked up on this sleepy, agrarian island. The best way to tour is to rent a car and drive the 56-km (35 mi) perimeter road. From **Cockburn** (pronounced Coburn) **Town**, head for a day or two of beachcombing, gazing out to sea from outlooks, poking around old Indian sites and cemeteries, or photographing historic markers and churches. Small museums are found at Cockburn Town and **Polaris Point**. Accommodations are at simple guest hou ses or at the commodious **Riding Rock Inn** resort, which has a pool, tennis courts, diving and dining.

Rum Cay is best known for its diving to the wreck of the *Conqueror*, which went down in 9 m (30 ft) of water in 1861. It is owned by the National Trust, so do not disturb any of the cannons and other artifacts.

Crooked / Acklins Islands

Crooked and **Acklins Islands**, separated only by **The Going Through**, are almost one big circular island surrounding **The Bight**. Sniff the air here and see if you can identify *cascarilla,* used to flavor Campari. If you ask a local what he is doing when harvesting the bark, he replies, "I is barkin', mon." The feeling of seclusion here is almost intoxicating. At **Pittstown Point,** on Crooked Island, an inn has been built around the ruins of what used to be the first post office in the islands. Near the **Bird Rock Lighthouse**

at Pittstown Point the land is punctured by enormous caves which are all a-shimmer with white stalactites. On Crooked Island there are other ruins too – old British forts and ancient homes including the ruins of **Hope House** (17th century). On Acklins you can discover an old lookout tower, and you can hire a boat to take you to **Castle Island**, south of Acklins, for a visit to the lighthouse at the southern end of the island.

Bahamasair flies once a week into **Colonel Hill** on Crooked Island or, for an even more complete feeling of escape, take the mail boat which also calls weekly. There are several guest houses, but arrange accommodation well in advance.

Other arrangements can wait until you get settled here. Like most of the more remote islands that see few tourists, these are unbelievably unspoiled. Simply express your interest in seeing the sights, ask directions and advice, and soon you will find yourself being shown around by some proud islander.

Bahamian Farms

Often you will read that an island's chief resource is farming, but do not expect to see waves of golden grain. Most islanders practice what is known as pothole farming, in which a cavity in the limestone is filled with whatever soil can be scraped together, then a seed or seedling is planted.

Often, water has to be carried on foot from miles away to nurture the little plants. Harvesting is equally laborious, and you will see women trailing back to their villages with baskets on their heads. Farmers use only one tool, a machete, for everything from clearing to cultivating.

If you are hiking in remote areas of the bush and come upon what appears to be a lush harvest, free for the taking, look but do not touch. There are no fences or other outward signs to identify this as someone's "farm", but it could be a family's livelihood. If caught, you will be brought before the constable, and probably fined heavily.

Getting Around

Hitchhiking is a well-accepted way of getting around the more remote islands. You cannot always get a ride, especially on islands where few people have cars, but if someone stops along a hot, dusty road and motions you into the back of a battered pick-up, it is probably not a mugger. If you can kick in a dollar or two for gas, it will be appreciated, but if you cannot, that is all right too.

Mail Boats

Do not confuse mail boat travel with anything you may ever have heard about posh and romantic freight boats. These boats are utilitarian, slow, and crowded with cargo, people, goats, chickens, fodder, oil drums and the thousand other things that make an island tick. However homely, they do maintain a reliable schedule between the islands, often serving settlements or islands that cannot be reached any other way.

Mail boat schedules are broadcast daily over ZNS radio in Nassau. Or, just go to **Potter's Cay** in Nassau to see what is available to go where. Boats for the most remote islands depart only about once a week. Check out the boat before sailing, to find out if you must bring your own food or bedding.

Right: If you take them home, make sure they are uninhabited.

Seashells

Because of its countless miles of gentle seacoast, the Bahamas offer some of the best seashell collecting in the world. Where the ocean crashes against land, shells are smashed as they are washed to shore, but there are beaches and flats in the Bahamas where you can walk for miles, picking up perfect tellins, scotch bonnets, pen shells, conchs as tiny as a thumbnail and as big as a bread box, tritons and chitons, sea biscuits, cowries, and periwinkles galore.

There is a system behind finding stranded shells. The best finds are made at falling tide, after a storm has unsettled the sea bottom. It is not necessary to take live shells as there are plenty of dead ones, cleaned out by nature and ready to take home. On the more remote islands you will find more big helmet conchs, sea fans and deer cowry than you can carry with you.

Give any shells plenty of time to air out. Even if their original inhabitants have long since vacated, a hermit crab may be living in the shell. Sealed in a plastic bag and left in your luggage, the resulting mess will create a sickening stench. If you are a serious collector and are taking live shells, observe the limits of undersea parks and other National

Trust areas where it is illegal to take living creatures of any kind – including coral. And remember, if it is coral you are after, restrict yourself to what you find washed ashore. Don't chip away at this submarine paradise, or it may quickly turn into a desert.

Out-island Survival Tips

Never forget that this island nation is held together by a tenuous supply line of mail boats, infrequent air service, CB radios and home generators. It is best always to have a Plan B in case Plan A is prevented by bad weather, a fuel shortage, a mechanical breakdown, communications failure, or a gap in the supply line.

You may not be able to use a credit card, and in the most remote areas it could create a hardship for your host if you use a traveler's check. Not all settlements have banks either, so have a reserve of cash with you. U.S. dollars are accepted readily in the Family Islands, but you may have to accept your change in Bahamian currency. A common mistake is to arrive at an out-island cottage in which you expect to do your own cooking, without knowing exactly what supplies are available on the island. It is best to bring supplies for at least the first day or two with you. You might also investigate in advance whether an out-island resort is in or near a local settlement, or is a complete, self-contained compound operated by foreigners for foreign tourists. There are plenty of choices in both categories.

The more remote the island, the more authentic and rustic the travel experience, but also the greater the need for the tourist to make arrangements well in advance. Out-island travel is not for the high-voltage jetsetter on a split second schedule. Relax and enjoy the Bahamas. Often the pace is infuriating, service inconsistent, weather whimsical and luxuries rare. But it all adds up to a unique, unpredictable, barefoot and Gauguin-esque getaway.

Access & Local Transportation

Air carriers into the Bahamas include Air Canada, American, Bahamasair, British Airways, Midway, Pan Am and TWA. Regional carriers include Aero Coach, Chalk's, Paradise Island Airlines and Comair. Family islands are served from Fort Lauderdale, Miami, West Palm Beach or Orlando by Comair, Chalk's, Aero Coach, Walker's Cay International Airline, American Eagle, and Air Canada. Taxis, rental cars, limousines and buses are available. Because the islands are small, it rarely takes more than 15-30 minutes to get from airport to hotel. Cab rates are metered and set by law. Plan to spend about $10 to get from Nassau's airport to Cable Beach, $12-$15 to downtown, and up to $20 to Paradise Island. Fare in Freeport from the airport to downtown costs about $6. Out islands' fares vary. Roads are often poor, cars and parts costly, and fuel very expensive, so rates may be high. Cut a deal in advance. Sightseeing rides in Nassau are $20-$25 per hour. Horsedrawn carriage tours around Rawson Square cost about $10 for 45 minutes for two. Negotiate ahead of time for a longer trip. Locals ride jitneys for fares in the $1 range, but consider them more an adventure than a serious way to get from Point A to Point B. Schedules are spotty, and routes hard for outsiders to understand. Freeport's double decker buses shuttle among the hotels and sightseeing attractions. Buses operate on Paradise Island. Budget and Avis rental cars are available in Nassau at the airport and in town. Driving is to the left and parking scarce, so it is best to do without a car if possible.

Night Life

Nights are quiet in the Family Islands while Nassau and Freeport sizzle with all the style of Las Vegas. Extravagant revues are presented at the casinos, sometimes as dinner shows. Disco at **Club Pastiche**, on Paradise Island. Piano and mellow vocals in the lobby bar of the **Britannia Towers**, or dance the night away at **Le Paon**, in the Sheraton Grand, on Paradise Island. In Nassau, **Peanut Taylor's Drumbeat Club** is the place to see a native show. Wednesday nights throughout Goombay Summer, native shows feature the famous Royal Bahamas Police Force Band when they are in town, spilling out on downtown Nassau streets, which have booths selling native foods and crafts.

Formalities & Currency

Citizens of the United States, Canada, the United Kingdom and its colonies should bring proof of citizenship such as a birth certificate or voter registration card. All others need passports. Each person age 3 and over pays a $7 departure tax on leaving the Bahamas. This is in addition to whatever ticket taxes you paid on your airline or cruise ship ticket. The room tax is a hefty 10%. Some hotels also add automatically a 15% service charge in lieu of tipping. There are no sales or value- added taxes in the Bahamas.

The Bahamian dollar is on a par with and interchangeable with the U.S. dollar. Use either, but do not leave the country with Bahamian funds, which may not be accepted at U.S. par outside the country. Leftover funds can be exchanged at Nassau airport. When using Bahamian money, do not go by size and shape alone because some coins could be mistaken for U.S. coins of lesser value. And in dimly lit nightspots, it is easy to tip with a $3 bill when you meant to leave $5. For collectors there is the $3 bill, fluted 10-cent pieces, and a square 15-cent piece. Major bank cards and gasoline cards are accepted throughout the islands, but do not count on using them at small, out-island guest houses.

Time Zone

The Bahamas observe the same times as the eastern United States. Eastern Standard Time is 5 hours later than GMT; Daylight Savings Time is observed in summer.

Tourist Information

Bahamas Ministry of Tourism, 255 Alhambra Circle, Coral Gables, FL 33134. 1-305/ 448-2084 or 1-800/346-7077. In Nassau, tourist information centers are found at the airport, Prince George Wharf, and Rawson Square. In Freeport, centers are at the airport, International Bazaar, and harbor. Bahamas tourist offices are also located in Montreal, Toronto, London, Paris, Milan, Tokyo, Frankfurt, and in the U.S., Atlanta, Boston, Charlotte, Chicago, Cincinnati, Dallas, Detroit, Houston, Los Angeles, New York, Philadelphia, San Francisco, and Washington DC.

Accommodation

It is best to arrange accommodations through a travel agent. Best packages include air fare, airport transfers and extras. Some include a cruise. Assume that your room in the Bahamas will be air-conditioned, unless otherwise stated. Unlike the trade wind belt, the Bahamas have many warm, still days when AC is a necessity. Toll-free reservations in the Bahamas can be made from anywhere in the U.S. at 1-800/327-0787.

NEW PROVIDENCE

LUXURY: **British Colonial Beach Resort**, P.O. Box N7148, 1-800-528-1234. The only beachfront 325-room resort in the heart of Nassau. Dining, private beach, tennis, pool. **Carnival's**

Cable Beach Riviera Towers, P.O. Box N-4914, 1-809/327-6000. Ultramodern 693-room highrise with dining, gambling, tennis, squash, private beach, golf. Suites available. **Carnival's Crystal Palace Resort & Casino,** 1815 Griffin Rd., Suite 400, Dania, FL 33004, 1-305/923-8448 or 1-809/327-6200. Enormous, 1559-room extravaganza. Avante garde decor. Golf, tennis, diving, private beach, boating, casino, two-story disco, lavish shows hourly all day. Adults-only show lounge. complete health club. **Le Meridian Royal Bahamian,** P.O. Box N10422, 1-800-543-4300. The most attractive hotel at Cable Beach, 125 rooms and 25 garden villa suites. Dining, healthclub, tennis, pool. **Wyndham Ambassador Beach Hotel**, P.O. Box N-3026, 1-809/327-8231. Full service 400-room hotel with private beach, diving, pool, boating, fishing. **Nassau Coral World Hotel**, Silver Cay, P.O. Box N-7797, 1-809/328-1036. Rooms have private pools. Private beach, dining at one of the Bahamas most unique tourist attractions. Suites have micro-wave, satellite TV. **Greycliff Hotel**, West Hill St., P.O. Box N-10246, 1-800/633-7411 or 1-809/322-2796. Swank, historic inn, downtown, continental service, famous dining room, beach privileges. **Divi Bahamas Beach Resort and Country Club**, P.O. Box N-8191, 1-809/326-4391. A new beach resort, 18-hole golf course, tennis, workout facilities, dive operation, fine dining. Rooms have TV, VCR.

MODERATE: **Nassau Beach Hotel,** 1-800/225-5843. 3000-foot beach, club concept with discount meals, free teatime and cocktails and other privileges, casino. *BUDGET*: **Buena Vista Hotel**, Delancy St., Nassau, P.O. Box N-564, 1-809/322- 2811. Six-rooms, bar and restaurant. **Colony Club**, St. Alban's Drive, Nassau, P.O. Box N-5420, 1-809/ 325-4824. Apartments with kitchens.

PARADISE ISLAND

LUXURY: **Paradise Island Resort & Casino**, P.O. Box SS-6333, 1-809/363-2000. Plush, full service, 1,110-room resort, dining in twelve specialty and gourmet restaurants, gambling, tennis, diving, boating and a fabulous beach. **Pirate's Cove Holiday Inn**, P.O. Box SS-6214, 1-809/363-2100. Beach-front, 535-room, full service hotel, pool, workout facilities, game room, children's playground. **Sheraton Grand Hotel & Towers**, Casino Drive, 1-800-325-3535. 360 room resort. 4 restaurants, 2 lounges/entertainment, pool, watersports, tennis. Dinner nightly except Mo. *MODERATE*: **Harbour Cove Inn**, P.O. Box SS-6249, 1-809/ 363-2561. Beachfront, 250-room hotel with tennis.

GRAND BAHAMA

LUXURY: **Bahamas Princess Resort & Casino**, Mall at Sunrise, Freeport, P.O. Box F-207 or 805 Third Ave., New York 10022. 1-809/ 352-6721 or 1-212/715-7090. Dining, boating, private beach, tennis, diving, gambling. **Lucayan Beach Resort & Casino**, Midshipman Rd., P.O. Box F-336 or 1610 S.E. 10th Terr., Fort Lauderdale, FL 33316, 1-305/463-7844 or 1-800/772-1227. Tennis, gambling, dining, boating, golf, diving, fishing. **Xanadu Beach & Marina Resort**, Sunken Treasure Dr., P.O. Box F-2438, Freeport, 1-809/352-6782. Private beach, tennis, golf, dining, pool. *MODERATE*: **Atlantic Beach Hotel**, Royal Palm Way, Freeport, P.O. Box F-531, 1-809/373-1444. Boating, fishing, golf, diving.

ABACO / HOPETOWN

MODERATE: **Abaco Inn**, 1-809/367-2666. Bar, dining room, pool, private beach, diving. *All-inclusive*: **Club Med** all-inclusive resorts are located on Paradise Island and Eleuthera. Call your travel agent or 1- 800/CLUB MED, or write Club Med, 40 W. 57th St., New York NY 10019.

Restaurants
NEW PROVIDENCE

LUXURY: **Greycliff**, West Hill St., 1-809/ 322-2796. World famous cuisine, colonial ambience, caring, unhurried service, superb dishes. Guests have included movie stars, royalty. Reservations, jacket and tie requested. Dinner nightly, lunch weekdays, breakfast for groups by arrangement. **Buena Vista**, Delancy St., Fresh Bahamian seafood in a restored old home, served on the garden patio or cozy dining rooms. Reservations, jackets for gentlemen recommended. **Frilsham House**, Cable Beach, 1-809/327-7639. Gracious old home overlooks ocean. **Sun and ...**, Lake-view Dr. off East Shirley St., 1-809/393-1205. Seafood with French accent.

MODERATE: **Blackbeard's Forge**, in the British Colonial Beach Resort, One Bay St. 1-809/322-3301, ext. 278. Tabletop grills for fish, chicken, steak. Touristy, but excellent value, nightly. **Bayside**, also in the hotel, has an all-you-can-eat lunch and dinner buffet. Open 7 a.m.–11 p.m. *BUDGET*: **Duff 'n Stuff**, Madeira St., and in the Nassau Arcade on Bay St, 1-809/ 328-2128. Eat in or take out native dishes. **Mandi's**, corner of Arundel St. and Mount Royal Ave., Palmdale. Conch served in every way – cracked, chowder, salad, fritters, and more. Open daily except Sunday, 11:30 to 11:30. **Sandpiper**, Bay Street near Elizabeth, 1-809/322-2486. Bahamian and Greek classics.

TURKS & CAICOS

Less than 960 km (600 mi) southeast of Miami and 144 km (90 mi) north of Haiti is a string of eight islands and many small cays which have been dubbed "the forgotten islands". As impossible as it may seem, these islands with their friendly people, some 368 km (230 mi) of perfect white sand beaches, pristine waters teeming with fish and coral which awe even the most experienced divers, have thus far escaped the overdevelopment and commercialism that has spread throughout much of the Bahamas and the Caribbean. Even the tourist literature asks the question: "Where on earth are the Turks and Caicos Islands?".

The Turks and Caicos have long had a real identity crisis. Chief Minister Oswalk Skippings was unnerved to discover during a visit to the office of a high-ranking London official in 1989 that the country was not even on the globe, despite its status as a British Crown Colony.

For years the original crest of the islands reflected the islands' first identity crisis. Back in 1860, all English territories were requested to submit a design for their colonial flag's crest. The Turks artist depicted a schooner in the background of two salt heaps and men raking the product. When the London flag maker saw the design, he assumed that the salt heaps were igloos and added his dash of authenticity with an entrance to one heap. For more than 100 years thereafter, the Turks and Caicos seemed to be some offbeat Arctic outpost of the British Empire. In 1967, the flag was changed to depict a crest with the country's spiny lobster, the queen conch and the Turks head cactus.

Left: Evening on the beaches, with a gentle sun and a calm sea, can be like a dream come true.

Stamp collectors might be familiar with these islands, for stamps are a major export. Space buffs might recall that, when United States astronaut John Glenn splashed down in 1962, he was debriefed in nearby Grand Turk. And back in 1974 the Canadian parliament debated making the islands a province of Canada. There was some excitement in the islands a few years ago because of the discovery of a wreck off West Caicos on Molasses Reef that divers say might be Christopher Columbus's *Pinta*, lost during a second voyage to the New World in 1500. Researchers from the Texas-based Institute of Nautical Archaeology have been diving and studying the wreck, which is the oldest yet documented in the New World.

Local legend and lore attribute the name of the Turks Islands to the native cactus flower, the scarlet blossom of

which was thought to resemble that traditional Turkish headwear, the fez.

The name Caicos was derived from either the Spanish word *cayos*, meaning cays, or from the map of della Cosa dated about 1500, identifying the islands as *Yucayo*, undoubtedly after the Lucayo Indians who settled there.

The islands' history has been tumultuous and contrasts with the peaceful nature of the people today. The Lucayo Indians were the first to inhabit the islands, but Spaniards enslaved them and killed them off. Some historians firmly believe that Grand Turk, and not San Salvador or Samana Cay in the Bahamas, was the site of Columbus's 1492 landfall. There are now two theories: First, that Columbus landed on a tiny cay now named in his honor off East Caicos; or that the site he called *Guanahani* was the Hawks Nest anchorage of Grand Turk in 1492. If he did come ashore in the Caicos Islands, Columbus encountered the Lucayan Indians who had a large settlement in Middle and North Caicos, and replenished the ships' water supply from the fresh water abundant on Pine Cay. Ponce de Leon is often acknowledged as the island's discoverer because of his official sighting in 1515.

Above: Old canons to protect the new treasury. Right: The service does use airplanes, however.

Pirates and Salt

During the 16th and 17th centuries, the islands sheltered some of the most notorious pirates, such as the Bloody Sisters, a band of women including Anne Bonney and May Reid. The first permanent settlers arrived in Grand Turk in 1678. They were Bermudans who established the salt industry which became the economic mainstay of the islands for over 250 years. The bright sunlight and drying winds had created natural salt ponds in the "salt" islands of Grand Turk, Salt Cay and South Caicos, which attracted the first permanent settlers.

The 16th century Spanish explorers had already made use of the natural salinas. The Bermudans created salt pans by walling the natural salinas with stone, which came with their schooners as ballast. At first they dredged channels to the sea and made sluices that could be closed to trap the seawater in the salt pans. They let the water evaporate, aided by the constant sun and 24-kmph (15-mph) tradewinds. The salt would accumulate up to 30 cm (12 in) high, then the raking began. Several men would use wooden rakes to heap the salt 40-50 cm (16- 20 in) high in rows 1.8-2 m (6-7 ft) long. Young men would shovel this into carts and take it to the beach to await shipment. The salt was then bagged – women often were the ones to tie the bags, two women working to one shoveler – and transported on donkeys or slaves' backs to the schooners and emptied into the holds. Each empty bag was proof for the paymaster of how much a man was owed. Some 10,000 bushels of salt could thus be shipped out in a day.

In later years, windmills were built to aid the process of carrying water off, and mechanical rakes were invented in 1860. A few windmills remain, especially on Salt Cay, where they make the salt-pans-turned-bird-sanctuaries look picturesque. The Turks Island salt even won awards in 1882 and 1891 in world fairs. A salt grinding machine was invented so that various grains of salt could be exported. Turks and Caicos salt was considered the best for preserving meat and U.S. General George Washington insisted on no other for his army's supply. Self-appointed historian Charles Hutchings described a South Caicos scene at the peak of production as "once the scene of wind pumps under sail, huge tidal floodgates, and a vast concourse of donkey and mule carts with men and boys engaged in draining pans, breaking up the salt, raking it, shoveling, carting, bagging". Britain nationalized the then-flourishing industry in 1951 and within twenty years salt production had ceased on the islands. Old salt sheds, dormant salinas, wind-

mills and a handful of donkey carts remain for visitors to photograph.

In 1787, Loyalists fleeing the southern American colonies in the wake of the Revolution arrived in the Caicos Islands with their slaves, where they established cotton and later sisal plantations. Other cash crops were tried but these plantations eventually failed.

The ruins of some of these old homes still stand, and the names of their original owners have become common Turks Island names: Forbes, Gardiner, Stubbs, Robinson, Hall and Williams, borne by descendants of the Loyalist settlers and their slaves. In the 19th century, a whaling industry developed on Salt Cay and ruins dating back to that period can be seen today.

The islands endured Spanish and French invasions prior to becoming a British possession. The islanders counteracted some of the attacks on them by wrecking. Blue Hills, now known as the island of **Providenciales**, or Provo, was the center of it. The settlers would lure ships with lights so that they would be wrecked on a reef as they approached what appeared to be a passing ship. Then the islanders would go out and loot the cargo, which they would use or sell.

Above: The old means of transportation still have a place in the rural Turks.

The islands were part of the Bahamas government administration from 1799 to 1848, when they were placed under the jurisdiction of Jamaica. In 1874 the islands suffered a terrible economic slump after rainy seasons ruined the salt industry. After being annexed by Jamaica in 1873, they remained a dependency until 1962, at which point they were lumped together with the Bahamas, whose governor they shared until the Bahamas themselves became independent. The British saw absolutely no strategic value here, no local economy developing which could help their economy. Today, the Turks and Caicos remain a British Crown Colony with a governor appointed by Queen Elizabeth and a local, elected, ministerial form of government.

The Islands Today

There are only 14,000 people scattered over these islands. The two groups of islands are separated by the 2,000-m (7,000-ft) deep, 35-km (22-mi) wide channel of the **Turks Island Passage**. From January through March, schools of humpback whales swim through the passage as they head south to the **Silver Banks** breeding grounds. Locked within a continuous coral reef estimated at 368 km (230 mi), together they occupy only 450 sqkm (193 sqmi) at low tide. The islands are a true tax haven, taking their clue from the Cayman Islands. There are no taxes on earnings, gifts, or estates, no matter what the source of income may be. There is no corporate or sales tax. The U.S. dollar is the official currency. Bank-

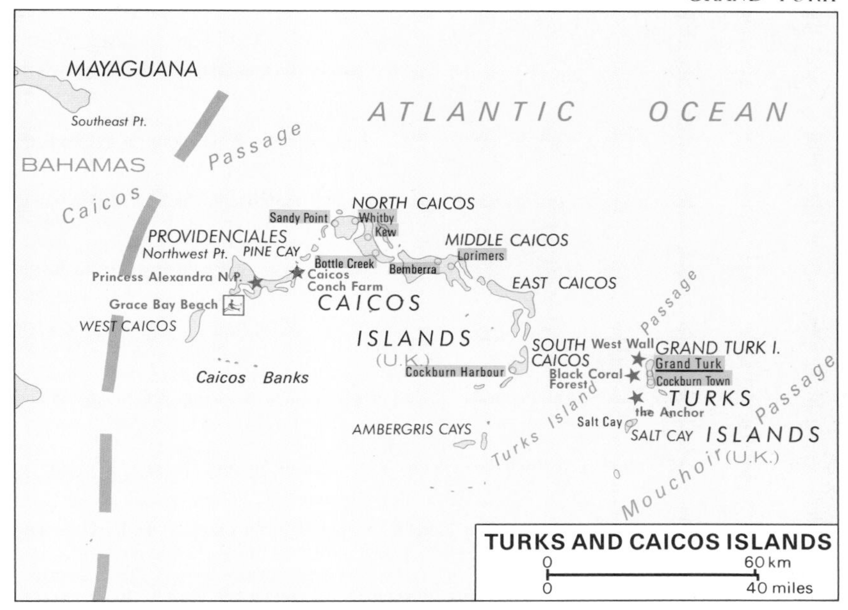

ing is a growing business, safe from the eyes of foreign governments and tax authorities.

Grand Turk

Grand Turk, with 20 sqkm (8 sqkm) and 5,200 people serves as the country's capital. A visit here is like a step into a tropical story by Somerset Maugham, without the lush vegetation of the South Seas.

The islands' capital and center of commerce is sleepy **Cockburn Town**. Rush hour here often means a few of cars cruising down the main street. Travelers who have visited Bermuda will recognize the style of houses that line the beach; limestone blocks were cut from the ground with the resulting hole used as a storage tank for the limited rain. The government buildings are here, as well as a large, whitewashed church with a bright red roof and some remnants of weathered gingerbread buildings of an isolated colonial outpost. The tiny bridges are grandly named Brooklyn Bridge and the White Cliffs of Dover. The island is treeless and brush-covered, with cliffs of limestone rising on its northern end.

There are striking contrasts to be found everywhere on Grand Turk; from modern telephones, highly sophisticated communications and banking facilities to 200-year-old limestone churches, a very old library containing such Lucayo artifacts as a 1,000-year-old stool and donkey-pulled buggies. There are small herds of "wild" donkeys roaming freely. It was one of these donkeys, or more specifically a black jackass, that gave rise to an all-time classic Turks newspaper headline a few years back. It seems that Buster, a frisky, three-year-old jackass was nipping unsuspecting pedestrians and cyclists on the backside. One evening a tourist was nipped and the Royal Police was called to apprehend the animal. Four motorcycle policemen sped the wrong way down Front Street but could not find Buster. That evening the local paper carried the headline: "Police Chase Black

Ass in Grand Turk." It instantly became a collector's item.

What Grand Turk lacks in land attractions it more than makes up for in incredible underwater beauty and a rich and healthy reef life. The coral walls drop-off dramatically and visibility reaches 46 m (150 ft). There are forests of black coral, schools of jacks, groupers, snappers, barracuda and all manner of smaller sea creatures. Some of the best sites are on the **West Wall**. One of the best known of these is called **McDonald's**. Two side arches, one of them big enough for three people to swim through, give the place its name. Another well-known site is the **Black Coral Forest** with, as the name suggests, a proliferation of black coral. South of the black coral is the **Anchor**, a large encrusted anchor, possibly of 17th century Bermudan origin. At a place called **Tiki Hut**, divers are likely to see schools of eagle rays. Despite the undersea beauties the area has not yet suffered the effects of over-diving that have hit some of the diving meccas to the south.

Above: Watch your language around this fellow. Right: Exotic shells and mysterious starfish.

Salt Cay is just 14 km (9 mi) from Grand Turk, easily accessible by boat and only five minutes by air. This tiny island is shaped like a wedge of pie and girded by beaches of pure white sand. It has two villages, a few churches, a grammar school, a store and several guest houses. The remains of the salt industry, which gave this island its name, can still be seen in the sluices and windmills formerly used in salt production and the many disused salt ponds. There has been some talk of resuming production.

The Turks Island Passage runs between the Turks Islands, principally Grand Turk and Salt Cay and the Caicos Islands that rim the broad **Caicos Bank**. West Caicos, Providenciales, North, Middle, East and South Caicos cap the Caicos Bank.

Caicos

The most developed of all these islands is **Providenciales**, or Provo as it is commonly known. Provo has the highest elevation of any of the isles and is regarded as the prettiest of all the Turks and Caicos. Development has transformed the island in the past decade and more changes are anticipated when a casino opens at the Ramada Turquoise Reef Resort. A popular Club Med facility features intensive diving programs.

Luckily for the fragile ecology of the islands, Provo is also home to PRIDE, the Society to Protect Our Reefs and Islands from Degradation and Exploitation. The organization is headed by Chuck Hesse who has crusaded for the past thirteen years for the creation of a national parks system to preserve and protect the country's environment and marine life. In 1988 his efforts were rewarded with the designation of 33 sites as National Parks and Sanctuaries. One area on Provo was

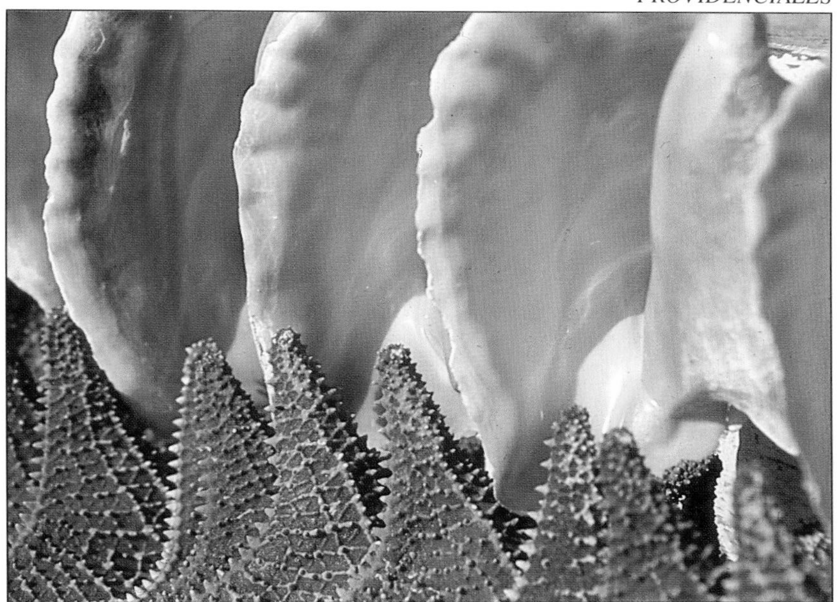

dedicated as **Princess Alexandra National Park** by the British princess herself. The sites also have scenic, historical or environmental importance. Many are important breeding or nesting grounds for some of the 150 species of birds which migrate through the islands.

Hesse has also been able to accomplish what most scientists thought was impossible: the establishment of the first commercial conch farm. The **Caicos Conch Farm** is breeding and raising queen conch for local use and for export. After many years of research Hesse and his team are able to produce a consumable conch in 28 months, from egg to adult conch. They estimate yearly production at about 700,000 animals worth $1 each.

The much cherished mascot of the island is an Atlantic bottlenose dolphin named JoJo. He is unique because he does not travel in a pod but seeks out human companionship off Provo's **Grace Bay Beach** instead. He is a wild dolphin who has never been trained and yet he seems to delight in playing with swimmers in shallow water or tagging along on a dive trips to deeper waters. Marine scientists from all over have come to Provo to study JoJo.

Diving in Provo is among the best of all the Caribbean and the Bahamas area. There are walls, caves, healthy coral reefs teeming with marine life and larger fish that have mostly disappeared in many diving areas to the south. One site looks like a rain forest, with green, fern-like black coral hanging from the ceiling of a grotto. Outside a school of jacks swim about. Gigantic purple and orange sponges abound. An occasional shark swims by. Midnight-blue parrot fish, puffer fish, French angels and the odd turtle add color and diversity to the reef along with scores of Nassau groupers.

No dive trip to Provo is complete without diving along the **Northwest Point**. Sleeping in the cuts in the wall you might find nurse sharks and turtles. Schools of snappers and grunts swim from pillar coral to mounds of brain

coral. Provo diving pioneer Art Pickering, who owns the country's oldest dive operation, claims he has not even scratched the surface of what is under the sea, even after thousands of dives.

Provo is also well known for its bonefishing on the flats. Bonefish are thin, silver fish that frequent the miles of flats that surround Provo and other islands and cays. Pound for pound they are rated the finest fighting fish in the sea. The fish must first be spotted in the shallows before casting the line just beyond them and reeling it in at just the right pace. Generally, the fish are released after landing them, although Turks and Caicos residents, who know how to get rid of the bones, say they are delicious.

Fishing for larger fish is also popular. The annual July Turks and Caicos Billfish Tournament at the Turtle Cove Yacht and Tennis Resort attracts a lively crowd who compete for prizes and record blue marlin, white marlin, wahoo, dolphin and yellowfin tuna. In keeping with the country's philosophy of conservation, all blue marlin under 90 kg (200 IG) must be released.

Above: A passing vision on the beach. Right: Idyllic living conditions but what about hurricanes?

The Caicos

From Provo, **North Caicos** is an easy hop either by boat or by Turks and Caicos National Airline (TCNA). Just remember that schedules are flexible and the airline seems to operate on island time. There are only two small tourist facilities on North Caicos. The larger facility, with 28 rooms, is elegant and visitors will experience the island in luxury surroundings. Those arriving in July can enjoy a real local festival – the annual *Festarama*, with excellent diving, beach picnics on isolated cays, trips into the island's interior, scouting for wild donkeys and flamingoes. This island offers a view of the rural Caicos lifestyle. The beach goes on for six uninterrupted miles and it

is not unusual that the lonesome beachcomber sees nothing but his or her own shadow. Some 4,000 permanent residents live in four tiny villages: **Bottle Creek** on its eastern edge, **Kew** and **Whitby** in the center, and **Sandy Point** in the northwest.

Middle Caicos can be reached by ferry from North Caicos. This is the largest island of the group but it is sparsely populated with only 400 residents. There are two two-bedroom villas for rent. Otherwise, there are no facilities for tourists. The secluded beach near the harbor is exceptionally beautiful. There are extraordinary limestone caves on the north coast with reflections of stalactites and stalagmites in the clear, salt pools. For the past decade, groups of U.S. archaeologists have been coming to Middle Caicos to explore the caves and ruins near **Bemberra** and **Morimers** for artifacts and relics of the Lucayo and Arawak Indians. They have also been exploring the ruins of plantations established by British Loyalists fleeing the American Revolution.

South Caicos is another island with potential but little development. It is anchored behind a sweep of coral reefs, which, along with wall and drop-offs, provide a number of diving sites. The town is small and uninteresting, but the harbor is the best natural harbor in all the islands. It is the focus of the fishing industry that exports conch and lobster, and also the scene of the annual Commonwealth Regatta held in late May each year. There is one sixteen-room hotel which attracts divers and fishermen.

Pine Cay is one of a chain of small cays that links North Caicos and Provo. It is privately owned by people determined to protect the fragile ecology of the land and surrounding sea. The Meridian Club is the social center for the enclave of some twenty homes that occupy the whole 324 ha (800 acre) island. There is a perfect beach, shelling, fishing, diving and just plain relaxing. Despite its private nature, rooms and homes are available for rent and there is a private airstrip for those who are interested in island hopping in a private plane.

Access & Local Transportation

Pan Am flies direct from Miami to Providenciales and Grand Turks several times a week. The country's flag carrier, Turks & Caicos National Airlines (TCNA), provides connecting inter-island service with arriving international flights and daily inter-island service between all inhabited islands. Flight time to Salt Cay from Grand Turk is a remarkable two minutes, ten minutes to South Caicos, or thirty minutes to Providenciales or North Caicos. Island-hopping within the group or farther afield can be arranged either through scheduled TCNA service to Nassau and Freeport (Bahamas), Cap Haitien (Haiti), or Puerto Plata (Dominican Republic), as well as through local air charter services, or through local boat owners. There is one international car rental agency, Budget, on Provo. Other local car rental firms include Island Rent-A-Car and Provo Rent-A-Car. On Grand Turk, there is a Hertz agency at the Island Reef Hotel and Dutchies Car Rental and Williams Motor Mart are locally owned operations. Rental cars cost about $40 per day, plus $11 insurance and $10 tax. Taxis are available at the airport of every inhabited island. Mopeds and scooters are available from Holiday Scooter Rentals on Provo and Kittina Hotel Scooter Rentals on Grand Turk. The cost is about $25 per day.

Customs Formalities

To enter the Turks and Caicos Islands, Americans and Canadians need proof of citizenship in the form of a current passport, or birth certificate plus a photo ID, for which a driver's license will suffice. Visitors from other countries need a passport. A return or ongoing ticket is also required. There is a $10 departure tax.

Currency

The U.S. dollar is the legal currency. Complete international banking facilities are available at Grand Turk, South Caicos and Providenciales. Traveler's checks are accepted at most hotels, the larger stores and at banks, although credit cards are accepted only rarely at business establishments.

Time

Turks and Caicos time is the same as the eastern seaboard of the United States during both Eastern Standard and Daylight Saving periods.

Festivals & Special Events

On Grand Turks islanders celebrate a Carnival that begins in late August and continues into September. The Commonwealth Regatta is the biggest event on the islands, taking place in South Caicos the last weekend in May. The Queen's Birthday is celebrated early in June. The Turks & Caicos Islands' International Billfish Tournament is held on Provo in July. Provo Days is a week-long annual celebration in August with races, parades, regattas, and a Miss Turks & Caicos beauty pageant at the end of July.

Tourist Information

The Turks and Caicos Tourist Board can be reached in the U.S. at 1-800/441-4419 or write 271 Main St., Northport, NY 11768. The Turks and Caicos Information Center, 255 Alhambra Circle, Suite 312, Coral Gables, FL 33134, 1-800/548-8462 handles hotel reservations. Bye-Coastal Tours, 1324 Boston Post Road, Milford, CT 06460, 1-800/227-2157, or 1-203/878-8854 is the authorized U.S. representative for complete travel packages to the Turks and Caicos. Or for additional information contact the Caribbean Tourism Organization, 20 East 46th St., New York, NY 10017, 1-212/682-0435.

Accommodation

Most hotels in the islands are small, individually owned places with a personal touch, the perfect get-away for those who find other parts of the Caribbean overdeveloped.

PROVIDENCIALES

Club Med Turkoise, operated by the French resort company, boasts 298 rooms on one of Grace Bay's best stretches of beach. Specials at this village include a dedicated dive center. All other sports and meals are included in the all-inclusive price between $850 and $1,500 per week, per person, double occupancy.

Island Princess is a friendly, family-owned beachfront resort. Its eighty rooms are surrounded by gardens. Rates are $80 to $100 for a double.

Third World Inn is the legendary thirteen- room inn on Turtle Cove Marina which has attracted celebrities of all sorts. The Seven Dwarfs bar is a popular watering hole for local characters and visitors alike. There is a full-service dive operation. Double rooms are $90.

Erebus Inn is perched on a cliff over-looking Turtle Cove Marina and the sea. Twenty-nine rooms, tennis courts, a pool and lovely bar. The award-winning restaurant specializes in seafood. Rooms range from $90 to $155.

Turtle Cove Yacht and Tennis Resort is located right in the heart of Turtle Cove. It hosts the annual July Turks & Caicos International Billfish Tournament. The club offers twenty-four rooms. Rates begin at $100 for a double.

Mariner's Hotel offers a quiet holiday on Sapodilla Bay in twenty-five rooms. It has one of the islands' most beautiful views. A water sports center with diving, boardsailing and sailing facilities is on the premises. Rates begin at $110 a day.

Le Deck Beach Club and Hotel is located on an isolated stretch of Grace Bay beach. It has twenty-five rooms and is decked out in pastel pink. Rates are $125, double.

The Ocean Club is Provo's first luxury beachfront condominium complex and is just south of Club Med. There is a pool and studios and two- and three-bedroom beach-front apartments. Units are also available for sale and daily rates begin at $110 for a studio.

Treasure Beach Villas is an attractive apartment alternative on Grace Bay Beach with twenty beachfront one- and two-bedroom units that are completely furnished down to the silverware. Rates are $110 for a double.

NORTH CAICOS

This little island has just a couple of small personality hotels. **Pelican Beach Resort** boasts fourteen units, six miles of powder white beach, snorkeling, diving, and getting away from it all. The owner is a first-rate pilot and offers flying excursions to nearby islands. Rates are $150 per day. **The Prospect of Whitby** is named after a London pub and strives for an intimate pub-like atmosphere. It has reopened under new owners and features twenty-eight rooms, pool, tennis, scuba diving miles of beach and plenty of seclusion. Doubles average $150 per night.

MIDDLE CAICOS

Currently there is just one small guest house with four rooms for visitors. **Taylor's Guest House** has four rooms and rates are $40 per double.

PINE CAY

This is a tiny private island and the home of the exclusive **Meridian Club** whose thirteen units attract a blue-chip largely American clientele. There is a small airstrip on the 800-acre island. There is a perfect beach, water sports and not much else here. Rates for doubles are $350 per night including meals.

SOUTH CAICOS

This island has plans for development and new hotels, but currently there is just one establishment for visitors. It is the sixteen-room **Harbour View** overlooking the sea. Rates are $50 for a double.

SALT CAY

The island has an old salt raker's inn – the **American House** – with seven rooms for visitors. Rates are $70 for a double.

GRAND TURK

This is the capital and has some of the islands' oldest establishments. The forty-eight room **Kittina Hotel** is the island's largest and liveliest resort. Owners Kit and Tina Fenimore attract the most interesting cast of characters on the island. Fenimore built the hotel himself and even quarried the stone. The twenty deluxe seaside beachfront suites, all with full kitchens, are the most prized rooms.

The restaurant and bar are both popular. Rates range from $90 to $200. A full-service dive operation is affiliated with the hotel. The nine-room **Salt Raker Inn** is a real country inn with a flowering garden. The 150-year-old former home has a popular Secret Garden bar and restaurant. It is just a short stroll from the center of town. Bikes and boats can be rented nearby and diving and swimming are across the road. Rates are $60 to $100. **The Island Reef Resort** is one of the island's newer and more comfortable spots with views of nearby cays and reefs and a pool, tennis courts, bar and restaurant on the premises. Suites and efficiencies with kitchenettes are $80 to $100. The tiny, four-room **Turks Head Inn** in a nineteenth-century house on Front Street offers simple accommodations for $50 a night for two.

Restaurants

With some exceptions dining is mostly in hotels, where island specialties as conch, lobster and other seafood are featured. Just about everything else is imported and dining is expensive. Expensive is over $60 for two without drinks and moderate is $40 to $59 for two. Inexpensive in these parts is under $40. On Grand Turk **Papillon's Rendez-vous** features casual seafood served by its French owners. Costs are moderate to expensive. **X's Place** on nearby Pond Street is an unusual establishment popular with British expatriates. It has an English pub atmosphere and is owned and operated by Frenchman Xavier Tonneau. Moderate. A must stop is **Peanuts Butterfield's Pepperpot Restaurant** for her legendary conch fritters and other local dishes. She will also entertain you with a rake and scrape recital. Inexpensive. On Provo **Alfred's Restaurant** is a local favorite featuring imaginative seafood. Moderate. **Dora's Restaurant** has great fish, conch and chowder. Moderate. **Henry's Road Runner** is one of the island's best dining spots with very good native dishes and the freshest seafood. Moderate.

PUERTO RICO

Little Puerto Rico is one of the Caribbean's most affluent islands and richest lodes of touristic pleasures, a tiny nugget measuring only 160 km (100 mi) in length and 56 km (35 mi) across. Yet within these few miles are enough hiking trails, caving, adventures, and beaches to spend a thrilling lifetime discovering them. Wooded slopes drop from a backbone of gently forested mountains, the Cordillera, to end in fertile plains and surf-washed seashore.

It is one of the Caribbean's most notable success stories. True, labor problems exist still, but even as recently as 1943 an American congressional subcommittee called Puerto Rico an "unsolvable" problem. For a long time, sugar barons lived like sultans while peasants, in the absence of any alternative income, worked for slave wages and lived in grinding poverty. Then the tide began to change. Programs such as *Operation Bootstrap* sought industrial investments and *Operation Amigo* trained local people in the various arts associated with the tourist trade. Multi-million-dollar resorts include those at Palmas del Mar and the Hyatt complex at Dorado, as well as entire strips of beachfront hotels at Condado, Ocean Park, Miramar and Isla Verde. Today, Puerto Ricans have one of the highest incomes in Latin America and a healthy life expectancy of 73.8 years.

Preceding pages: A solitary haven in the jungle. Left: The San Juan guard, an almost medieval reminder.

Puerto Rico's history, with its centuries of destruction and rebuilding, mirrors that of most of the West Indies. It began as a Spanish colony. The French destroyed San German in 1528. The English attacked in 1595, were routed, and their commander, Sir John Hawkins, died of his wounds. They had more success three years later when they captured San Juan, but a mere three months later they in turn were forced to surrender the town. In 1625 San Juan was burned by the Dutch and in 1702 the English pounded Arecibo to rubble. Although the British tried again and again, they never got another toehold on the island and Puerto Rico remained Spanish until 1898, when it was ceded to the United States.

Sugar cane was introduced to Puerto Rico, via Hispaniola, by the Spanish in 1515 and for centuries it was the major crop. The colony already had a labor force of servant-slaves, or *encomendados*, made up of captured Indians. African slaves were added in 1518. By the time the Indians were freed in 1544, in a royal decree that announced they were equal with any Spaniard, their ranks were

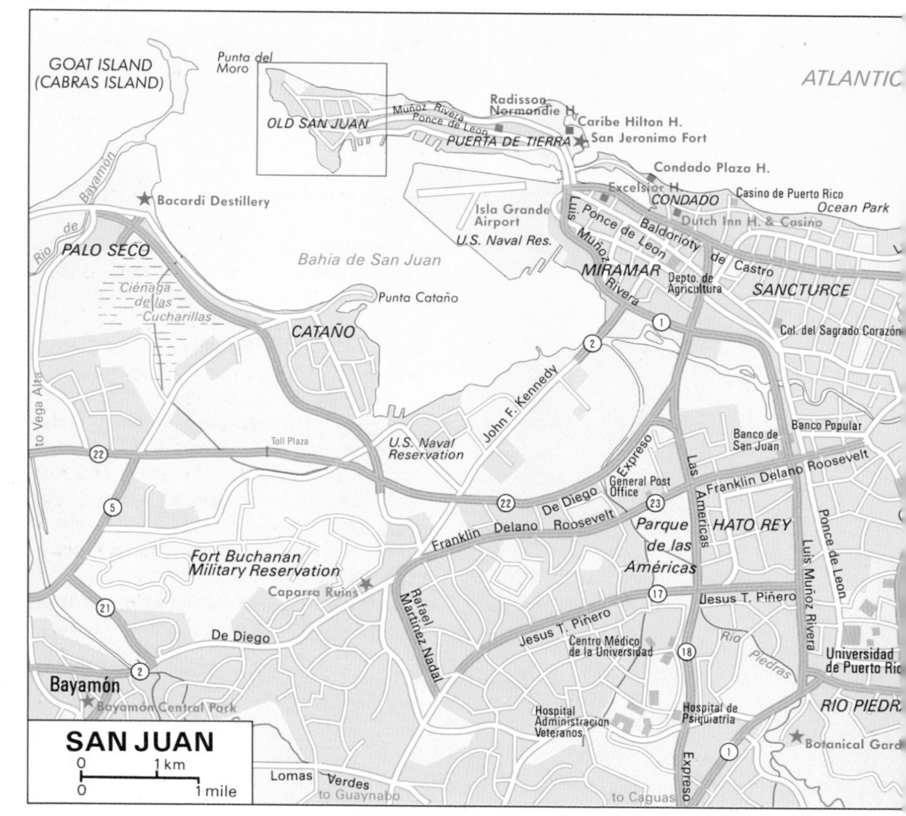

already thinned by disease and execution. Those remaining amalgamated with the new population. It was not until 1873 that emancipation came to black slaves.

Exploring Puerto Rico

Most tourists think of the island in two parts: San Juan with its riviera of white beaches lined with luxury hotels, and everything else, known to locals as *en la isla*, which means "out on the island". This consists mostly of a hilly region with beaches, canes and friendly guest houses offering lodgings. The Puerto Rican province is as slow-paced and verdant as San Juan is showy and alive. Everything begins and ends, of course, in historic San Juan where the first surprise is that everything can be so exotically Hispanic, yet so American at the same time. Whatever your country of origin, it is almost impossible to feel out of place in a land where Coke and a burger, shrimp as big as tomcats, *mofongo* on the side and *guava* ice cream share a menu cheek-by-jowl. Through it all, you are serenaded by the happy shriek of the *coqui*, a small frog that has become Puerto Rico's symbol, mascot, nuisance and joy. Its impudent tweeting wakes you in the morning and serves as your lullaby at night.

Do not leave Luis Munoz Marin International Airport without stopping at the tourist information office near the main

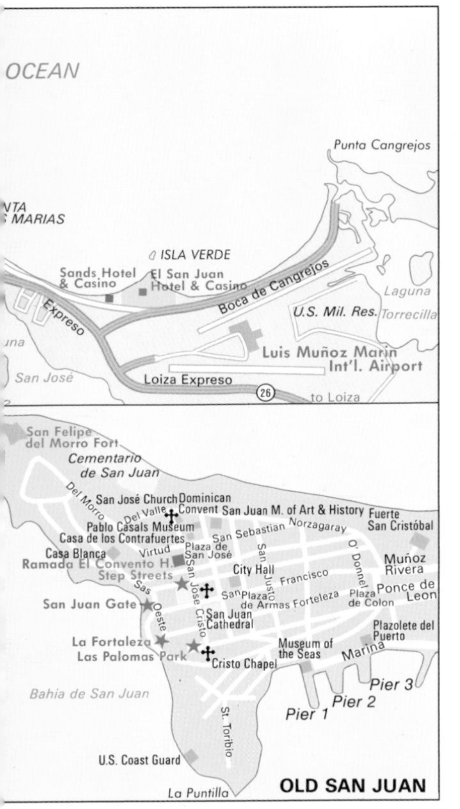

entrance. It offers the invaluable monthly publication *Que' Pasa* free of charge; a wealth of other publications and brochures are available, too. And if you have arrived without reservations (it is unwise, but it happens), friendly staff will help you find a room.

San Juan

Old San Juan is a city in itself, a seven-block enclave that was once a walled city protected by the mighty fort San Felipe del Morro and by the city walls themselves. Two 13 m (42 ft) high sandstone fences were built parallel to each other, then the space between them was filled with sand. At nightfall, six mammoth wooden doors were closed and sentries were set to keep a lookout from the heights. Thus the San Juan of the 17th century slept safe from marauding Dutch and English.

San Felipe del Morro, now a national historic site administered by the National Park Service, is an impressive sight – six stories high and so powerful that it withstood repeated attacks as late as the Spanish American War in the 20th century. Even when the city itself was conquered, *El Morro* held firm. The fort is open daily 8 a.m. to 6 p.m. and entrance is free. And if your heart goes out to old fortresses, **San Jeronimo**, behind the Caribe Hilton in the *Condado* area has a well-supplied military museum. The fort itself was nearly blown to irretrievable smithereens by the British in 1797, but it has been restored, and is a pleasant place for a stroll.

It was at the **San Juan Gate**, north of *La Fortaleza*, where arriving VIPs were met by locals, to be escorted up the hill to the cathedral and the saying of a *Te Deum* mass in thanks for a safe passage. In later years, the ceremony shifted to the San Justo Gate, but only the San Juan Gate remains.

Do not try to drive in the old city. It is best seen on foot. Spare two or three days for the tour if possible. On a one-day tour, there is only time to walk the centuries-old blue ballast-stone streets and lose yourself in the subsequent time warp. Two of the streets are just series of steps, the only ones remaining from an era when people went everywhere on foot. Where pathways were too steep, steps were added instead of paving.

With the luxury of more time, you can visit the many small museums and galleries, and shop in a galaxy of boutiques. Also enjoyable is a stop for morning coffee – hot and strong in a tiny cup – then a cooling rum drink and a leisurely luncheon at places ranging from chic to shabby, expensive to dirt cheap. A good

place to make reservations for dinner is **La Mallorquina** on San Justo Street. It has been in operation since 1848, and serves the definitive *asapao*, Puerto Rico's national dish.

Now restored, the **San Juan Museum of Art and History**, at the corner of MacArthur and Norzagaray, was built in 1855 as a marketplace. It is a fine example of the open air architecture of the period, with an immense patio often used for festivals and special events. The two galleries display local art; audio-visual programs tell the history of San Juan. In the **Pablo Casals Museum**, at 101 San Sebastion, are manuscripts, photographs, and memorabilia relating to the famous cellist. Included in the collection are videotapes of Casals Festivals, the island's internationally attended annual classical music event. It is open Tues. through Sat., 6 a.m. to 5:30 p.m., Sun. 1 p.m. to 5 p.m.

Above: Detail of leatherwork on a chair in the Casa Blanca, San Juan. Right: El Morro fortress in San Juan.

On the same plaza is the **Casa de los Contrafuertes**, believed to be the oldest surviving private residence in the old city. It is now a graphics museum open Wed. through Sun., 9 a.m. to 4 p.m. Even if you are not interested in the graphics, the building itself is worth a visit.

On the Plaza de San José, the **San José Church**, which was begun in 1532, is one important cultural attraction. With its vaulted ceilings, it remains a superb example of medieval architecture transported to the New World. It was once the church of the family of Ponce de Leon, and his body was enshrined here for 350 years. On the same plaza the **Dominican Convent**, which is even older than the church, dating back to 1523, once sheltered women and children from Carib attacks in its dungeons. It now functions as a museum with galleries and a pleasant courtyard, and is open to the public from Wednesday to Sunday, from 9 a.m. to noon, and from 1 p.m. to 4:30 p.m.

One of the other fine examples of medieval architecture in the West Indies is

San Juan Cathedral, at 153 Cristo. The first cathedral was built of lumber in the 1520s and it had a humble thatched roof. The rather flimsy structure was destroyed in a hurricane and rebuilding started in 1541. Threatened for centuries by hurricanes and predacious English soldiers, the cathedral has undergone many refinements, repairs and additions; most of its features date from the early 1800s or later. It is here that Ponce de Leon's body lies in a magnificent marble tomb. The cathedral is open daily. A little further down Christo, at number 253, is a small art museum. The neighboring house has a collection of rare books on public display.

The **Casa Blanca**, or White House, at 1 San Sebastion, is the original governor's palace, dating to the early 16th century. It was occupied by the Ponce de Leon family for 250 years, and is now kept as a living museum showing family life as it was in the 16th and 17th centuries. **La Fortaleza**, however, is the seat of the oldest executive mansion in the western hemisphere. It was completed in 1540, in a rush to raise defenses against the Carib Indians, and has been home to Puerto Rico governors for 400 years. It was occupied briefly by the British, and by the Dutch, who burned it in 1625. It was rebuilt in 1640 and again in the 1840s; now it is a World Heritage Site. La Fortaleza is open weekdays except holidays.

Another government building, the **City Hall**, is a small-scale replica of its analogous edifice in Madrid, Spain. The San Francisco St. entrance has a tourist information center offering maps for self-guided walking tours of the city, among other things. Its main entrance is on the **Plaza de Armas**, at one time the city's center, where citizens once drilled to keep themselves ready for enemy attack. One of the best free shows in the old city is the march of the **Colonial Guard**, with drums and bracing military music, Tuesday through Saturday at 10:45 a.m., noon, and 2 p.m. The parade route goes from the Plaza de Armas to the **Plaza de Colon** (plaza of Columbus) and back,

Above: The ornate façade of the old customs house in San Juan. Right: Taking it easy in Old San Juan.

along San Francisco and Fortaleza streets. While you are at the Plaza de Colon , study the bronze tablets depicting the life of Christopher Columbus. (If you are coming from an outlying hotel, the bus terminal here is a good place to begin or end a walking tour of Old San Juan).

The view of the harbor is good from **Las Palomas Park** and its legend is beguiling. It tells of a young horseman who, while participating in the feast of St. John in 1723, failed to control his horse and plunged over the edge. A friendly onlooker vowed to build a chapel here if the young man's life could be spared. Although historical records show that the youth died, the faithful man contributed money anyway for the building of this charming little **Cristo Chapel**. Its elaborate altar and paintings can be seen through the glass door at all times. It is open Tuesdays from 10 a.m. to 4 p.m.

From the first Spanish footsteps, San Juan's life has centered around the **harbor**. A boat tour offers a panorama of the city as it was seen by its visitors for centuries, until the air age. Sight-seeing, dinner and disco cruises, and the Catano ferry leave from Pier Two. Nearby, at Pier One, the **Museum of the Seas** is open only when cruise ships are in port. On display are old maritime instruments, charts and ship models. Across from Pier Three in the **Plazolete del Puerto**, local handicrafts and produce are sold in a colorful, if somewhat touristy, marketplace. From the bus terminal here, you can return to your hotel.

Shopping

The city is famed for the number and quality of its professional galleries. The Butterfly People for example, offers a wide range of butterfly arrangements and murals. Galeria Botello exhibits a permanent Botello collection, and works of local and overseas artists. Que'Pasa

offers a full list of Old San Juan's art galleries. But regular shoppers with varying budgets can also enjoy some consumerism in San Juan. All the usual cruise ship shopping is found in the old city, from emeralds and perfumes to leathers and linens. Imports from all over the world have been gathered here – silks and cottons from India, woven mats from the Philippines, handicrafts from Haiti. Breezing in and out of shops, looking for duty free bargains, is one of the fun sports in San Juan.

One of the best buys on the island is rum, which is produced here by the barrel in every flavor from a delicate white rum (white rum Martinis are very "in") to a deep, wood-aged rum as rich as brandy. If you are a smoker, Puerto Rico is famous for its hand-rolled cigars made from locally grown tobaccos.

Greater San Juan

Metropolitan San Juan is as hectic and traffic-congested as any other major modern city, but many visitors enjoy getting around for a day or two by rental car or by local *publicos* (small buses). Most hotels can arrange a sight-seeing tour, and it is well worth taking one – both to avoid having to drive in San Juan traffic and because the guide's narration always provides spicy little details not mentioned in most guidebooks. In addition to local tours, a one-day shopping trip to **St. Thomas**, by air, can also be arranged.

Points of interest in Greater San Juan include **Rio Piedras**, home of a botanical garden where more than 200 species of tropical plants flourish. Here you can lose yourself in an orchid garden, sit by a lotus-filled lagoon, or wander down a bamboo-lined pathway. Puerto Rico itself is a tropical garden inhabited by a zoo of twittering birds.

All kinds of plants grow on the island, from the flamboyant pink and purple queen-of-flowers to pink cedar, audacious immortelle, orchid-like tulip trees, and intoxicatingly fragrant frangipani. Flamboyant is also both the name and description of one of the tropics' boldest and most beautiful trees, so crowded with flame-colored blossoms that hardly a leaf can be found. The garden at the intersection of Routes 1 and 847, is open Tuesday through Sunday, from 9 a.m. to 4 p.m.

The **farmers' market** in downtown Rio Piedras is the island's largest. It is a crowded, colorful hodgepodge, run by and for locals so it is a good spot to sample fresh pineapple or shop for Puerto Rican coffee.

On the edge of town, the **Luis Munoz Marin Archives, Museum and Gardens** are of interest to historians and scholars. The archives are devoted to papers and memorabilia of Marin, who was a popular governor. The library at the nearby university is the island's largest. The route back, along traffic-laden **Ponce de Leon Avenue**, follows the **Golden Mile** financial district.

On the way, the **Sacred Heart University** in Santurce, has also become the repository of a Museum of Contemporary Puerto Rican Art and a Fine Arts Center. Also in Santurce is the **Jewish Community Center**, housed in a fine example of turn-of-the-century architecture.

Hato Rey breathes a sense of gaudy entertainment. It has a modest theme park with rides, restaurant, playground, miniature golf, and water slides. Hours vary, with the park areas and aquatic areas not always open at the same time. Call 1-809/754-9500 for information.

It also boasts the largest shopping mall in the Caribbean, a colossal, American-style shopping center complete with numerous shops, restaurants, theaters and pharmacies.

In the **Bayamon area** with its old and romantic streets you can find the remains of Ponce de Leon's first settlement, **Caparra**, that was founded in 1508. You can still see the remnants of foundations, and a small museum showing exhibits from the era. Bayamon's Central Park offers tours on an old schoolhouse and a sugar

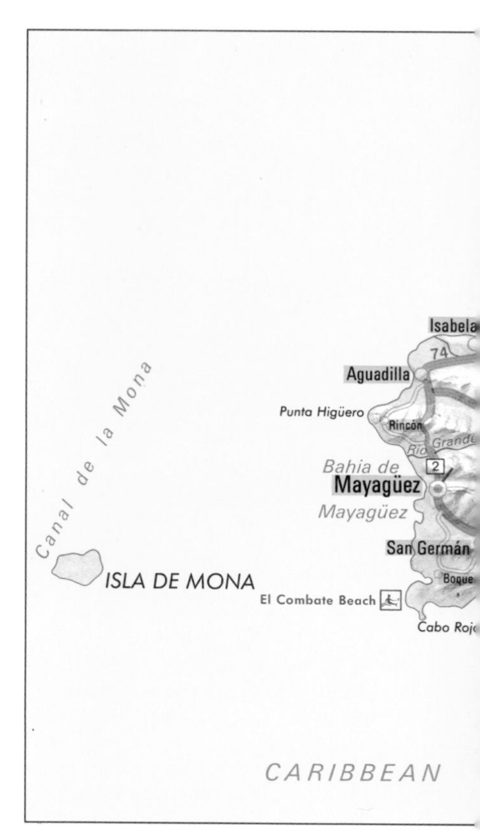

cane train. Northwest of town are some museums which are devoted to science and archaeology.

Continuing to the city of **Catano** (which can also be reached from San Juan by ferry), you will pass a 150-year-old windmill, a rum distillery and a centuries-old home.

The Bacardi distillery gives tour and free sample, before the journey continues to **Goat (Cabras) Island** for a superb view of El Morro. The island's own current ruins are not those of the fort that stood here in 1608, but rather of a fortress-like building used by the Spanish as a jail. Afterwards there is swimming at **Punta Salinas**, and picnicking at Cabras Island.

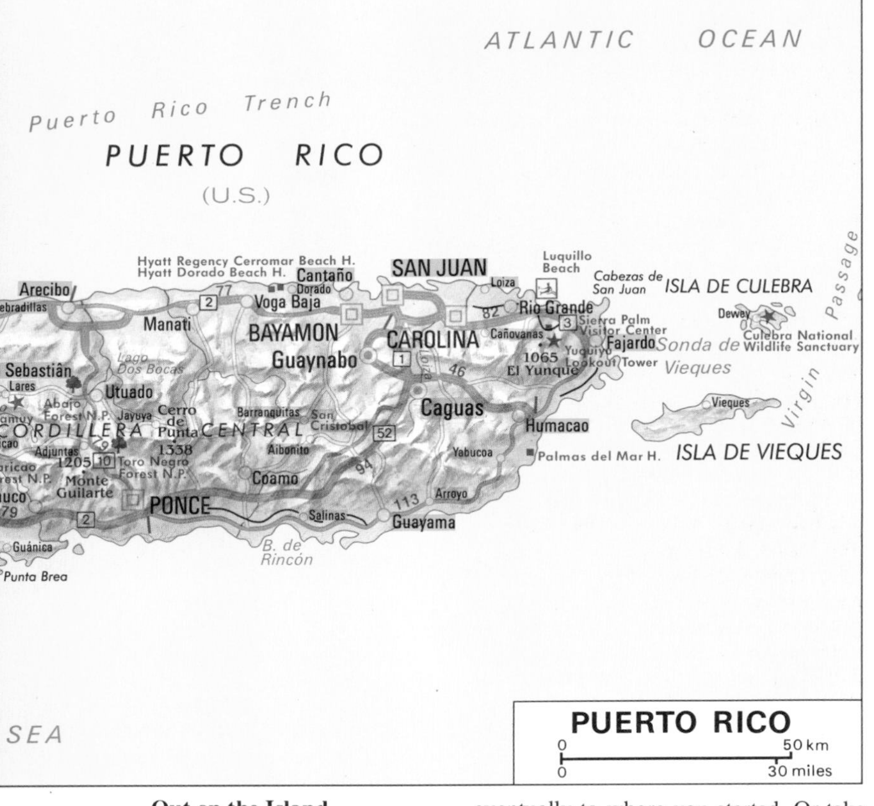

Out on the Island

To head away from the steamy city and into the countryside is to shed the cacophony of civilization and discover another side of Puerto Rico. There are the mountains where coffee is grown, so fragrant and special that it is sent to the Pope. You pass farms where rare and elegant *paso fino* horses are trained, and a rain forest alive with birds and rushing waterfalls.

The island contains miles of good roads, and a labyrinth of meandering secondary roads where tourists can get lost in a second. There are three major routes to use to avoid this. One follows the perimeter of the island, and brings you back eventually to where you started. Or take off on the good expressway that runs north and south between San Juan and Ponce. It is fast, safe and offers sweeping views of the countryside. The third choice is the Panoramic Route, a network of roads that follows the spine of mountains east and west across the island. It is rugged going, and well worth it, but do allow at least three days to follow the entire route. It leads through villages where people live as their grandparents did, farming, harvesting coffee, carving wooden animals, or making citron.

Deep in the Cordillera, near **Utado**, an ancient Taino Indian ceremonial center has been unearthed. There is a small museum here, and a shop selling relics. It

is probably the best archaeological site in the West Indies, and one of a handful that today still seems to remember the flesh-and-blood people who lived here. The site covers 5 ha (13 acres) and has been landscaped to show how it might have looked 800 years ago. Stone walkways lead around the ten ceremonial ball courts, or *bateyes*, much like those used by the Taino Indians. Royal palms and guavas are among the present trees that could have been growing here then; stone petroglyphs look as though they are waiting for Taino worshippers to return.

Two of the island's best *paradores*, or guest houses, are along this route: the old coffee plantations at **Jayuya** and **Maricao**, which have been turned into rustic inns. Another *parador* is at the ancient bath site at **Coamo**. In all, there are sixteen such country places, all modestly priced and in beautiful areas.

Above: Harmless reptiles even approach people. Right: Orchids also thrive in the tropical climate.

El Yunque

For centuries, this tangle of gnarled trees and rushing rivers was a hideaway for Taino Indians, escaped slaves and daring adventure seekers. Even today it is not wise to venture into **El Yunque,** the United States' only tropical national forest, without a guide – not so much because of the dangers but because you might miss some of the most significant birds, rock formations, waterfalls, orchids, peaks, and trails. A highlight is the **Yuquiyu lookout tower**, with its see-forever views.

El Yunque begins at the **Sierra Palm Visitor Center** on Route 191 which is open every day. Here you can get a camping permit, latest condition reports on hiking trails, topographical maps and sage advice on the safest spot to leave your car while you are gone. Take along a picnic lunch, or splurge at the landmark **El Yunque Restaurant** where the forest view is outstanding and the food ranks with the very best in local cuisine.

Most one-day bus tours to El Yunque only scratch the surface, but they do give a sampling of the mountains and they include a stop at **Luquillo Beach** for a cooling dip after a day in the damp, steamy woods. Fringed in coconut palms, this picturebook beach also has tent sites if you want to camp. For more information, call 1-809/887-2875 or 1-809/766-5335; or write to the Caribbean National Forest, Box B, Palmer, PR 00721.

Camping is also permitted, with prior permission, in most of the island's forest preserves. Always stop at the ranger station first, for permits and advice on local conditions. The dozen or more national forests include the majestic **Abajo Forest** with its mahogany and teak, the sere **Maricao Forest** with its wealth of raptors, and **Toro Negro Forest** with its ocean views. It is best to visit the forests during the week, when they are less crowded. For information, call the Department of Natural Resources at 1-809/722-1726. Between Utuado and the Rio Abajo Forest lies **Lake Dos Bocas** with its sporty freshwater fishing and pleasant boat rides. Nearby is **Lake Caonillas**, which has a nice *parador* to spend a few nights in.

Rio Camuy

Rio Camuy Park is one of the Caribbean's most dazzling nature shows. Centuries ago, the Camuy River disappeared into the **Blue Hole** near Lares and began carving one of the largest underground river systems in the world – an elaborate network of caverns, tunnels, and sinkholes that has never been fully explored. For years it was a private preserve of daring spelunkers, but in the 1980s it opened as a public park. After viewing an orientation movie, visitors climb aboard trams for the long, tortuous spiral deep into a lushly forested sink where gapes the mouth of an enormous cave. From here you strike out on foot, with a bilingual guide, to see caverns, underwater pools filled with blind fish and huge, echoing sinkholes. Admission is charged

for the main trip and for side trips to a private cave and to a 198 m (650 ft) deep sinkhole. If you are an experienced spelunker, and can link up with one of the local caving groups, you may also be able to go along on one of their outings. Call ahead for information, 1- 809/756-5555 or 1-809/898-3100; the park is enormously popular and has a capacity of only 1,500 visitors a day. It is open Wednesday through Sunday and on holidays. The premises have been provided with picnic tables, a food concession and a playground. Cave tours, a painless way to see one of the island's most important sites, can be booked from San Juan hotels.

The Out Islands

Ferries to Puerto Rico's two major out-islands leave from **Fajardo**, a sun-splashed fishing village suffering – as most of Puerto Rico is – from crowding and over-population. Still, it is a quaint place to stop for a seafood meal, boating, swimming and a visit to **Casa Roig**, a museum and cultural center. The Casa, designed by a disciple of Frank Lloyd Wright, dates to the 1920s.

Both out-island groups, the **Culebras** and **Vieques**, are still recovering from the pounding they took from Hurricane Hugo in 1989. Nature's resilience can be surprising, but it may be some time before the **Culebra National Wildlife Sanctuary** is what it was in 1909, when it was set aside as a refuge by Teddy Roosevelt. Its fame rests on the bird colonies and on the snorkeltours on gaudy reefs. Take the short boat or plane ride to **Vieques** to enjoy the beaches and a picnic, photograph the old lighthouse, check into a quaint *parador,* camp, or sit on the shores of Mosquito Bay on a moonless night to observe its mysterious phosphorescence. It is not, as you might think, reflections from stars or the moon but rather billions of micro- organisms producing the glow.

Above: The palm trees come alive in the evening sun and breezes. Right: A smiling face for the camera.

Other Cities and Villages

In alphabetical order: **Aquadilla** supplied fresh water to Christopher Columbus and his Spanish sailors, whose first footsteps on Puerto Rican soil were in this area in 1493. The area is still known today for its waters, those that lap against brown sugar sands shaded by coconut palms. For surfing, some of the best beaches lie between **Rincon** (where the world surfing championships were held in 1968) and **Isabela**. Off Isabela, you can snorkel or scuba on brilliant reef gardens. Several *paradores* at **Quebradillas** offer accomodations; guests are trolleyed around free of charge to local points of interest such as beaches (including some with pirate legends), a few ancient railroad tunnels, and the best places to buy the area's famous *mundillo* lace.

Arecibo is a working scientific laboratory rather than a tourist attraction – the largest radar/radio telescope in the world. Arecibo Observatory attracts visitors from all over the globe. Scientists here monitor emissions from distant galaxies in hopes of learning more about outer space. The grounds, and a platform overlooking the telescope, are open on Sunday afternoons. Tours are given only Tuesday through Friday at 2 p.m. Arrive early. Tel. 1- 809/878- 2612.

Arroyo and **Guayama**, once a smugglers' paradise, can be toured on an inexpensive trolley that operates daily out of Arroyo. The **Casa Cautino** is a fine little museum, and you will also see a sugar mill, beaches and the ultra-modern Olympic training lodge at **Salinas**.

Cabo Rojo: This sleepy fishing region on the southwest corner of the island is a hideaway popular with Puerto Ricans themselves, who come for the white sand beaches, superb seafood restaurants, (eighteen in **Joyuda** alone) and simple, small town street festivals. There is a waterfowl refuge in **Boqueron** and a wildlife refuge administered by the U.S.

Fish and Wildlife Service just beyond **El Combate Beach**. The lighthouse at the end of Route 301 rises impressively from a cliff-rimmed coast. **Caguas** lies halfway between San Juan and the south coast, neatly perched in the highlands. The water park here operates water slides, paddle-boats and canoes, swimming pools and a restaurant. It is usually closed during the week, so check ahead at Tel. 1-809/747- 4747.

Catano is really part of San Juan, but the best way to get here is by ferry, which is as much fun, as good a view, and as good a bargain as riding the Staten Island ferry in Manhattan. Tours of the local Bacardi Rum Distillery are as usual available free, with samples on the house.

Dorado is just a small fishing village, but this area west of San Juan has become home to two of the Antilles' best hotels, the Hyatt Regency Cerromar Beach and the Hyatt Dorado Beach.

The estate of the **Livingston family** constituted a flourishing plantation during the first half of this century. Clara

Livingston became famous as an aviatrix during the same years that Amelia Earheart (1898-1937) earned her wings. The old family home is now a cozy gourmet restaurant, **Su Casa**. Developed by Lawrence Rockefeller, these resorts have lavish swimming pools, golf, a myriad of beaches, fine dining and an away-from-it-all ambience. If you have seen San Juan on previous visits, and want only to get out of the city and into a Utopia of vacation pleasures, arrange ahead of time to go straight from the airport to the resort using the Hyatt's own transportation.

Humacao: Nearby is a stretch of seashore that, like Dorado, is a former plantation turned playground, complete with villas and hotels, golf and tennis, boating, diving, deep-sea fishing, watersports instruction, swimming pools (but no beaches), restaurants, a casino and a complete health center and spa. And, like Dorado visitors, guests usually drive or fly here directly from the airport at San Juan. The complex is handled by one reservation center at Tel. 1-800/221-4874, 1-212/983-0393, or 1- 809/852-6000.

Above: Where land and sea meet. Right: The famous delicious langostinos del Caribe of Sabana Grande.

Mayaguez is a stately port city despite its not-so-pretty tuna canning factories. Although it was almost completely wiped out by an earthquake in 1918, the city was consientiously restored with pleasant plazas and a tropical park that spills over onto the grounds of the Mayaguez Hilton. It has one of the largest tropical collections in the hemisphere. A zoo is situated in a park filled with ponds and scenic, shaded pathways lined with flowers and foliage. Animals on view include a collection of capybara, the world's largest rodent, a Bengal tiger and a condor. Admission is $1 for adults and 50 cents for children. The zoo is closed Mondays.

The port at Mayaguez is a casting off point for visiting wild and windswept **Mona Island**, a wildlife refuge where 91 cm (36 in) iguanas share the spotlight with color-splashed reef fish, long-

legged shore birds and rare plants. Call ahead for permission to visit, 1-809/722-1726. Then charter a boat or plane. The 80 km (50 mi) wide **Mona Passage** can be rough, so be picky about the boat you hire. Camping is permitted by prior arrangement, but you must bring everything you need, including water, and take everything back out including garbage.

Ponce is a major city with an impressive art museum containing more than 1000 paintings and 400 sculptures. Nearby the **Tibes Indian Ceremonial Center**, where the oldest cemetery yet discovered in the Antilles was uncovered in the 1970s. Indian skeletons, plazas, and dance grounds have been excavated, and a Taino village has been replicated. The museum is open daily except Monday.

Sabana Grande is the home of Langostinos del Caribe, the largest freshwater prawn artificially bred in the United States. Tourists are welcome to see the culturing, harvesting, and processing of these luscious shrimp, daily 8 a.m. to 5 p.m.

San German was Puerto Rico's second city in 1528, when it was sacked by the French. Its Porta Coeli Church, which dates to 1606, is a museum of religious art. It is open Wednesday through Sunday and admission is free.

Rincon: Also see Aquadilla above. In addition to its surfer ambience, Rincon is a place to keep an eye peeled for humpback whales in winter.

San Cristobal area: The deepest canyon on the island plunges 231 m (700 ft) down vine-covered cliffs between the communities of **Aibonito** and Barranquitas. The canyon is a natural wonder containing, among other awesome sights, a 30 m (100 ft) waterfall. The area has no facilities for tourists yet, but you can get a view of it from a point near Km 17.7 on Route 156. To the south is **Coamo**, which has been revered since Indian times for its healing hot springs. You can stay at a cozy *parador* here, and soak your weariness away in the spa. The other point of interest at Coamo is a picture-book church, the very model of an 18th century

Spanish mission. There is also a small museum off the plaza. At **Barranquitas**, a charming little cliff-clinger village north of here, a museum and library are devoted to Munoz Rivera, father of Luiz Munoz Marin whose museum and library is at Rio Piedras. Both are buried at Barranquitas.

The Artisans of Puerto Rico

The crafts of Puerto Rico make meaningful souvenirs, and smart artists have also saddled the tourist trade by turning their work into a free show as well. Call the Tourism Artisan Office at Tel. 1-809/721-2400, ext. 215, for information about those craftsmen who welcome visitors to their shops, including their addresses and hours. For further information call the Fomento Crafts Program, Tel. 1-809/758-4747, ext. 2291.

Above: Woodcarving is among the important handicrafts in Puerto Rico. Right: An evening stroll on the beach.

Among the islands' most treasured relics are *santos*, small carved wooden religious figures made by *santeros*. Each family has its own motifs and techniques, and has passed the craft down for generations, making these figures truly unique specimens of a time-honored folk art. Bobbin lace, which had a great vogue in the United States a century ago but has become almost a lost art, thrives among the country women of Puerto Rico. You can watch them at work on their *mundillo* frames, turning out lace collars, dresser scarves, and delicate tablecloths. One island center for the craft is **Quebradillas**, but you can find *mundillo* in the countryside as well as in some of the most chic city shops.

Ancient fishermen's skills are still put to work in knotting hammocks for sale to tourists. The hammock was unknown to the world before the Spanish arrived in the New World and found them in use by aborigines. They immediately became the accepted sleeping mode for sailors and are today the backyard loafer's favorite napping spot. One shop where hammock makers welcome tourists to watch their work is in **San Sebastian**, at the mouth of the Anasco River – northeast of Mayaguez.

When the Spanish arrived in the West Indies, the native Indians had a well-developed sense of music and dance, but no stringed instruments. At first, dried gourds were strung with gut to create the songs brought from Spain by lonely sailors. Such *guiros* are still made here, for sale to informed tourists. Another native instrument, the *cuatro*, has five double strings. Made from native trees, using skills that have been handed down from father to son for centuries, *cuatros* are not only collectors' items but are serious musical instruments with a sound somewhat like a mandolin. *Cuatros* might be found anywhere, but one center for the craft is Utuado, deep in the Cordillera – north of **Adjuntas**.

Hand-rolled cigars are still being made in some of the tourist-traveled parts including the **San Juan Bus Terminal**. Cigar-making is an interesting craft to observe, and the product is world famous among cigar aficionados.

Other ancient crafts still practiced on the island are basket making, and the making of *vejigantes*, ceremonial masks made from coconut shells. Traditionally, they are used in saints-day celebrations at **Loiza** on the northeast coast. Authentic papier mâché masks of the type used during carnival in Ponce are also sold.

Many of the same local markets that are the happy hunting grounds for souvenir seekers are also the best places to buy locally grown fruits and vegetables. They are best eaten and savored under Puerto Rico's sun, besides, your home country may prohibit importing agricultural products. You have to go through an agricultural inspection on the way out of the country. At present, it is permitted to take avocado, papaya, coconut and plantains to the States but not mango, soursop, passion fruit or any potted plants. If you are in doubt, call the Puerto Rican branch of the U.S. Department of Agriculture at 1- 809/253- 4505 or 253-4506.

Watersports

Bounded by the Atlantic to the north and the Caribbean Sea to the south, and located on the edge of "marlin alley", the Atlantic's miles-deep **Puerto Rico Trench**, the island could be no better situated for sportfishing. Scuba diving, sailing, surfing, snorkeling, waterskiing, and all the other watersports, plus deep-sea or reef fishing by the day or half day, can be arranged through your hotel.

Horseback Riding

To riders who know and respect the finest in horses, Puerto Rico could become a mecca. Leading thoroughbreds race at **El Comandante**, at Canovanas, and spectators watch from a modern and comfortable clubhouse while dining

sumptuously. An even better show, though, is that put on by the island's beautiful and splendidly trained *paso fino* horses. Look out for notices of local horse shows and events.

To tour the beaches and rain forest trails by horseback, contact Hacienda Carbali, 1-809/795-6351 or 1-809/887-4954. *Paso fino* horses are available. Riding horses and instructions are also available at the **Palmas del Mar Equestrian Center**, a part of the enormous Palmas del Mar Resort, at Humacao.

Paradores

Paradores are too special, too uniquely Puerto Rican, too hard to categorize, to be listed among hotels. They are not always the most lavish lodgings but they are located in the island's best scenic or historic spots – often in places where no other lodgings are available. To be listed by the Puerto Rico Tourism Company, they must meet certain standards in cleanliness and comfort so you are assured of dependable quality even in the most remote areas. All offer meals at modest prices. Rates vary, but average less than $60.

Above: Welcoming faces from children. Right: Puerto Rico also offers great opportunities for aquatic activities.

For information about any of the island's sixteen government- inspected *paradores* call 137-800-462-7575; outside San Juan, 1-800/443-0266 in the U.S., or 1- 809/721-2400 or 721- 2884. Prices depend on location. *Paradores* are found in Coamo, Boqueron, Utuado, Mayaguez, Quebradillas, Juyaya, Maricao, Fajardo, Luquillo, San German, Cabo Rojo, Lajas, Rincon, and Vieques.

What to Wear

Although Puerto Rico is mere millimeters away from the Virgin Islands on the map, it is Hispanic. And that makes for a few differences in dress. The pleated, embroidered *guayabera* shirt is almost al-

ways suitable dinner garb for a gentleman. Jackets are rarely required, and ties almost never. Local men seldom wear shorts, but no one will be offended if you wear them at resorts and beaches. Otherwise, "resort chic" is the order of the day.

Ocean Sports

Oceanfront camping is available at Anasco, Boqueron, Cerro Gordo, Fajardo, Luquillo, Punta Guilarte, Punta Santiago, and Sombe. Information about overnight stays at these beaches is available from the Department of Recreation and Sports, 1-809/722-1551 or 721-8000, ext. 225 or 275.

For scuba diving, contact Aquatica Underwater Adventures, 1- 809/890-6071; Carib Aquatic Adventures, 1-809/724-1882 or 1-809/765-7444; Caribbean Divers, 1-809/724-3292 or 793-8585, ext. 1047; Caribbean School of Aquatics, 1-809/723- 4740 or 728-6606; Castillo Watersports, 1-809/791-6195 or 726-5752; Coral Head Divers at Palmas del Mar, 1-809/850-7208 or (800) 635-4529; La Cueva Submarine Training Center in Isabela, 1-809/872-3903 or 872-1094; San Juan Water Sports at the Condado Plaza Hotel, 1- 809/ 721-1000, exts. 2105 and 2106; Scuba Shoppe, Fajardo, 1-809/863-8465; or Mundo Submarine, 1-809/791-5764.

For sportfishing charters, call Aquatica Underwater Adventures, 1-809/890-6071; Benitez Deep-Sea Fishing, 1-809/723-2292 or 1- 809/724-6265; Castillo Watersports, 1-809/791-6195; or Markeira Hunter, 1-809/755-3050 or 793-5221.

For snorkeling charters, call any of the scuba outfitters listed above and aboard the *East Wind* catamaran, 1-809/863-2821 or 863-4267, or the Micana Loujour, 1-809/765-1212, ext. 2004.

Boat rentals can be arranged through Club Nautico at Fajardo, 1-809/860-2400. A glass-bottom boat trip is available out of Lajas. Call 1-809/899-4565. Sail and snorkel is offered aboard Captain Jack's Catamaran, Fajardo, 1- 809/863-1905; Captain Jayne Sailing

Charters, 1-809/791-5174; or Carib Aquatic Adventures, 1-809/724-1882. The latter also offers jetski rentals.

Festivals

Puerto Ricans love to gather together at anything from a christening to some city-wide wingding. **Carnival**, held in Ponce in springtime, always on a Thursday and lasting through the weekend, is presided over by *King Momo,* a figure who in early European carnivals was the village idiot. He was wined, dined, and executed. Today only the wining and dining remain, after which *King Momo* is unmasked. Carnival consists of a joyous blowout of dancing, feasting, parades, and a 12 m (40 ft) *pinata*.

The summer-long **LeLoLai Festival** was manufactured by the tourism department, but that does not make it any less boisterous or less appealing. Packages during this time are discounted to the bone, and you get long lists of extras such as side tours, a rental car, or golf plus fiestas, *jibaro* dances and other folk events. Call tel. 1- 809/723-3135 or 722-1513.

When you are on the island, keep abreast of local events because festivals are held often, usually in celebration of a saint's day. The musical festival held in honor of the great but late Spanish cellist Pablo Casals in June is internationally recognized.

Above: Coconuts are among Puerto Rico's natural products.

Puerto Rican Cuisine

Caribbean food in general is covered in another section of this book, but some foods are unique to Puerto Rico, where Carib and African elements mix with Spanish tastes and tropical seafood and produce. From Spain came cattle, goats, wheat flour, raisins and olive oil. To them were added fresh fish, vegetables and fruits in a list that grew everlonger as the seeds brought from around the world flourished here.

Asopao, the national dish, is a soupy stew that may be made with chicken, meat, or crab. It is traditionally served with cold, sliced avocado. *Pinon* is a tomato type casserole made with strips of plantain. *Tostones* are plantain slices that are fried twice, for crunchiness. White cheese, ideally served on plain soda crackers with a slice of guava paste or candied papaya, is a dessert fit for the gods.

Other sweets include the traditional flan, rice pudding (*arroz con dulce*) and a coconut cake winningly named *bien-me-sabe* (it tastes good to me). *Pionono* is a piquant hamburger wrapped in a strip of plantain. Salt cod, also called *bacalao*, is a legacy of pre-refrigeration days and it is served here in a tomato-based stew and in fritters. Finally, street vendors sell fragrant taro root *alcapurrias*, filled *surrilitos* and *morcillas*, fried sausages.

Tourist Information

Tourist information booths are at the airports in San Juan and Aguadilla, El Centro Convention Center in Condado, La Casita in Old San Juan and in Ponce. In most other communities, a Tourist Information office is in City Hall.
Puerto Rican tourism offices are at Coulsdon, Surrey, in England and in Chicago, Dallas, Denver, Frankfurt, Houston, Los Angeles, Madrid, Mexico City, Miami, Milan, New York, Orlando, Paris, Philadelphia, St. Louis and Washington.

Access

Direct flights from major cities throughout the United States, South America, and Central America, as well as from Madrid, Rome, Paris, Frankfurt, and London. Also, San Juan is a major hub for flights to and from other Caribbean islands.

Currency and Regulations

Currency: U.S. funds are used. Other currencies can be exchanged at the airport, any branch of the Scotia Bank or the Banco Popular, or at the Caribbean Foreign Exchange in Old San Juan. Puerto Rico is a territory of the United States, so U.S. money and postage are used. No duty is charged on articles taken to the mainland from PR, but an agricultural inspection is required. Certain produce and plants cannot be taken to the U.S.

Accommodation

LUXURY: **Caribe Hilton**, Fort San Jeronimo, Pta. de Tierra (San Juan), 1-809/721-0303. Beachfront resort in historic setting. Formal or casual restaurants, lounge with live music, pool, tennis, casino. **Condado Plaza**, 999 Ashford, Condado, (San Juan), 1-809/721-1000. Beach, pool, health club, casino, tennis, watersports, casual or fine dining. **El San Juan Hotel & Casino**, Avenida Isla Verde, San Juan, 1-809/791-1000 or 1- 800/468-2818. VCR, tennis, pools, spa, restaurants, biggest casino in Caribbean, lounges, show clubs. **Hyatt Regency Cerromar** and **Hyatt Dorado Beach**, Dorado (thirty minutes west of San Juan), 1-809/796-1234. Full resort facilities in lavish beachfront setting. Pool at Cerromar is 548 m (1,800 ft) long, includes waterfalls, grotto with whirlpool. Golf, tennis, spa, casino, cafes, elegant dining in an old plantation home. MAP available and recommended. Free shuttles between the two hotels; guests enjoy privileges of both. **Mayaguez Hilton**, Rt. 2, Mayaguez, 1- 809/831-7575. Beach, pool, tennis in garden bower setting. Superb chef, lounge with entertainment, golf privileges, casino, fitness paths. **Ramada El Convento**, 100 Cristo St., Old San Juan, 1- 809/723-9020. Heart of historic area, walk to shops and points of interest in old city. Pool, dining, health club. **Sands Hotel & Casino**, Route 37, Isla Verde, San Juan, 1-809/791-6100. Plush decor, enormous pool with water-falls, famous restaurants, prestige wing Plaza Club has garden suites and regal pampering. *MODERATE*: **Dutch Inn Hotel & Casino**, Ashford at Condado Ave., Condado, San Juan, 1-809/721-0810 or 1-800/468-2014. Pool, restaurant, lobby bar, cable TV, apartments available. *BUDGET*: **El Canario**, 4 Condado Ave. and 1317 Ashford Ave., both Condado, San Juan. 1-809/722-8640, 724-2796 or 1-800/533- 2649. Air-conditioned bed and (continental) breakfast inn. Private baths.

Restaurants

SAN JUAN AND ENVIRONS

EXPENSIVE: **El Batey del Pescador** in the **Caribe Hilton**, Pta. de Tierra, 1-809/721-0303. Seafood serenaded by sea view, dinner only, closed Sun. **El Zipperle**, Hato Rey, 1-809/763-1636. Classic paella, Spanish and German dishes, extensive wine list. **La Casona**, 609 San Jorge, Santurce, 1-809/727-2717. Turn-of-the-century mansion serving international menu with Spanish accent. **Scotch 'n Sirloin**, 1020 Ashford Ave., Condado, in **La Rada Hotel**, 1-809/722-3640. Dine on best beef while overlooking lagoon.

OUT ON THE ISLAND

LUXURY: Dorado: **Su Casa**, in the **Hyatt Dorada Beach Hotel**, 1-809/796-1600. Full island flavor in old family home. *Mayaguez:* **Hilton Hotel**, 1-809/831-7575. Continental dining in grand manner. *Ponce:* **Tanama**, **Holiday Inn**, 1-809/844-1200. Local and continental favorites. *BUDGET*: Look for the designation **Mesones Gastronomiquos**, indicating that the restaurant is part of a tourism-sponsored program of quality restaurants that feature native cuisine. Restaurants include: *Aquadilla:* **Dario's Gourmet**, 1-809/890-6143. *Aguas Buenas:* **Sirimar**, 1-809/732-6012. *Aibonito:* **Piedra**, Route 7718, KM 0.8. *Cabo Rojo:* **Perichi's**, 1-809/851-3131. *Caguas:* **Paraiso**, 1-809/747- 2012. **Cayey**, Jajome Terrice, 1-809/ 738-4016 and **Miramelinda**, 1- 809/738-9031. *Coamo:* **Banos de Coamo**, 1-809/825-2186. *Dorado:* **Ladrillo**, 1-809/796-2120 and **Terraza**, 1-809/796- 1242. *Guyanilla:* **Pichi's**, 1-809/835-4140. *Hatillo:* Buen Cafe, 1-809/898-3495. *Humacoa:* **Tulio's**, 1-809/852- 5471. *Jayuya:* **Dujo**, Route 140. Km. 8.2 or **Hacienda Gripinas**, 1-809/721-2400. *Juncos:* **Tenedor**, 1-809/734-6573. *Lajas:* **Villa Parguera Parador**, 1-809/899-3975. *Maricao:* **Hacienda Juanita**, 1-809/838-2550.

DOMINICAN REPUBLIC

The Dominican Republic is the second largest country in the Caribbean, surpassed in size only by Cuba. Characterized by white sand beaches, the tallest mountains in all the Caribbean, rain forests, damp lowlands, cactus-studded deserts and coastal swamps, it occupies 18,700 sq mi on the island of Hispaniola, which it shares with Haiti. As part of the Greater Antilles, the Dominican Republic lies 800-miles southeast of Florida, and 150-miles southeast of Cuba. Jamaica is 300-miles to the west and Puerto Rico to the east, across the sixty-mile wide Mona Passage.

Despite tremendous growth in the tourist trade, much of the country's impressive coastline has remained undeveloped. One can still move off the beaten path inland to discover arid plains atop the Caribbean's tallest peaks, forests of dwarf grasses and tenacious little ferns and dense rain forest undergrowth. Here one finds mahogany, lignum vitae, and the prized satinwood used in cabinet making, all draped in tangled vines that are home to a host of birds: the Hispaniola parrot, rufous-throated solitaires and the elaenia. Descending farther, one encounters woodpeckers, humming-birds, the *zumbadorcito,* one of the world's smallest birds, herons, ibises, flamingoes and impressive frigatebirds. Other animals include a range of tiny lizards, through geckos, iguanas and crocodiles. Fist-sized tarantulas are thankfully less common than small biting insects. Insect repellent and mosquito coils should be part of any traveler's gear.

Preceding pages: Guards at the Pantheon in Santo Domingo. Left: The waterfall near Jarabacoa.

The country has a number of national parks, including major ones at Parque Nacional del Este, Isla Cabritos on Lago Enriquillo, Los Haitises on Samana Bay, and two located in the Cordillera Central, where one finds **Pico Duarte**, the Caribbean's highest mountain, at 10,416 feet. Hikers can spend days in this area, although access to the national parks is by permit only. These are sometimes available at individual parks, but best obtained in advance at the park office in Santo Domingo.

On the Beaches

Along the coast, developed areas alternate with solitary. Among the best on the north coast is the beach at Punta Rucia, on a hard-to-reach bay between Puerto Plata and the Haitian border. East of Puerto Plata, in Playa Dorada and Sosua, resort life gets into full swing along several miles of beachfront. Cabarete's beach is popular with windsurfers due to powerful winter winds. The beach at Playa Grande, near Cabrera, is known for its swells and privacy-seekers heading to the beach at Playa la Preciosa. The Samana Peninsula has a good share of nice beaches outside town, at Puerto Escondido, Las Galeras, Playa las Terrenas and the quiet beach at Playa Bonita. Twenty miles east of Santo Domingo, a quintessential Dominican beach, popular with the locals, is located at Boca Chica. Beaches are virtually continuous south of Punta Cana to Miches.

By far the greatest cultural influence in the Republic is Spanish, with a smattering of French, and while other parts of the Caribbean revel in their African heritage, this country represents the major repository in the Caribbean of Spanish history and customs, dating proudly back to the New World of the fifteenth century. Columbus himself provided the name Hispaniola when he established his first American settlement on the Atlantic coast at La Isabella, on December 5, 1492. It is only fitting that the seaside near where this early international tourist first set foot ashore is now the modern-day site of the booming resort area around the city of Puerto Plata.

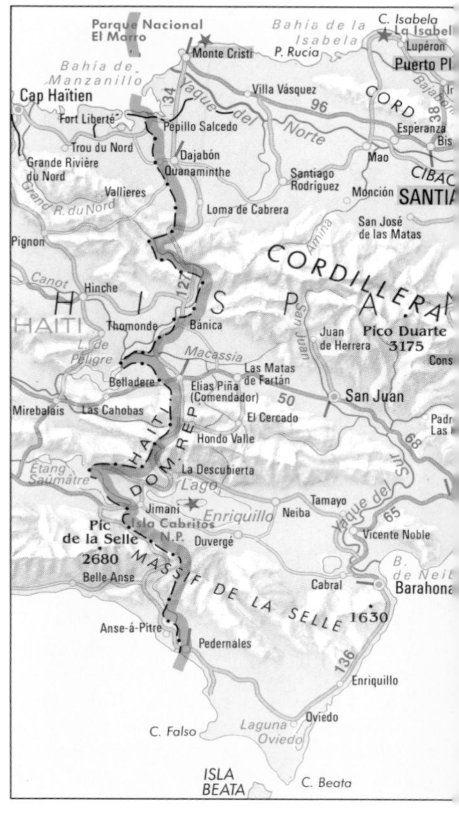

The Way of Life

In a traditionally rural agrarian culture now promoting industrial growth, where old and new exist side-by-side, it is not unusual to see a farmer slowly towing a goat on a rope alongside a busy highway filled with cars and trucks zipping by at frightening speeds. The nature, its mountains, coastal stretches and eternal forests clash with the sensuous rhythms of the merengue, whose music seems to pound from every car, storefront and radio. Visitors and locals alike flock to the great Merengue Festival that takes place in Santo Domingo in the third week of July. The changes wrought by modern life are nowhere more apparent than in the rapid development of tourism and baseball. Throughout the country every village, no matter how small has a baseball field. *El beisbol* is a national obsession. The country's winter and summer leagues, scheduled from October to January and April to September, provide a high-calibre of professional play at large stadiums located in Santo Domingo, Santiago, Puerto Plata, La Romana, San Cristobal and San Pedro de Macoris, while offering a scouting turf for the major leagues.

Other sports such as cockfighting and wrestling are popular with Dominicans and thus worthwhile excursions for the visitor seeking cultural insights. The

other insistent prod toward the fast lane comes from tourism. Motivated in part by favorable tax incentives, the Ministry of Tourism expects tourism-generated revenue to balance foreign trade deficits by the time of the 500th anniversary of Columbus' discovery of the Americas in 1992, good news for the nation's seven million predominantly poor residents.

Santo Domingo

Despite the tremendous growth that continues on the north coast, the cultural hub of the country is still the capital city of **Santo Domingo**, situated in the middle of the south coast at the mouth of the Ozama River, less than a half-hour from Las Americas International Airport. Here, a modern city of two million people, replete with predictable urban ills of overcrowding and traffic jams, as well as international cuisine, fine arts, a national symphony, hotels and resorts, spreads north and west beyond the ancient city walls of the old colonial city where the flavor of Spanish colonial history infuses narrow streets and restored architecture. Foremost among the city's attractions are the following historic sights, some dating back to the 1490's and the founding of the New World's first city. **Calle Las Damas**, the first street in the New World, was named for ladies of the royal court and today showcases many examples of 16th century colonial

Above and right: The shopping strip El Conde and a much quieter area.

architecture. These include the **Fortaleza Ozama**, which was a fortress and prison that incorporated the Torre del Homenaje (Tower of Homage), where the condemned awaited death as far back as 1503. Various occupying nations that ruled the country from 1505 to 1844 used the complex, whose restored structures dwarf nearby historic sites in size, though not in significance. On the same street, and surviving from the same era, is **Casa de Bastidas**, now a complex of interesting shops, galleries and museums. **Museo de Las Casa Reales**, also on Calle Las Damas, is the Museum of Royal Houses. For three centuries it provided government offices. Today it houses exhibits extolling the very history created within its walls. Such modern touches, such as an illuminated map of the world in the time of Columbus, lighten up the fascinating and skillfully displayed rare 16th century artifacts.

A walk along Calle Las Damas creates the necessary ambience for a visit to **Columbus Square**, where a bronze statue of the explorer greets you. **The Cathedral of Santa Maria la Menor** is also on this square, completed in 1523 and considered to be the first church in the New World. The church claims to be the final resting place of Columbus, although several other countries also claim that distinction. No one is likely to ever know the truth, but with or without an illustrious skeleton, the bronze and marble crypt warrants a visit. Another interesting building gracing the square's sky-line is the **old city hall**, now occupied by a bank. Staying with Columbus, however, **El Alcazar de Colon**, a palace carved out of coral rock in 1510, was the first residence originally built for the family of the sea- farer's son, Diego, and later serving for sixty years as the seat of the Spanish government and as residence to conquistadors Francisco Pizarro, Hernando Cortes, Juan Ponce de Leon and Vasco Nunez de Balboa. It was restored to its original grandeur in 1957 with stones from the original quarry, and today houses a museum of 16th and 17th century furnishings and tapestries.

La Atarazana, close-by, is a cluster of eight 16th century buildings used long ago for munitions storage. The street is now lined with pricey, tourist-oriented shops, galleries and cafés surrounding evocative courtyards. The more cost-conscious shopper is likely to discover good buys on **Calle de Conde**, the New World's first shopping street and now a bustling pedestrian mall with bargains for traders willing to haggle. Here, one can watch a veritable parade of Dominicans including persistent hustlers offering to exchange money at above posted rates, or sell drugs and services not worth risking. Other historic sites of special note include **Casa del Cordon**, the temporary home of the Diego Columbus family, the oldest home in the New World.

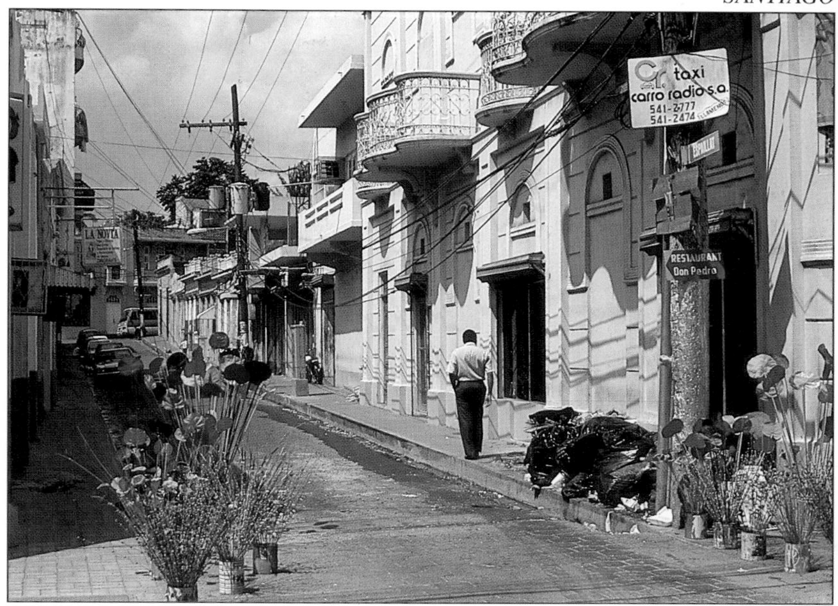

El Conde Gate leads into Independence Square and modern Santo Domingo. Among the must-see attractions in this part of the city are the modern structures of the **Plaza de la Cultura** on the site of the home of the former dictator Rafael Trujillo. He ruled the country for thirty years until his assassination in 1961, and though his reign was far from benevolent, he is remembered in this complex that houses the **National Library**, a **Gallery of Modern Art**, a **Museum of Natural History and Science**, a **Museum of the Dominican Man**, as well as the highly regarded **National Theatre**.

In addition, nearby are the **National Zoo**, and **Botanical Gardens**. The **Malecon**, the main street along the sea, shaded by towering royal palms, is possibly the liveliest street in town at night, when everyone comes out to enjoy the soothing evening breezes. The **Faro a Colon** is a huge light-house set to open in 1992 in honor of Columbus' discovery of the New World in 1492.

To Santiago and the North Coast

The road to Santiago from Santo Domingo cuts through two mountain ranges, the Cordillera Central and the Cordillera Septenrional, divided by the Cibao Valley, dotted with subsistence farms. **Costanza** and **Jarabacoa** are cool upland mountain towns growing in popularity with Dominicans seeking relief from torrid coastal areas. Near Costanza, are two pretty waterfalls, the **Aguas Blancas**, in an area offering pleasant hikes and swimming. **Jimenoa Waterfall** splashes 100-feet near **El Salto** just outside Jaracaboa, where climbers traditionally begin their ascents to the summit of Pico Duarte. Guides are available in town. **La Vega** is the biggest town in the Cibao valley. Outside town are the ruins of **Vega Real**, another long-abandoned settlement dating to the Columbus era.

Santiago, the country's second largest city, is considerably less active than the capital, with stately old homes, few tourists and therefore fewer hustlers. The

Museo del Tabaco displays steps in the processing of cigars, which are on sale locally. A **Museo de Arte Folklorico** displays arts and crafts.

By the time one reaches the town of **Monte Cristi**. The land between Santiago and the Haitian border turns to desert. Northeast of the town is the **Parque Nacional El Morro**, a sanctuary to a diverse birdlife. This is the start of the 150-mile stretch eastward containing the country's primary touristic zone.

Puerto Plata

The city of **Puerto Plata** has developed as a major destination for tourists over Santo Domingo for one compelling reason. There are no decent beaches in the capital city which spreads along a rocky southern coast. Less cosmopolitan than Santo Domingo, this city retains a certain Old World charm reflected in courtyard gardens, colonial architecture and ethnic dining. Major points of interest include the **Amber Museum**, a 16th century fort at San Felipe, and a cable car that carries passengers to a botanical garden atop a 2,850 foot mountain named **Isabella de Torres Peak**, which pierces the sky less than one mile from the sea. The **Fundaçion Dominicana de Desarrollo** is a school for artisans where apprentices learn from master ceramists, stonemasons and wood workers. This is a good place to see some of the nation's finest works in jewelry, pottery and sculpture, and helpful in gauging the quality of goods you will be offered throughout the country.

Above: Who needs a barber pole? Right: In storms this catwalk is not advisable.

Playa Dorada, Sosua, Cabarete

Playa Dorada is a modern resort area a few miles east of Puerto Plata which has only been developed since the late 1970s. With more than 4,000 hotel rooms already built and a Robert Trent Jones-designed golf course, the resort enclave is trying to enter the big league in terms of accomodation in the Caribbean.

The **Playa Grande**, just east of the Playa Dorada, by contrast, still exudes a breath of the old, paradisical, natural way of life. Unfortunately it too will probably have to give way to the expanding tourist trade. For the moment, however, it is a relatively quiet place where nature and the human being can hold an undisturbed conversation.

Sosua, ten-miles east of Puerto Plata, is of two minds. One section, **El Batey**, is built-up, noisy and touristy. Across the bay, **Los Charamicos** was established by Jewish immigrants fleeing Hitler's Germany in the 1940s and inuited to the Dominican Republic by the ex-dictator Trujillo still quite popular with Europeans seeking a cheaper, more laid-back, indigenous approach to the nation.

The beaches between Puerto Plata and Sosua are mostly vacant and enticing.

Sosua Beach, though far from pristine and vacant, has become the meeting place of a culturally fascinating amalgam of local business-people hawking all manner of goods, ranging from ceramics and jewelry to idiosyncratic local fast food that far surpass anything certain international chains offer in chain meal fare, unless your local establishment of this type serves up spicy fresh barbecued chicken, or oysters, or fresh tropical fruits. Add small hotels and unpretentious resorts, quality restaurants and evocative street-side cafés, and the result is an unsung, though well-beloved money-saving Caribbean destination.

Cabarete is known for its beaches with a three-mile stretch now facing the rising tide of progress.

Samana Peninsula

This peninsula northeast of Sosua is slated for tourist development, but currently still serves as a relatively remote, unspoiled home to mountain-dwelling farmers and fishermen, as well as several touristic complexes whose planning died in infancy.

Samana was for a long time a sleepy fishing village, but it turned into a stop-over port for cruise ships, and its old town was replaced by characterless box-like structures housing a variety of shops catering to cruise passengers. This is by no means a recommendation for a visit, but stop for an experience of the country-side, a wildland bordered by sandy beaches, seaside stands built of coconut palms, wild mango and bananas sprouting from dense thickets of forest greenery, tiny offshore islands gleaming in the sunshine like Caribbean jewels. Humpback whales mate fifty miles off-shore, with excursions available to match these phenomenal creatures. **Rio Limon Waterfall** tumbles 160 feet out of the hills. **Los Haitises National Park** features unusual karst limestone geography as well as dense mangrove swamps. Off-shore islands are a treasure trove for bird-watchers.

Boca Chica, La Romana, Punta Cana

East of Santo Domingo, **Boca Chica** has good beaches that attract overhealed Domingans on weekends. One-hour south of Punta Cana and a two-hour seacoast drive from Santo Domingo is **La Romana**, harboring one of the Caribbean's top resorts, the 7,000-acre **Casa de Campo**. A private airport serves corporate jets and is set amid three golf courses. Wealthy luxury seekers come to Casa de Campo for golf, to play tennis or polo, or to try a hand at sport fishing. The village of **Altos de Chavon** nearby is a recreated 15th century village that includes galleries and craft shops, as well as restaurants and cafés. A 5.000 seat open-air amphitheater holds occasional concerts by international performers such as Frank Sinatra and Julio Iglesias. A regional museum of Taino Indian history displays a wide variety of artifacts, including ancient native cooking tools, jewelry and ceremonial objects. Schedules for special events, such as music festivals and crafts shows are available through Casa de Campo.

Above: The artists colony tucked away in Altos de Chavon.

Also worth visiting is a **sugar mill** that is still, despite mass tourism promoted by the local resorts, the number one local industry. Farther east, and only three-hours by car from Santo Domingo, near the spot where the Atlantic Ocean and Caribbean Sea combine their watery bodies, is **Punta Cana**, the second fastest growing resort area in the country. Noted for casually elegant resorts, it still boasts some of the best beaches, including **Macao** and **Bavaro** to the north. The main east coast beach at Punta Cana once stretched for 31 pristine miles, but has long since been sub-divided and bisected by inevitable development. Nevertheless, the stretch from Punta Cana to Macao still covers almost 25 miles of wind-swept beach, and despite interruptions along the way, it is still probably the widest and longest beach in the country. And the beach is a traditional launching point for small boats braving the treacherous Mona Passage to Puerto Rico, where Dominicans gain the easiest access to the United States.

The southwestern part of the country is perhaps the most adventurous and individual. Dry and barren in spots, it has been overall bypassed by the tourist storms and offers a fairly genuine slice of Dominican life and culture. **San Cristobal** is where Trujillo was born. There is a large plaza and church, as well as the Casa las Coabas, his home, and Castillo del Cerro, one of his several palaces. Canefields, cactus-spiked hills and poor fishing villages with quiet beaches lead the way to **Jaragua National Park** and Beata Island offering unspoiled desert scenery and birdlife. **Lago Enriquillo**, a saltwater lake 140-feet below sea level, surrounds **Isla Cabritos**, a national park housing alligators, iguanas and birds.

Access & Local Transportation

International airports: Las Americas International, in Santo Domingo, and Puerto Plata International. Small airports in Punta Cana, La Romana, and Portillo Airport, in Samana. Service from New York, Miami, San Juan or the Caribbean is on Continental, Pan American, Dominicana, American, ALM and VIASA. Limousines (inexpensive, infrequently scheduled), taxis (negotiate the price first), buses (cheap, colorful), or rental cars (Hertz, Avis, Budget, local firms).

Formalities & Currency

Visitors need a valid passport and US $10 tourist card available at the airport. A US $10 departure tax is charged. Shops close from noon till 2:30 p.m. Many do not re-open until 5 p.m. Currency: Dominican peso, averaging around 6.5 to US $1.

Tourist Information

Dominican Republic Tourist Information Centers are located at 485 Madison Ave., New York, NY 10022, 1-212/826-0750; 1300 Ashford, Santurce, Puerto Rico 00907, 1-809/725-4774, 29 Bellair St., Toronto, Ontario, Canada M5R 2CB, 1-416/928-9188; 156 Arzobispo Merino, Santo Domingo, 1-809/687-8038.

SANTO DOMINGO

Accommodation

LUXURY: **Santo Domingo Sheraton**, 365 Av. George Washington, 1-809/686-6666. Good service. **Santo Domingo**, Avenida Indepencia, 1-809/535-1511. Design by Oscar de la Renta. **Jaragua Resort**, 367 Av. George Washington, 1-809/686-2222. *MODERATE:* **Gran Hotel Lina**, Av. 27 de Febrero, 1-809/686-5000. Central location. **Hispaniola**, Avenida Indepencia, 1-809/535-7111. Use Hotel Santo Domingo facilities, but pay less to stay here.

BUDGET: **San Geronimo**, 1067 Av. Indepencia, 1-809/533-8181. For those who speak Spanish. **Nicolas de Ovando**, 53 Calle las Damas, 1-809/687-3101.

Restaurants

LUXURY: **El Alcazar**, in Santo Domingo Hotel. **Il Buco**, 152-A Arzobispo Merino, 1-809/685-0884. **Lina's**, Gran Hotel Lina.

MODERATE: **El Bodegon**, 152 Calle Arzobispo Merino, 1-809/682-6864. **Jai-Alai**, 411 Av. Indepencia, 1-809/685-2409. **Vesuvio II**, 17 Tiradentes, 1-809/562-6060. Italian.

PUERTO PLATA / PLAYA DORADA

Accommodation

LUXURY: **Eurotel Puerto Plata**, in Playa Dorada, 1-809/586-3663. **Heavens**, Playa Dorada, 1-809/586-5250. All-inclusive.

MODERATE: **Costambar Beach**, 17 El Penon, 1-809/ 586-3828. **Victoria**, Playa Dorada.

BUDGET: **Hostal Jimmeson**, Calle Beller. In-town, local color.

Restaurants

LUXURY: **Los Pinos**, Av. Hermanas Mirabal, 1-809/586-3222. **Neptune**, Av. Malecon, 1-809/586-4243. Seafood. **De Amando**, 23 Av. Mota, 1-809/586-3418.

MODERATE: **Jimmy's**, 72 Calle Beller. *BUDGET*: **Porto Fino**, Av. Hermanas Mirabal. Bargain Italian/Dominican.

SOSUA / CABARETE / SAMANA

Accommodation

LUXURY: **Los Caballeros**, Sosua Beach, 1-809/571-2645. Villas. **Sand Castle**, Puerto Chiquito Beach, 1-809/571-2420. New, well-equipped. **El Portillo**, Samana, 1-809/689-6191. All-inclusive.

MODERATE: **Los Almendros**, Sosua, 1-809/571-3515. **Lora**, Av. Dr. A. Martinez, 1-809/571-3939. Cozy inn. **Punta Goleta**, Cabarete, 1-809/571-0700. Quiet.

BUDGET: **Hotel Sosua**. In-town. **Cabarete Beach Hotel**. Cozy. **El Portillo**, Las Terrenas. Rustic, ox-cart carriage.

Restaurants

MODERATE: **Cafe Sosua**. Menu varies with local market specialties. **Marco Polo Club**, Av. Martinez. *BUDGET*: **El Jardin**, Cabarete. Patio dining. **Mama Juana**, Cabarete. Hearty.

PUNTA CANA

Accommodation & Restaurants

Self-contained resorts dominate here. Guests tend to dine on property. *LUXURY*: **Bavaro Beach**, 1-809/682-2162. Large, sports-oriented resort. **Punta Cana Beach**, 1-809/541-2714. Nearly 1/2 mile of beachfront. Active, all-inclusive. *MODERATE*: **Club Med**, 1-809/687-2767.

LA ROMANA

Accommodation

LUXURY: **Casa de Campo**, 1-809/523-3333. 7,000 acres, golf, tennis, polo. Private airport. Latin ambience, no beach.

MODERATE: **La Posada**, Altos de Chavon. Small, elegant inn.

Restaurants

LUXURY: **La Piazetta**, Altos de Chavon, 1-809/523-3333. Elegant and romantic. *MODERATE:* **Casa del Rio**, Altos. Seafood. **De America**, 52 Calle Castillo Marques, La Romana, 1- 809/556-4582. Good value. *BUDGET:* **Cafe del Sol**. Cheap eats. **Mama Nena**. Fresh, local cuisine.

HAITI

Haiti has beaches, but visitors do not go there for the sun and the sand. It has one of the Caribbean's largest cities, but visitors do not go there for sleek shops or sophisticated nightlife. They go to experience an exotic Third World atmosphere and are willing to sacrifice typical touristic luxury to do so. Haiti is the western hemisphere's most African country, and as such, it feels more "foreign" and more primitive than anyplace else in the region. The people are closer to their roots than those on other islands. Ninety percent of them are black, and most of the remaining ten percent are Haitian Creoles, upper-crust mulatto descendants of black slaves and white masters.

Haiti's poverty and political turmoil have been well documented, and headlines trumpeting various violent coups d'état have served to eclipse all that is unique about this country.

The country itself occupies the western third of the island of **Hispaniola**, after neighboring Cuba, the Caribbean's second-largest island. This mountainous, Maryland-size country is known for its vibrant art, Afro-Caribbean mysticism and French-inspired cuisine– astonishing in the face of its long, sad history. Haiti is a country that charges you up rather than calms you down – a compelling cross-cultural odyssey that excites, and sometimes overwhelms, the senses.

Preceding pages: The painter painting himself painting a depiction of a local marriage.

Columbus dropped anchor near **Cap Haïtien** and discovered Hispaniola on December 5, 1492, during his first voyage. Early attempts at colonization were frustrated by dissent and disease, but eventually the Spaniards managed to conquer the island. After enslaving, slaughtering or deporting some million Arawak natives in the relentless quest for gold, they replaced the indigenous peoples with African slaves who worked the plantations of this lush island.

In 1697, the Spanish ceded western Hispaniola to the French, who continued importing slaves but not treating them any better than the Spaniards had. The ideals of fraternity and equality promulgated during the French Revolution may not have been intended for the colonies across the Atlantic, but the slaves nevertheless got the word and were inspired to begin their own battle for freedom. Just as the sansculottes had burned on their ex-masters in the mother country, rebel Haitian slaves took bloody revenge on the French plantation owners.

Toussaint L'Ouverture, a slave with regal roots, being the grandson of an African ruler, emerged as a natural leader.

He headed a black militia which defeated the French troops sent over to quash the violent revolt and took advantage of successive conflicts between the French and the Spanish and the English to solidify his rule. He first had the blessing of France, which was happy just to have peace restored, but once he went about abolishing slavery and writing a constitution, Napoleon Bonaparte declared L'Ouverture's concepts to be treason and sent a huge army to return the colony to the fold. While the Haitians at first resisted, L'Ouverture was willing to negotiate an armistice. On his way to French headquarters, he was captured, sent to France and ultimately died in prison on a cold Alpine mountain. Other Haitian leaders – Henri Christophe, Alexandre Pétion and Jean-Jacques Dessalines – took his place.

On January 1, 1804, Haiti declared its independence, becoming the world's first Black republic and the second nation in the western hemisphere, after the United States, to shake the yoke of European colonialism. It was a republic with a self-proclaimed royalty. Dessalines, L'Ouverture's lieutenant and successor, was the first monarch, but upon his death in 1806, the young country was divided in two. Henri Christophe, who became the model for Eugene O'Neill's *The Emperor Jones*, ruled the north, calling himself King Henri I and again enslaving much of the population.

Haiti has always suffered from political instability. Throughout the 19th century one dictator followed the other., while the Spanish Creoles on the eastern side of the island struggled for their own independance which they achieved in 1844 with the founding of the Dominican Republic. In 1915, in the wake of another, American Marines occupied Haiti, bringing a modicum of stability and simultaneously paving the way for U.S. business interests, whose interest lay in cheap raw materials, cheap labor and corruptible officials.

When the Americans left in 1935, the political wrangling resumed. In 1957, fearing its "vital interests" were being threatened, the Eisenhower government helped François "Papa Doc" Duvalier to power. In 1964 he elected himself president for life. He and his son Jean-Claude "Baby Doc" (who took power as a teenager in 1971) were to become among the most egregious tyrants in the western hemisphere. Their power rested on the brutality of a paramilitary police force known as the *Tontons Macoutes*. The Duvalier dynasty ended in 1986, but not the political unrest. The tug-of-war between military regimes and civilian rule, however, has continued to plague the nation while the people sink deeper and deeper into an economic and social abyss.

This achingly beautiful land, once the richest tropical colony of its size in the world, is now the western hemisphere's poorest country, with a per capita income of under $400 a year. With steep mountains rising to 2,438 m (8,000 ft) and a low coastal plain, arable land is limited, yet 80 percent of the population live in rural farming villages. Agricultural practices remain primitive, with subsistence farming prevalent, and coffee, sugar, rice and sisal raised as cash crops.

Efforts at promoting a cheap labor pool for light manufacturing, assembly and sewing have been thwarted by years of political uncertainty. Overpopulation, illiteracy, disease and infant mortality are the difficult framework within which most of the population must live. The impoverished people skid from one political cauldron to another and from one health crisis to another, while the economic situation worsens, with foreign debt growing faster than the economy.

Close to six and a half million people try to exist in a land that, for all its lushness, cannot support that many. For visitors, the grinding poverty evident in the cities and in the country villages is heartbreaking in human terms, as is the relent-

less destruction of the rain forest in ecological ones. It takes determination to find forests that have not been demolished for building material or firewood. Tourism was once an important source of revenue, but with the combination of political unrest and a highly publicized AIDS scare, it has fallen off drastically. In recent years many cruise lines took Haiti off their itineraries or modified their traditional stopovers.

While Haiti continues its own struggles, visitors discover an energizing and exciting, but not unstressful destination. The air services, accommodation and other data in this guide were correct at the time of writing to the best of our knowledge, but as the country is in constant disarray, nothing is firm and any travel plans should be re-confirmed.

Despite this dismal list of national ills, there is a strong faith, touching friendliness and unquenchable spirit about the place. These characteristics are commonly expressed in Haiti's music and especially in the brilliant, albeit primitive paintings which seem to celebrate a life on canvas that has no basis in reality.

Above: Four friends or an accessory engine? Right: The busy, bustling Iron Market attracts all of Port-au-Prince.

Haiti is not a country where you want to rough it. You should get your vaccinations before you visit and avoid drinking the water while you are there. Sanitation is poor in all but the top places, so caution is advised. It is also good to have a middleman accompany you on your adventures. When you sightsee or shop, you will want to engage a guide or a driver-guide who does far more than just show you around. Any of these energetic young men will, by their presence at your side, proclaim you off limits to the persistent peddlers, beggars and pleading children who continually pester unaccompanied tourists. With someone to clear the path and help you negotiate for those things you really wish to buy, you can concentrate on becoming acquainted with other compelling aspects of this Carribean

country. The guide will also be getting a commission from any shopkeeper he steers you to.

Port-au-Prince

Port-au-Prince is Haiti's capital and largest city by far. Nearly one and a quarter million people live in a crowded and vibrant metropolis at the end of a deep, well-protected bay called the **Golfe de la Gonâve**. The main business district is located in close proximity to the harbor.

Pretentious government buildings are the only structures that can be called modern. Otherwise, Port-au-Prince retains the look of a Third World city. Fanciful gingerbread houses in various states ranging from restored to dilapidated are the most striking architectural notes in a place where most residents live in shacks and only a minority resides in fancy outlying neighborhoods.

Just a couple of blocks from the waterfront is the **Iron Market**, a two-block-long covered hall, which is an experience more than simply a sight. This intimidating, teeming, noisy and sometimes noisome place is not for the faint of heart, but for those with an adventurous spirit and a penchant for excellent values in crafts – especially needlework and straw work – which can be found among a labyrinth of stalls heaped with meats, canned goods, soaps, tools, sewing supplies, jewelry, religious icons, toys, salves and handicrafts. It makes particularly good sense to enlist a local guide to help in the bargaining procedure and to stave off the aggressive pleas and pitches by every merchant in the market.

Most of the capital's other attractions are far more tame. They are located for the most part on a north-south strip about ten short blocks from the harbor. Closest to the Iron Market is the **Cathedrale de Port-au-Prince**, actually an imposing complex of buildings consisting of a main cathedral and chapels of various sizes, and it astonishes most visitors to see an amalgam of Catholic and African derivative worship in so traditional a cathedral. The nearby **Cathedrale de la St. Trinité**, an Episcopal cathedral with thirteen murals depicting biblical tales interpreted by leading Haitian artists, has been called the "Sistine Chapel of the Caribbean". *The Miracle of Cana* was painted by Wilson Bigaud when he was still a young disciple of the immortal Hector Hippolyte, considered one of the great masters of Haitian art. Art critic Selden Rodman called Bigaud "the Breughel of Haiti".

The **Musée d'Art Haïtien du College St. Pierre**, familiarly and plainly referred to as *Le Centre d'Art,* is the country's leading showcase for museum-quality paintings, as well as sculpture and fine crafts. Founded in 1944 as a workshop for local artists by DeWitt Peters, an American conscientious objector who went to Haiti as a teacher, the art center today displays some of the world's finest naive-style art. It was relocated into a modern museum in 1972 and is now both an exhibition and sales facility. The collection includes works of such "classic" Haitian painters as Philome Obin, Hector Hippolyte and Castera Bazille, as well as their disciples. Next door is **La Maison Defly**, a turn-of-the-century mansion once occupied by a Haitian general and now restored as a house museum.

The **Place des Héros de l'Indépendance**, commonly called the **Champ de Mars**, is a large city park in and around which several prominent attractions are found. Notable are the fine statues of Haiti's early heroes, as well as the famous sculpture of *The Unknown Slave*, his head tilted back as he blows on a conch shell to commemorate his country's independence. The **Musée du Pantheon National Haïtien** is the country's national museum. Located in a former presidential mansion, it features an eclectic collection of historical objects, costumes and documents, but its most noteworthy artifact is the anchor from Columbus's *Santa Maria*. Across a spacious bou-

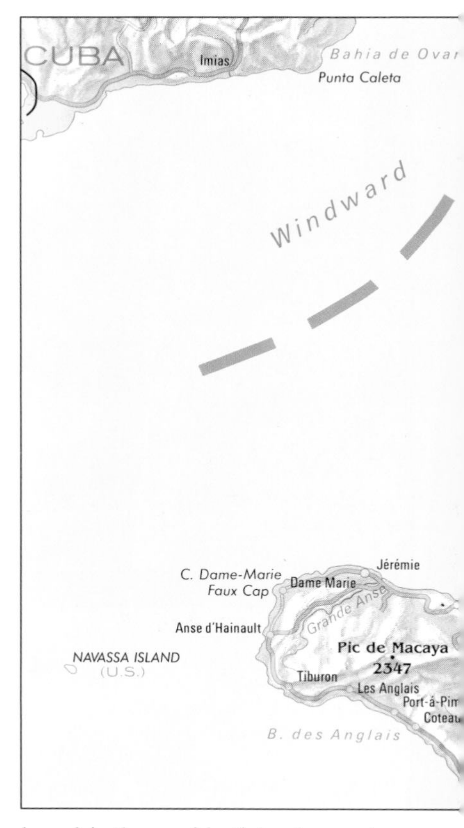

levard is the presidential palace, a low-slung white mansion.

To the east lies **Pétionville**, Port-au-Prince's most elite suburb. Perched on a cool hillside nearly 609 m (2,000 ft) above the teeming city, this district features fine hotels, restaurants, boutiques and night-spots. In nearby **Boutillier** the Jane Barbancourt Distillery makes some twenty kinds of rum, including varieties flavored with coffee or various fruits and flowers. The setting, in a spotless building looking rather like a castle, and with wonderful views of the steep hills and gorges, is refreshing. The samples are free, and the rum is a good bargain.

Beyond Pétionville – and some 1,219 m (4,000 ft) higher – is **Kenscoff**. The

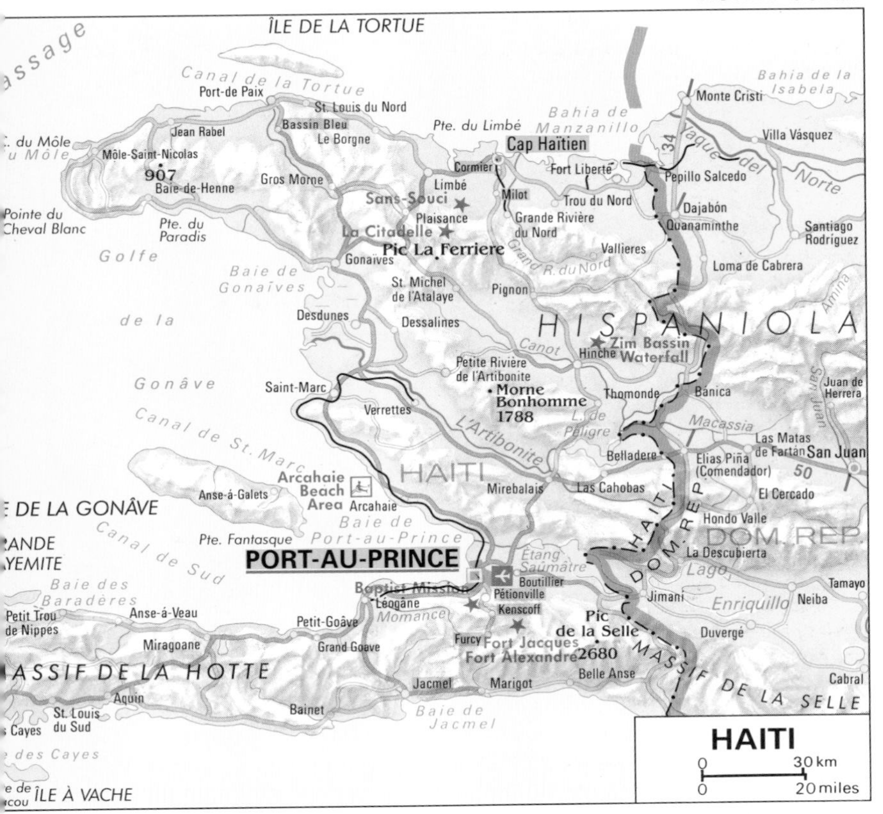

drive there offers spectacular scenery and opulent flowers along the way. The town's colorful outdoor market every Tuesday and Friday morning is both smaller and easier than the giant daily Iron Market down in the city. The **Baptist Mission**, between Pétionville and Kenscoff, has a store offering inexpensive crafts in an uncharacteristically tranquil atmosphere. An unpaved side road leads to two ruined forts, **Fort Jacques** and **Fort Alexandre**, which can be explored. The main road continues past Kenscoff to **Furcy**, 300 m (1,000 ft) higher, and ends at the **Pic de La Selle**, Haiti's highest mountain close to 2,744 m (9,000 ft), near the border with the Dominican Republic.

The North Coast

On the north coast, a five-hour drive from the capital, is **Cap Haïtien**, a somewhat downbeat colonial-style city. With the decreasing number of cruise ship visits to Port-au-Prince, this city of 65,000 inhabitants, now gets a larger percentage of the seafaring tourist traffic than before. Passengers on shore excursions join vacationers at two of the most astonishing man-made wonders to be found anywhere in the Caribbean.

Palais Sans Souci, near the town of **Milot**, was built by Emperor Henri Christophe I to rival Versailles. Marble floors, crystal chandeliers and a court modeled after Europe's most pretentious one char-

acterized Sans Souci of the early 19th century. Destroyed in 1842 by an earthquake, the palace is a megalomaniac dream in ruin. By contrast, **La Citadelle**, perched 910 m (3,000 ft) above sea level atop **Pic La Ferrière**, is grandiosity incarnate. This vast fortress, built over a thirteen-year period for Henri by 20,000 enslaved laborers, has been called the Eighth Wonder of the World. With walls up to 6 m (20 ft) thick and a stockpile of 400 cannons, it was designed like a medieval fortification, and intended to withstand and repel an invasion from Europe which never came. Henri ordered a suite of 40 rooms for his use, but eventually his reintroduction of slavery to carry out his construction projects and his hunger for power inspired a palace revolt. He was executed using a golden bullet, and is buried in the center of La Citadelle. To best sense the majesty of this mighty fortress, hire a horse or hike up the steep road and approach it one step at a time. Another close sidetrip is a three-hour hike or horseback ride from **Hinche** to the **Zim Bassin Waterfall**.

Above: Emperor Henri Christophe's Sans-Souci. Right: La Citadelle offers its plunging view onto a sea of mist.

Jacmel

Two hours south of Port-au-Prince is **Jacmel**, a quiet coffee plantation town with attractive beaches of black sand, which is seeking to usurp Port-au-Prince's role as a tourist destination. As a more relaxed town with far fewer of the capital's obvious and overwhelming problems, it offers quiet resort atmosphere. Well-maintained traditional buildings, many with iron filigree balconies and some of the best coffee in the Caribbean add to the local appeal. The best scenic excursion in Haiti is the day trip from Jacmel to the **Bassin Bleu**, a complex of pools, grottoes and waterfalls. The journey takes one and a half to two hours each way on horseback, with a half-mile walk at the end.

Beaches

Just because there are better beaches elsewhere in the Caribbean does not mean that Haiti's are no good. A number of beaches are within an hour of Port-au-Prince. Most of them levy an entry fee, and unless you are staying at a resort with beach privileges, it is advisable to bring your own refreshments and supplies.

In the **Arcahaie Beach** area, north of Port-au-Prince, extend several separate beaches, each with a small resort. These include the gold-sand stretches of **Ibo Beach**, **Kyona**, **Ouanga Bay**, **Mai-Kai** and **Amani-Y**. **Taino Beach** and **Sun Beach** are southwest of the city at **Grand Goave**. **Cormier** and **Labadie** are near Cap Haïtien. Labadie is a deserted beach near **Cormier**, which you can reach by rowboat. In addition to normal sand-and-sea activities, there are colonial ruins to explore. You can negotiate hiring a row-boat and oarsman yourself. **Raymond les Bains**, **Congo** and **Cyvadier Cove** are in or near Jacmel.

Art

Sotheby's in New York sold a painting by Hector Hippolyte for $36,000, and a German collector purchased a Hippolyte for twice that. But for most visitors, Haiti gives new meaning to the term "affordable art". In addition to the acknowledged masterpieces that sell for five figures in top galleries around the world and the best examples of Haitian art available in local galleries and museum shops, literally thousands of enchanting paintings can be found in the $10-$50 range. They may not be fine art, but they will be original, hand-done, bright and a wonderful souvenir of this astonishing country.

Food and Culture

Haitians' languages may be French and Creole, but their body language is African, and their beliefs combine Christianity and Voodoo. Voodoo is an exotic and mystifying religion springing from time-

less African beliefs and rituals. The *hougan* (priest) or *mambo* (priestess) performs ceremonial rites infused with magic, music and dance to implore the *loas* (gods) to enter the worshippers' bodies and souls. Brought from Africa with the slaves, Voodoo is the most elemental and spiritual aspect of Haitian life.

Voodoo has not yet been turned into a tourist spectacle, and visitors are generally not permitted at ceremonial sites where music, dance and trance are combined to communicate with the spirits. It may be possible to visit a Voodoo priest if accompanied by a Haitian, so it pays to inquire – carefully – if this is of interest.

Haitian music and art will remind you of Africa, and its food will remind you of France, with a distinct Caribbean overlay. Pepper steak, French bread and French pastries are commonly found in finer restaurants. Indigenous Creole dishes include seafood (especially lobster) and *lambi* (conch), *griot* (fried pork), *poulet creole* (spicy chicken), or *tasse* (marinaded turkey). These dishes are invariably served with *poua*, Haitian red beans. The true gourmet will top the meal off with an *assiette de fruits,* a sumptuous platter of fresh tropical fruit, and a cup of good, strong coffee.

Above: Haitian family eking out a living in Kenscoff.

Sports

Most of the hotels have swimming pools, many have tennis courts and all but the Port-au-Prince properties have access to beaches and can arrange picnic lunches, and snorkeling or scuba gear. In addition, the new JOTAC tennis center opened near the airport in early 1990, with seven courts, aerobic center, fitness room, massage facilities, men's and women's locker rooms and restaurant.

Scuba diving is best at the **Arcadins**, a trio of islands in the **Golfe de la Gonâve**, which are being incorporated into an underwater preserve and a national park under the auspices of the World Wide Fund for Nature. Other major dive sites include **La Gonâve Island**, a day-trip offering eight challenging dive options to deep canyons, mammoth basket sponges and centuries-old wrecks. The best diving near Cap-Haïtien and most facilities in Haiti are at **Kyona** and **Kalico Beaches**. Reef trips, horseback riding and tropical mountain hiking are also possible.

Nightlife

Port-au-Prince once rivaled Havana for wild nightlife, but the fall-off of tourism and fear of AIDS tarnished Haiti's image as an entertainment capital. Larger resorts have their own shows, and most of the remaining nightlife now centers around the top hotels in the city and in Pétionville. The discos, clubs and handful of rudimentary casinos that still exist keep relatively late hours, but the luster and glamour are gone.

Access & Local Transportation

One of "Papa Doc" Duvalier's better acts was to create a modern jetport less than 16 km (10 mi) from Port-au-Prince, although through Haiti's troubled years, international air service has been inconsistent. Flights from North America are usually from Miami and sometimes also from New York and San Juan. At present, international services are via Air France, ALM, Air Canada, Air Jamaica, American Airlines, Copa Air, Eastern Airlines, Haiti TransAir and Pan American World Airways. Haiti Regional flies between Port-au-Prince and Santo Domingo. There is an airport departure tax of $15, payable in gourdes or dollars. Rental cars can be booked, but with confusing, poorly signed roads, private taxis, shared taxis (called *publiques*) and taxi guides, useful for sightseeing and shopping excursions, are best for visitors. Tap-taps are brilliantly painted, always crowded trucks with board seats which are great to photograph but too gamey for most foreigners. Tap-taps carry passengers and cargo around the city and throughout the country.

Currency

The Haitian gourde, which is divided into 100 centimes, is fixed at 5 to US $1, although American currency is always welcome and a black market exists, too. Travelers' checks and credit cards are accepted in major hotels.

Accomodation

LUXURY: **El Rancho Hotel & Casino**, Ave. Pan-Americaine, P.O. Box 71, Petionville, Tel. 7-2989/41. Elegant Mexican-style hotel, pool, tennis courts, MAP option. **Villa Creole**, 95 Bourdon, P.O. Box 523, Petionville, Tel. 7-1570, 7-1571. Shares facilities with neighboring El Rancho. **Club Mediterranee**, P.O. Box 1575, Commune de Montrouis, Tel. 2-5131, 2-3118. Tried-and- true formula in Haitian setting; best bargain of Club's Caribbean villages. **Jacmelienne Beach Hotel**, Jacmel. Mailing address: P.O. Box 916, Port-au-Prince. Tel. 5-0810. Friendly beach hotel, pool. *MODERATE:* **Grand Hotel Oloffson**, 60 Ave. Christophe, Port- au-Prince, Tel. 2-0139, 2-5180. Eccentric Victorian charm pool lush gardens model for site of Graham Greene's *The Comedians*. **Plaza Holiday Inn**, Rue Caprois, Port-au-Prince, Tel. 2-9821, 2-3722. Central in-town location.

BUDGET: **Beck Hotel**, P.O. Box 48, Cap-Haitien, Tel. 2-0001. Small hotel, pool, restaurant and bar. **Villa Kalewes** Guest House, 99 Rue Gregoire, Petionville, Tel. 7-0817. Tiny guesthouse, pool, dining. **La Griffone**, 21 Rue Jean Baptiste, Canape Vert. Tel. 5-4095, 5-3440. Clean, comfortable, overlooks city.

Restaurants

Au Petit Louvre, 27 Rue Gregoire, Petionville, Tel. 7-1543. **Ghala**, Hotel Splendid, Port-au-Prince, Tel. 5-0166. **La Belle Epoque**, 23 Rue Gregoire, Petionville, Tel. 7-1530. **La Recif**, 430 Route de Delmas, Delmas, Tel. 6-2605. **Le Steak Inn**, 31 Rue Magny, Petionville, Tel. 7-1822. **La Terrasse**, Rue du Champ de Mars, Port-au-Prince, Tel. 2-0855.

Festivals / Seasonal Events

Carnivale, celebrated for three days preceding Ash Wednesday, is the liveliest festival. *Independence Day* celebrations fall on January 1-2, capping a holiday season that starts with *Discovery Day* on December 5 and lasts through Christmas and New Year.

Most other holidays are Catholic in nature, with Good Friday, Easter, Corpus Christi, Ascension Day and assorted saints' days all celebrated, many as public holidays. The most mystical is the pilgrimage in honor of The Virgin in Ville Bonheur, in the mountains northeast of Port-au-Prince, on July 16. March marks Pestel's annual *Sea Festival*, while Jacmel puts on a special folkloric show on May Day. The anniversary of Henri Christophe and Dessaline's deaths are commemorated on October 8 and 17 respectively.

Museums / Art Galleries

The leading museums are the **Musee d'Art Haitien** and **Musee du Pantheon National Haitien**, both in Port-au-Prince. According to the national tourist office, they are generally open during weekday business hours, but check to be sure.

Top galleries are **Issa's**, **George Nader**, **Claire's**, **Galerie Monnin** and **Galerie Marassa**, all in Port-au-Prince or Petionville, and **Renaissance II** in Jacmel.

Shopping

Haiti is not a shopping country in the commonly accepted Caribbean sense. There is no major-league duty-free shopping and very few imported goods. The best selection and best buys are crafts found in markets, craft shops, museum shops, boutiques and even on the streets. Embroidery, crochet work, wood carving, straw goods, jewelry and wrought iron are produced in varying degrees of quality and at various prices, ranging from inexpensive trinkets to exquisite work.

Tourist Information

Haiti National Office of Tourism, 18 E. 41st St., New York, NY 10017, 1-212/ 779-7177. **Haiti National Office of Tourism**, Ave. Marie Jeanne, Cite de l'Exposition, Port-au-Prince, Haiti, Tel. 2-1729.

JAMAICA

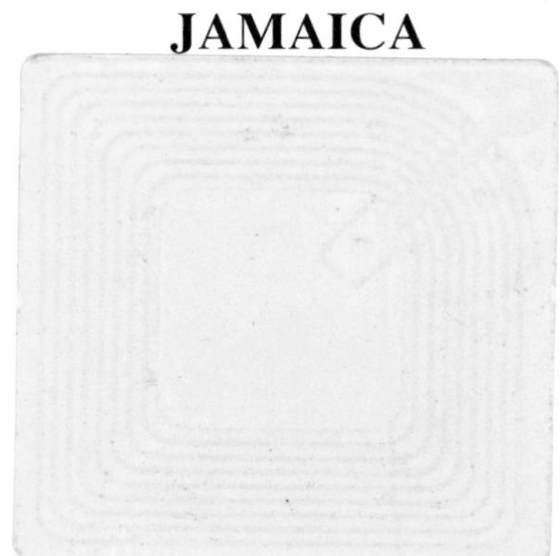

Jamaica, third largest island in the Caribbean and one of the most popular vacation spots of the western hemisphere, has a very special kind of ambience. Few visitors have wishy-washy feelings about this place that Columbus discovered and called "The fairest isle the eyes have ever beheld." That quote, by the way, has also been claimed by the Dominican Republic, which Columbus saw first.

Fair still to this day, its overwhelming tropical beauty continues to lure visitors. Sun-soaked beaches slope up from the sea. Vegetation, including bananas, coconut palms and towering shady mangoes combine in a heavily forested backdrop with exotic tropical fruits and spices. Roadsides are crowded and tin-roofed homes shaded by edible foliage such as sweetsop, soursop or *ortanique* (a Jamaican-bred cross between an orange, a tangerine and the word unique). *Otaheiti* apples came from the South Pacific along with breadfruit. Fragrant allspice grows profusely and is called *pimento* here; pimento wood is used for cooking jerk pork, another Jamaican specialty. Thyme, basil, lemon grass and lime leaf cloak the sea coasts and fill the mountainsides, lining fertile river valleys that splash down in jungle waterfalls from the central mountain spine bisecting the country from east to west.

Preceding pages: Living from the sea requires patience. Left: Jamaica rum, as famous as reggae.

The highest point in Jamaica is the fabled **Blue Mountain Peak**. Being over 2,255 m (7,400 ft) tall, it frequently lies shrouded in a misty haze that gives the **Blue Mountain Range** its name, a scant 16 km (10 mi) from teeming **Kingston**. This city of more than a million is the cultural, governmental and business hub of the island, and one of the most interesting and misunderstood capitals in the whole of the Caribbean.

Historical Background

Many flags have flown over Jamaica. The early Spanish cultivated the island's fertile topography, bringing in the first horses, cattle and pigs, as well as introducing many species of flora that thrive today. They also enslaved the proud Arawak Indians found living here in Columbus's day, many of whom committed suicide rather than submit to slavery. The brutality of Spanish slavemasters and new diseases soon killed off all Arawaks anyway. Several caves containing petroglyphs and the **Arawak Museum** in Spanish Town show the traces of their existence. The British, who

the fertility and strategic military location of Jamaica, easily wrested control of the country from the diminutive Spanish population in 1655. They were aided immensely by buccaneers, pirates hired by the British Crown in place of a more disciplined and costlier navy. Payment to these mercenaries was a percentage of whatever wealth could be captured from Spanish ships carrying gold and jewelry. Spoils such as women and wine went solely to the buccaneers.

Henry Morgan was the most famous of all Jamaican pirates. This 17th century man's public image underwent a radical transformation over time that may hold clues to one strand of the roots of the Jamaican character today. Morgan was first considered a criminal, then, after numerous successes against the Spanish, he became a Jamaican governor, and finally a wealthy landowner and national hero. If there is such a thing as a national character, it is reflected in those on whom immortality is bestowed. The spirit of Henry Morgan begot a slave revolt led by Sam Sharpe, who was hanged for his crimes, yet is still remembered today in Sam Sharpe Square, the central city square in the heart of downtown Montego Bay, Jamaica's second largest city.

Above: A beautiful head of hair. Right: No need to rush, the sun and air will take care of drying the tobacco.

Marcus Garvey, a Jamaican hero, was an early black-power advocate whose provocative writings in the 1930s got him thrown into an American jail. And reggae superstar Bob Marley, a towering figure in Jamaican history, who put this little island on the map for good with his internationally acclaimed music, was a pot-smoking Rastafarian who spent time in Jamaican jails. Sprinter Ben Johnson, another Jamaican hero, who was disqualified for using steroids after breaking all records in the 1988 Olympics, has yet to redeem himself, – but his story is not over yet. Jamaicans persevere, they are not quitters, and they admire a little larceny in their heroes, ever hopeful that a new

spin on the ball will move things along. After all, the shackles of slavery would never have been broken otherwise.

Slavery escalated dramatically with intensifying sugar cultivation and milling in the 17th and 18th centuries. At one point a ruling class of 20,000 British, mostly bureaucrats, plantation-owners and their families, controlled 300,000 black African slaves. Every Jamaican is aware of this history, which led through British Commonwealth status to Jamaican independence only in 1962. It is no surprise that Jamaica experienced all the growing pains of a new nation these last 30 years, complete with political violence during emotional election campaigns.

Jamaica remains predominantly poor, with rampant unemployment and high inflation. That these circumstances make for a high cost of living for Jamaicans, while providing relative bargains to visiting tourists, is but another of the contradictions of this country. The government vigorously sponsors tourism, and for good reason: it is the number one source of foreign exchange. Not all Jamaicans feel the same way. To an angry Jamaican the tourist represents impossible attainments, and though there may be no real danger, at certain times and places in Montego Bay, Ocho Rios or Negril, the main tourist haunts, many visitors have unsettling encounters with Jamaicans who have little to lose.

Mostly this takes the form of rather insistent attempts to sell some unwanted item or service, a T-shirt, hair braiding, a shell necklace, or something illegal, such as marijuana or cocaine. A firm "no" is usually all it takes to continue on one's way, but that "no" may have to be repeated numerous times to numerous Jamaicans, which is one reason why some prefer the uncrowded Jamaican countryside to its tourist towns.

Where people do not depend on tourists to earn their living, Jamaicans, who are by no means all the same and can be strongly opinionated, are some of the friendliest, most hospitable and charming people on earth.

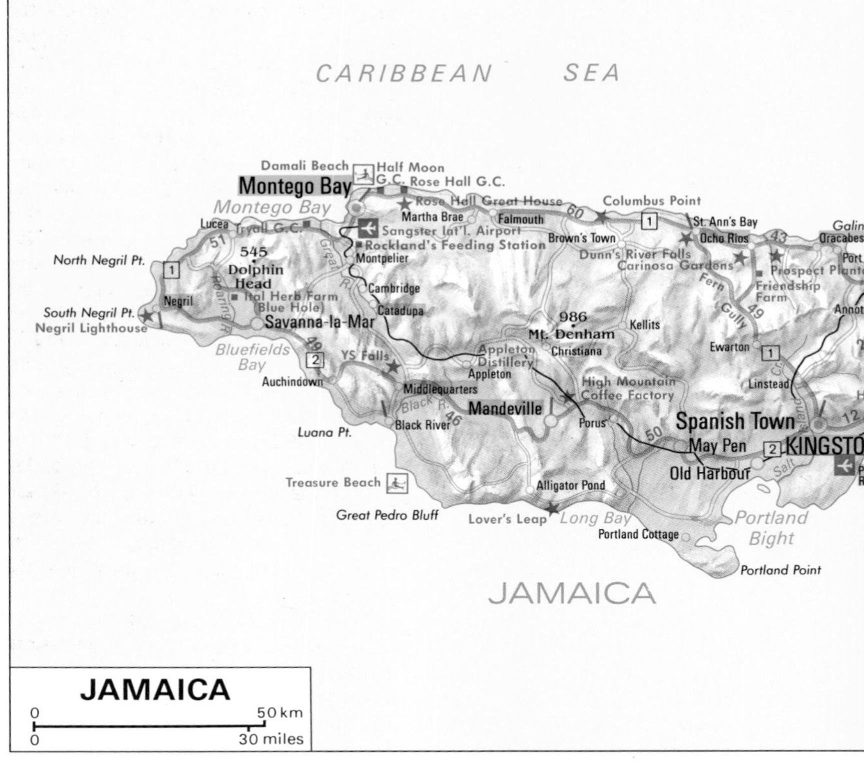

Jamaica, No Problem

The frequently uttered response "No problem" can mean anything from no problem to no way, depending on the speaker's body language and intonation and on the context of the question. Another variant is "Soon come", meaning *in progress, completion expected*, as in waiting two hours for a fresh seafood dinner on the docks of Port Royal, not knowing in advance that the chef would first have to catch the fish. When this sort of thing happens, as it will frequently if one ventures far from beaten tracks, there is not much one can do but to sit back, drink a few of the locally brewed *Red Stripe* beers, watch the fishing boats come and go and pretty soon one will be relaxed to the point where it really is no problem. And the fish dinner, likely to be served *escoveitched* (cooked in a Jamaican marinade of vinegar and hot peppers), will prove to be worth waiting for.

Anything Goes

Jamaica's casual reputation as an "anything goes" sort of place can be traced back to Morgan's day, when Port Royal, the 17th-century pirate capital and now a quiet fishing village, was known as "the wickedest city on earth". An earthquake in 1692 ended that city's notorious preeminence, and periodically other natural disasters, the latest being Hurricane Gil-

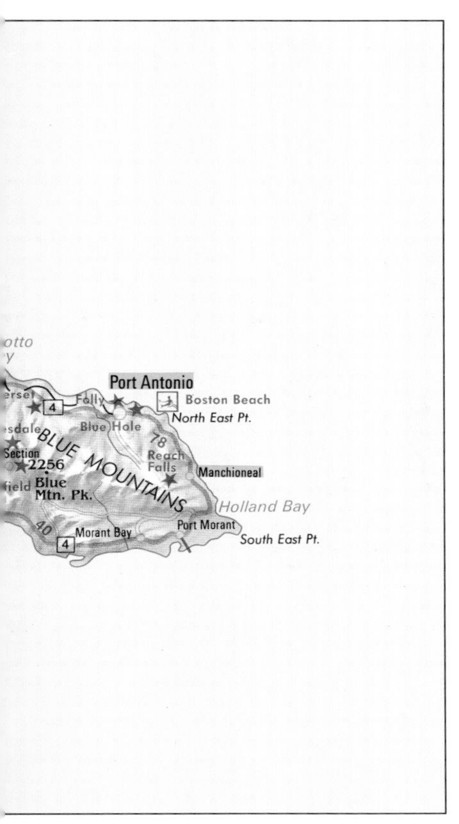

bert in 1988, have left their damaging mark on the country, yet without dampening the spirit of the people. A population of 2.5 million, comprised of a thorough mixture of black Africans, white Europeans, Asians and a smattering of others, knows deep in its national consciousness what it means to start all over again, and nothing – neither slavery, political turbulence or natural disaster – has ever kept them down for long. With a time and place for everything, just about anything does go at one time or another.

Discovering Jamaica

Columbus "discovered" Jamaica, then called *Xaymaca* by the Arawaks, in 1494 on his second voyage to the New World. In 1503 his ship was wrecked off the coast and he and his crew spent a year living in Jamaica before another ship was sent for them. Today you can visit the spot where he landed at **Columbus Point**, situated on **Discovery Bay**, on the island's most tourist-intensive north coast. This 104-km (65-mi) stretch between the city of Montego Bay *(Mo'Bay* to the locals), with its busy **Sangster International Airport**, on the northwest coast, and Ocho Rios, in the center of the north coast, contains the majority of major tourism properties on the island.

Negril, 80 km (50 mi) and an hour-and-a-half-drive south of Mo-Bay, is a relative upstart in the big-time tourism field. Formerly attractive mainly to the 1960s counter-culture because its 11-km (7 mi) beach was undeveloped and hard to reach, it is now catching up with a number of luxury properties, lavish resorts of recent vintage curving around the island coast.

Port Antonio, 96 km (60 mi) east of Ocho Rios, resists major intrusions wrought by development, combining a laid back provincial appeal with a number of smaller elegant properties; while Kingston, 96 km (60 mi) southeast of Ocho Rios, simmers in its own hot juices, producing a stew too spicy for most tourists' appetites, but one that adventurous travelers might savor.

Add the Caribbean's most impressive "all-inclusive" resorts – a concept originated in Jamaica and now much copied elsewhere, where one pays a set fee for all accommodation, meals and most activities – top-flight hotels, hundreds of luxurious villas, small guest houses or Jamaican-style hotels, colorful coastal or inland villages populated by fisherfolk or farmers, sugar mill workers, hotel staff or idiosyncratic Jamaican entrepreneurs, and you have a recipe for contrasting tropical delights with enough diversity to please indulgent sun worshippers or

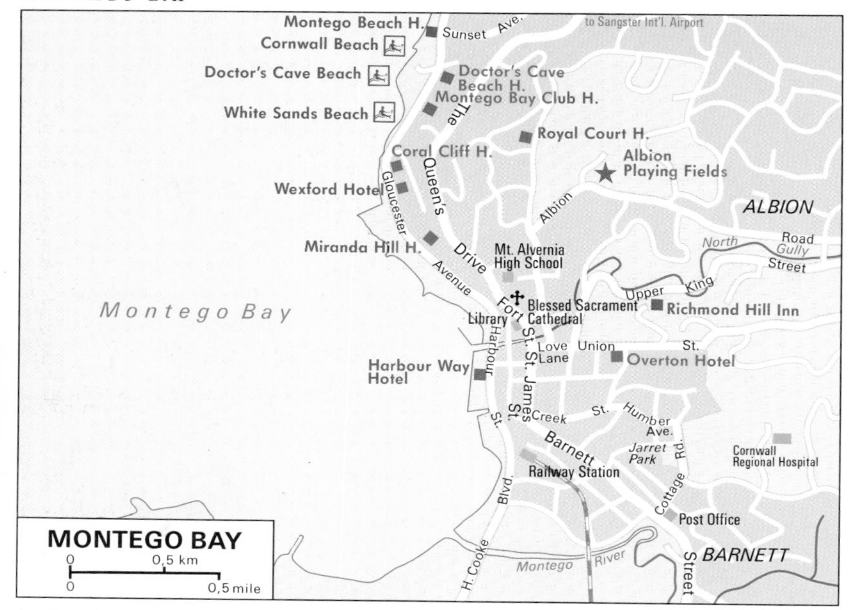

backpackers, resort lovers or hard- boiled camping buffs. It is just these contrasts that make Jamaica special. From beachside to the Blue Mountain Peak, from blasting reggae pouring forth from dilapidated Kingston storefronts to the white-gloved tropical elegance of world-class resorts, from the fresh market produce sold for pennies on street corners to imported food and drink served in the most expensive restaurants, from lying back to bake in the sunshine to getting out and about with the people – Jamaica has it all.

Montego Bay

The second largest city in Jamaica is also its main tourism destination. Visitors are greeted with a free rum punch while awaiting customs formalities, courtesy of the **Appleton Distillery**, before dispersing in various directions for hotels in the city, to the south toward Negril, or eastward toward Ocho Rios or Port Antonio. Montego Bay has more hotel rooms than any other part of the island, more restaurants and the biggest concentration of tourist-oriented facilities. These include watersports such as sailing, scuba diving or snorkeling; golf at **Ironshore**, **Rose Hall**, **Half Moon**, or **Tryall;** tennis; horseback rides; restored plantation manors, called *Great Houses*; tourist train rides on the **Governor's Coach**, or **Appleton Express**; bird-watching at the **Rockland's Feeding Station**; gentle bamboo raft trips down the scenic **Great River** or the **Martha Brae**, near **Falmouth**; and some good, though comparatively commercialized beaches.

Doctor's Cave Beach is the best-known of them, at its downtown location on **Gloucester Avenue**. **Cornwall Beach** nearby has made a name for its deep sugary sand and beachside bar beneath the generous branches of a spreading almond tree. For a peaceful beach, just a little out of town heading east, next door to the

Right: The view of Montego Bay – Mo'Bay to the locals – from the sprawling Tryall Golf and Country Club.

Holiday Inn, there is **Damali Beach**. The Holiday Inn lost its roof in Hurricane Gilbert in 1988 and the beach was hard hit, but it remains a quiet curving expanse along a reef-protected shoreline. Great snorkeling, glass-bottom boat rides and parasailing are available.

Close to Damali, most visitors will want to see the **Rose Hall Great House**, headquarters of an old sugar plantation. Guides tell the story of Annie Palmer, a former resident and the notorious White Witch of Rose Hall, who is thought to have murdered three husbands and buried them beneath three swaying palms visible from the veranda of the large stone structure looming high on a hillside overlooking the sea.

Montego Bay, nicknamed Mo'Bay by the locals, is considered "the most beautiful swimming resort in the world". This, however, only accounts for one of the facets of this tourist mecca. The other side of the glittering coin consists of slums that stretch up to the slopes of the North Gully from **Sharpe Square** in the city center, the location of such historical buildings such as **The Cage**, a onetime prison (built in 1806) and the **St. James Parish Church** (from the mid-18th century). Hardly any tourist ever ventures into these regions. It is probably easier to meet with locals in August at the annual *Sunsplash Festival* that takes place in the **Bob Marley Performing Center** on the artificially created peninsula of **Freeport**, where the cruise ships also berth. The event lasts all of four days during which thousands of fans have the opportunity to honor the old and new stars of the reggae scene.

The **Appleton Express** or the **Governor's Coach** rail tours are also recommended excursions on Jamaica's rail system, which runs from Montego Bay to Kingston. You pass through villages and wooded areas, stopping to visit a cave on the edge of the **Cockpit Country**, a unique part of Jamaica composed of steep limestone formations, which are honeycombed by underground caves and waterways.

In the village of **Catadupa**, where the train stops on the way to the Appleton Distillery, seamstresses displaying bright, colorful bolts of fabric take the measurements of passengers for custom- tailored dresses or shirts, which can be picked up and paid for, after returning from the tour of the destillery, which will inevitably include a certain amount of time in the Appleton tasting room.

Ocho Rios

Ocho Rios is the main tourist town on Jamaica's north coast, a booming cruise ship port and the location of a number of hotels and resorts. It is also probably the least Jamaican of all the country's towns, catering primarily to up-scale tourists who enjoy resort amenities and good beaches, and do not mind sharing them with many other visitors as well as many, many Jamaicans trying to make a few dollars. In recent years complaints about the throng of vendors, cab drivers and hustlers who surround cruise ship passengers on shore excursions has caused the authorities to tighten licensing restrictions and build a fence to separate visitors from the locals.

The result is that although travelers are protected, many local people are cut off from their only source of income. Bad feelings along the lines of "haves" versus "have-nots" are now common and certain elements of the local population can be less than forthcoming with tourists, at times even unfriendly or frightening.

Nevertheless, there are things to see in the area, the most famous of which is probably **Dunn's River Falls**. This waterfall tumbles 183 m (600 ft) out of the hills above the town, cascading over tiers of smooth rocks, before running into the sea.

Tour guides lead visitors on a climb of the falls, which, though not dangerous, is assuredly one of the more popular tourist attractions anywhere in Jamaica. In fact, most brochures of the island usually include a photo of tourists in bathing suits holding hands and creeping along these rock ledges.

Not exactly a tourist site, but simply a beautiful drive, is a road called **Fern Gully**, which connects to Kingston on the other side of the island. Gigantic ferns, some with leaves the size of a car, hang out of the dense, damp forest hugging the narrow roadway. It rains frequently, and even when clear it is mostly impossible to see the sky through the intertwining tree cover.

More trees and flowers may be viewed on several plantation tours in this area. Guests pay a fee to be driven in open-sided vehicles while a tour leader describes the flora of Jamaica, including bananas, coffee, pimento, sugarcane, coconuts, pineapple and other tropical fruits. It can be pleasant to spend an hour

Above: The unique beauty of the Dunn's River Falls. Right: The settlement of Port Antonio on the east coast.

or two at **Prospect Plantation**, **Carinosa Gardens**, or **Friendship Farm**. Also available at Friendship Farm are horseback rides, and accommodation above Fern Gully, outside of town, in buses that have been converted into motorless motorhomes with flower gardens.

Harmony Hall, just outside of town, is one of Jamaica's top art galleries. The one-time plantation house now contains a small restaurant, as well as some of the best examples of Jamaican crafts and paintings. For literary buffs, two sites east of town are worth visiting. The first is at **Oracabessa**, where Ian Fleming lived in a house called **Goldeneye** while writing the James Bond stories. It is privately owned though, and the only way to get inside is by renting this villa property that overlooks the sea from a secluded end-of-the-road perch above the north coast.

Not far from Fleming's retreat is the one-time home of the British playwright Noel Coward. His modest whitewashed stone cottage, called **Firefly**, is now owned by the Jamaican government and is open for tours. Nothing has been changed since the death of Coward here in 1973. Originally owned by Henry Morgan, the pirate and Jamaican politician, the property overlooks the seacoast from a tall hillside and is one of the many spectacular sites in Jamaica.

Port Antonio

The farthest eastern community on the north coast was a busy shipping port for the United Fruit Company in the days when Jamaica's banana exports were big business. Today, **Port Antonio** is a quiet, low-key tourist town, thanks largely to a visitor in the 1940s. Filmstar Errol Flynn made his last home here and his widow still maintains a house on the island.

Among Flynn's contributions to the local economy was the establishment of one of the most popular tourist activities on the island, rafting the **Rio Grande** river. The story goes that he observed banana planters from high up in the hills

using narrow bamboo rafts to bring their produce to market and decided it would be fun to ride such a raft. Today, there are a hundred or more raftsmen who build their own vessels to transport visitors on the two-and-a-half hour journey through rain forest scenery along the usually gentle river. Although this trip is memorable at any time, it is at its best on nights with a full moon.

Another Flynn legacy is **Navy Island**, situated in one of Port Antonio's twin harbors and once owned by the actor. Stories abound about the Hollywood party crowd that used to flock to the area, including tales of inebriated swimming races across the quarter-mile expanse to the mainland. Today, Navy Island is the site of a small, upscale resort, the **Admiralty Club**, and guests do not have to swim since they can travel on a boat leaving from the heart of downtown area.

Above: A means of carrying freight has become a tourist attraction. Right: The sport arena tells its own story.

Nearby is an unusual architectural ruin called **Folly**, consisting of the crumbled remains of a concrete mansion overlooking the sea, that was made with sea water early in this century. Over years, the salt in the water rusted out the steel supports until the building collapsed.

Also close by is the **Blue Hole**, an allegedly bottomless body of water. A number of local businesses offer watersports and there is a restaurant too.

On the west side of town are the tiny **Somerset Falls**, far smaller than the more popular and spectacular Dunn's River Falls in Ocho Rios. For a small obolus a boatman punting a bamboo raft will give you a ride, and the swimming here is cool and other-worldly amidst the luxuriant jungle growth. On the other side of the town are the **Nonsuch Caves** and **Athenry Gardens**. For a single fee, visitors can explore both sites.

Farther along the coast lies **Boston Beach**, arguably one of the finest beaches in Jamaica. It is also the birthplace of "jerk" cooking, the slow method of bar-

becuing meats and fish that has become popular island-wide. Open-air butchers prepare cuts of pork, chicken or spiny lobster by dousing them in a fiery pepper marinade, then cooking them for hours over a smoky green pimento wood fire. Stop by early for the best selection to enjoy this delicacy. Late in the day you may be out of luck. A good idea is to come out in the morning for a pleasant swim, and then to splurge at lunchtime.

Not exactly in Port Antonio, but outside the coastal village of **Machioneal**, midway around the east coast toward Kingston, are **Reach Falls**. One must drive up a long road passing through cane fields and banana plantations, then hike down a steep path to the falls. There is excellent swimming and good hiking in the area and very few tourists to obstruct one's experience of nature.

The fishing village of Machioneal is a good place for fresh seafood that one can buy direct from fishermen. Local chefs will prepare it for you in exchange for a little money.

Kingston

This city is the hub of Jamaican government, business and culture, the capital and a lively place that is usually bypassed by tourists. Hot, urban, with its share of crime and decay as well as beauty, it does indeed include parts in the slum areas of **Trench Town** or **West Kingston** where tourists are unwelcome without a Jamaican escort. Nevertheless, there are a number of fascinating things to do in and around town that are far from most tourists' ideas of sun and sand. Kingston's best beaches are outside town at **Hellshire Beach**, a long strip of sand west of the city, and frequented primarily by Jamaicans, not foreign tourists. The little stalls strung along the beach offer fantastic seafood and afford an opportunity to mingle with Jamaicans at play. If you come at the right time you can listen to live reggae at **Fort Clarence**.

Speaking of reggae, the home and recording studio of the late Bob Marley is now a museum in Kingston. *Tuff Gong*,

as it was known when Marley was alive, is now the **Bob Marley Museum**. Inside are mementos and press clippings, concert posters, and there is always good music playing. A tip for reggae lovers: If you want to bring home the music but do not want to carry records, stop in at a record shop with a blank cassette tape. The proprietor will make you a high-quality recording for a small charge. A good spot for the latest recordings is at **High Times Ltd**, in the **Kingston Mall**, across the street from the **Oceana Hotel**, a centrally located business hotel. Also nearby is the **National Gallery of Jamaica**, featuring works by the most prominent Jamaican artists. Within walking distance is the docking site for the **Port Royal Ferry**.

A ride across **Kingston Harbor** to the former private capital cost somewhere below a dollar. There, you can see **Fort Charles**, which once protected the city; the **Naval Hospital**, which is now an archaeological museum; as well as several other sites of historic interest. More lively are the fishing boats based at **Port Royal**. Several small waterside shacks house restaurants serving excellent Jamaican food, and you can negotiate for a boat ride out to the **Port Royal Cays**, several small islands just beyond the harbor offering undisturbed swimming, sunbathing or snorkeling.

Above: Sucking pig is a speciality on many Caribbean islands like Jamaica.

After returning by ferry back to Kingston it is only a few short blocks to the **Kingston Crafts Market**. This is where you can find the largest selection of T-shirts, straw goods, wooden carvings, shell jewelry and many other souvenirs.

Other sites of interest in Kingston include: the **Institute of Jamaica**, repository of the largest library and research facility for Jamaican and Caribbean history; **Devon House**, a restored 19th- century home that is now part museum, featuring antiques and period furnishings, with several restaurants and the **Things Jamaica** shop, featuring high-quality but expensive goods unlike those found in the crafts market; **Hope Gardens**, a pretty botanical garden with a small zoo; the **University of the West Indies**, which is another good spot for hearing live reggae shows on weekends. For theater buffs, the **Ward Theatre** and **Little Theatre** are recommended.

If you get as far as the university, you will be at the base of the **Blue Mountains**. Numerous homes and small villages flank the mountainsides, most obscured by thick forests. The best hiking and backpacking can be found in these heights, and this is the home of world-famous Blue Mountain coffee, which sells for $35- $45 per pound in the U.S., and nearly as much at tourist shops in Jamaica. If you know where to go, you can buy the same beans direct from small growers for a fifth of that price, or less. Although the government certifies coffee factories throughout the island to package the coffee, including one at **Mavis Bank**, outside Kingston, the very best of the Blue Mountain crop can be found in the small village of **Section**, at the home and farm of James Dennis, or on the **Brooks River**, at the store of Joseph Wolfe. These places are admittedly harder to reach, and will probably require a rental car, but are well worth the effort for the authenticity of the cultural experience, as well as the fresh coffee.

In this same area are two national forest reserves that are quiet sites of humbling beauty, **Holywell** and **Clydesdale**. Both offer modest lodging facilities, long hiking trails and views to the horizon, as well as swimming holes. The more adventurous traveler can consider a hike to the top of **Blue Mountain Peak**, the highest point in Jamaica at a height of 2,256 m (7,402 ft). The classic experience consists of overnighting at a rustic guest house and coffee plantation called **Whitfield Hall**, where there is no electricity and the horse-hair mattresses are not too comfortable. It matters little as one rises at 1 a.m. to start the climb with a guide in the darkness. The path is steep and rocky in parts, perfectly accessible for the modestly fit, but a flashlight is necessary. Mules can also be hired, although it is debatable which mode of transport is rougher on one's body. If timed right, the 11-km (7-mi) hike should be completed just before the sun breaks through at dawn. On clear days at the peak, one can see Kingston and the south coast as well as Port Antonio's twin harbors to the north. And on even clearer days one can see Cuba 144 km (90 mi) away, a thin landline floating on an emerald sea.

Mandeville and the South Coast

This area is frequented far more by vacationing Jamaicans than by tourists, which means the prices are generally more agreeable than popular north coast resort areas. **Mandeville** is located at 609 m (2,000 ft) and best known for flower gardens and retirement homes. It is a slow-moving community, cooler than the coastal cities and not heavily developed for tourists. One of the interesting things to do is visit **Marshall's Pen**, a 250-year-old house filled with antiques and a fine collection of books on Jamaican history. About 121 ha (300 acres) of grounds offer hiking and horseback trails of particular interest to birdwatchers (by reservation only). Not far from town is the **High Mountain Coffee Factory**, good for purchases of Blue Mountain coffee, or the milder, less expensive High Mountain beans, which are blended from other local coffees.

Heading for the south coast and some of Jamaica's best uncrowded beaches, the main road passes through **Bamboo Avenue**, a short stretch bordered by thick stands of bamboo. If you get out of the car and turn off the engine to listen to the clattering in the gentle breeze you can hear the roots of Jamaican music in the hollow clacking of the swaying bamboo.

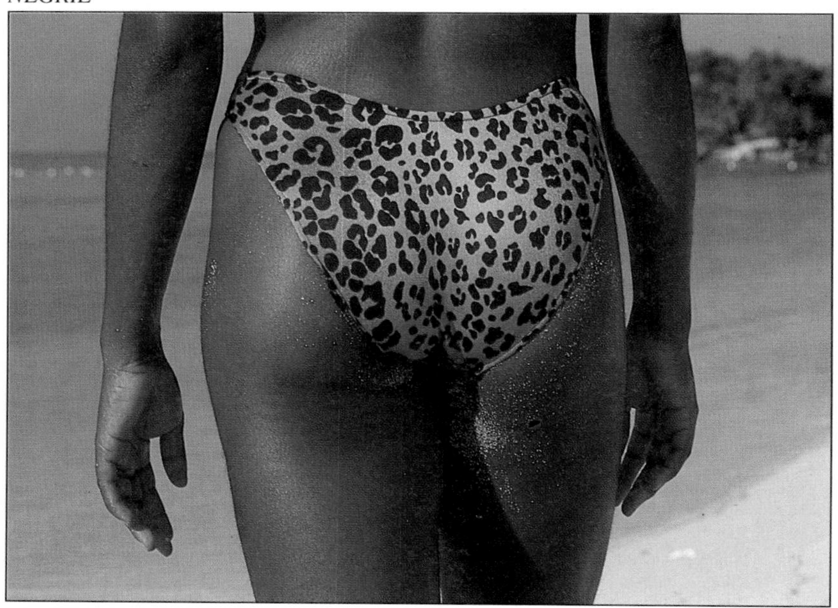

Roads through the south coast are in poor shape but worthwhile for those looking for modest alternatives to the run-of-the-mill tourist experience. **Treasure Beach** is one of the best in the country, with several lively discos, and **Lover's Leap** is a scenic cliff 518 m (1,700 ft) above the sea. Rivers in this part of the island are famous for rafting and there are now commercial boat tours of the **Black River**, Jamaica's longest and largest, flanked by mangroves and grassland. Numerous small fishing villages mark the sea coast and this is another area for fine, fresh seafood. In the town of **Middlequarters** roadside entrepreneurs surround passing cars offering small bags of hot-peppered shrimp, which are really crayfish. Hot, salty and crispy, they provide a delicious taste of the real Jamaica. Other vendors sell roasted *yams* or cashews.

Above: An attractive instance in the landscape. Right: A shot at the fish market.

Inland, a short way from this area, is the **Roaring River**, another little-known spot with its own **Blue Hole** for swimming located at the **Ital Herb Farm**. *Ital* is Jamaican for *vital and natural*. When you see the word outside a restaurant you can count on vegetarian cuisine, modest prices and generally the freshest food served on the island. There is also an Arawak cave located here, and nearby is the most beautiful waterfall in all Jamaica, the **YS Falls**. They are located on private property, and one must ask permission to hike down the sloping hillsides, through the fertile river valley to the secluded and powerful falls. The trek might be somewhat strenuous and not to everyone's liking, but those who do try it will get a glimpse of the other, non-tourist side of Jamaica.

Negril

Negril keeps growing faster every year and is not exactly the laid-back, out-of-the-way place it was just a few years ago.

Still, it attracts a mainly younger crowd who crave its 11-km (7- mi) beach and casual approach to life. Along the beach one can see people who live in hammocks or shacks sharing beachfront space with elegant resort hotels.

Among the things to do besides simply hanging out and enjoying the sun and sea, is to walk up a serpentine staircase to the top of the **Negril lighthouse** to view the coastline from a bird's eye perspective. It is situated on the cliff side of Negril, away from the beach and a good bet for finding a place to stay away from the main beach activity. The cliffs are peppered with small guest houses and modest resorts run almost exclusively by Jamaicans rather than foreign investors. One exception to this is **Rick's Café**, which is owned by an American who has built this bar and restaurant famous among sunset watchers as the place to be when the sun sinks into the sea.

Other than these few sites and a fairly deteriorated **Crafts Market**, the joys of Negril are all associated watersports. Do not be surprised if an ambitious salesman offering the famous Jamaican herb *ganja* swims up to you on the beach proposing a sale. The herb is illegal, although far from hard to find, and Negril, like everywhere else in Jamaica, seeks to provide what the customer wants. A firm, polite "no thanks" is all it takes to send such a small business-person scurrying to the next available tourist. For those who wish to partake of the herb on the island, remember the penalties can be unpleasant jail time at worst, which is very bad in Third World Jamaica, or an intimidating court appearance, complete with legal fees and a fine that will most definitely put a serious dent in your vacation money. The days of Rastas strolling down the street, dreadlocks bouncing to the rhythm of reggae, smoking big *spliffs*, cone-shaped marijuana cigarettes the size of a large cigar, are over. Of particular note to travelers who plan to visit several areas of the country, are police road blocks which appear suddenly, hidden around blind curves on the main roads.

Access & Local Transportation

International airports: Kingston, Mo-Bay. Service by Air Jamaica, Continental, American, Eastern, Northwest, Jamaica Shuttle Air Canada, Aeroflot, ALM, BWIA, British Airways and Pan Am. Trans-Jamaica links Kingston, Ocho Rios, Montego Bay, Mandeville, Negril and Port Antonio. Ground transport: Taxis (negotiate fee in advance), tour buses (with a/c, tapedecks), city buses (big, slow, cheap, colorful), minibuses (cheap, small, crowded and quick for long hauls), trains (fine if you have time for probable delays), and thirty-five rental car firms including Hertz, Avis, Budget, and most big ones, as well as locally-owned firms. Moped and bicycles are available in resort areas.

Tourist Information

Jamaica Tourist Board: Kingston, Mo-Bay, Ocho Rios, Port Antonio, Negril, Mandeville. Main office: 21 Dominica Drive, PO Box 360, Kingston 5, Jamaica W.I., 1-809/ 929-9200.

Also in New York, Miami, Los Angeles, Chicago, Atlanta, Dallas, Boston, Mexico City, Montreal, Toronto, Frankfurt, London, Paris, Rome, Tokyo. Jamaica Reservation Service, 1320 S. Dixie Highway, Coral Gables, FL 33146, 1-305/666-0447.

Jamaica has the widest variety of accommodations in the islands, from approved resorts, hotels, guesthouses and fully staffed-villas, to tiny, officially unacknowledged cabana and campsites. The Sandals Resort Group originated the all-inclusive concept of one-price-pays-all properties with every vacation need filled on premises.

Note: Room tax of US $2-$10 added daily, plus service charge 10%-15%.

MONTEGO BAY

Accommodation

LUXURY: **Half Moon Golf, Tennis & Beach Resort**, PO Box 80, Montego Bay, 1-809/953-2211. The best. **Round Hill Hotel & Villas** PO Box 64, Montego Bay, 1-809/952-5150. **Tryall Golf, Tennis & Beach Club**, PO Box 1206, Montego Bay, 1- 809/952-5110. **Sandals Montego Bay**, PO Box 100, Montego Bay, 1- 809/ 952-5510. **Sandals Royal Caribbean**, PO Box 167, Montego Bay, 1-809/953-2231. All Sandals are all-inclusive for couples only.

MODERATE: **Chalet Caribe Hotel**, PO Box 365, Montego Bay, 1-809/952-1364. Diving. **Coral Cliff Hotel**, PO Box 253, Montego Bay, 1-809/952-4130. **Richmond Hill Inn**, PO Box 362, Montego Bay, 1-809/952-3859. Overlooking a panoramic city view. **The Wexford**, PO Box 108, Montego Bay, 1-809/ 952-9854. Jamaican-owned buisiness-person's hotel on Gloucester Ave.

BUDGET: **Caribic House**, 1 Gloucester Ave., White Sands PO, Montego bay, 1-809/ 952-5013. **Harbour Way Hotel**, 1 Harbour St., Montego Bay, 1-809/952-6560.

Restaurants

LUXURY: **Marguerite's by the Sea**, 1 809/ 952-4777. Seafood. **Richmond Hill**, 1-809/952-3859. Hill-top terrace dining. **Sugar Mill Restaurant**, at Half Moon golf course, 8 miles east of Mo-Bay, 1-809/953-2211. Superb romantic dining alongside an ancient water wheel.

MODERATE: **Front Porch**, at the Wexford, 1-809/ 952-9854. Stick to Jamaican dishes.

BUDGET: This is where Mo-Bay shines, with a variety of options. **Pork Pit**, on Gloucester Ave. Jerk pork and chicken. Take home a bottle of their peppery sauce. **Whitehouse Village**, on Kent Ave., behind the airport. No tourists. Freshest seafood in town. Bevins & Barnett Sts. evening street market from 4 p.m. to 2 a.m., sugarcane, water coconut, steamed peanuts, jerk chicken, cooked to order, on the spot. Rock-bottom prices.

OCHO RIOS

Accommodation

LUXURY: **Sandals Dunn's River**, PO Box 51, Main St., Ocho Rios, 1-809/972-1610. Newest and nicest all-inclusive. Opened Jan. 1991. Mediterranean-style villas. Five room/price categories. **Sandals Ocho Rios**, 1-809/974-5700. Sandals reservations: Unique Vacations, 7610 SW 61st Ave., Miami, FL 33143, 1-800/SANDALS. **Boscobel Beach Hotel**, PO Box 63, Boscobel, 1-809/974-3331. All-inclusive, accepts families. **Couples**, PO Box 330, Ocho Rios, 1-809/974-4271. Only couples, all-inclusive. Private islet for nude sunbathers. **Sans Souci Hotel Club & Spa**, Box 103, Ocho Rios, 1-809/974-2353. Natural mineral spa. *MODERATE:* **Casa Maria Hotel**, Box 10, Port Maria, 1-809/994-2323. Quiet, Jamaican-style. **Turtle Beach Towers and Apartments**, PO Box 73, Ocho Rios, 1-809/974-2801. Good value, apartment-hotel. *BUDGET:* **Arawak Inn**, Arawak PO, Mammee Bay, 1- 809/972-2318. Diving. **Hibiscus Lodge**, Box 52, Ocho Rios, 1- 809/974-2676. Attracts European budget travelers.

Restaurants

LUXURY: **Casanova**, at Sans Souci Hotel, 1-809/974-2353. Seafood. **Moxon's**, at Boscobel, 1-809/974-3234. Dinner only. **The Ruins**, 1-809/ 974-2442. Oriental dining beside a waterfall. *MODERATE:* **Almond Tree**, Hibiscus Lodge, 1-

809/974-2813. **Parkway Restaurant**, 1-809/974-2667. Jamaican menu, mostly locals. *BUDGET:* **Ruins Snack Shop**, Jamaican patties, spiced meat in flaky dough. **Jerk Center**, jerk pork, chicken, fish. **Lobster Pot**, Main St. Bargain seafood downtown.

PORT ANTONIO

Accommodation

LUXURY: **Jamaica Palace Hotel**, PO Box 277, Port Antonio, 1-809/993-2020. Eighty-antique-filled suites. **Trident Villas & Hotel**, PO Box 119, Port Antonio, 1-809/993-2602. Exclusive, ultra-deluxe.

MODERATE: **Admiralty Club & Marina**, Navy Island, Port Antonio, 1-809/993-2667. Once Errol Flynn's island. **Bonnie View Plantation Hotel**, PO Box 82, Port Antonio, 1-809/993-2752. Harbor views. **Goblin Hill Villas**, at San San, 1-809/993-3286. Townhouse apartments on a 700-acre estate. *BUDGET:* **DeMontevin Lodge**, 1-809/993-2604. Victorian-Jamaican-style landmark.

Restaurants

LUXURY: **Trident**, Formal, expensive, good. 1-809/993-2602.

MODERATE: **Admiralty Club**, 1-809/993-2667. **DeMontevin Lodge**, 1-809/993-2604. Jamaican home-style cooking.

BUDGET: **Early Bird Restaurant**, take-out. **Kingslee Bar & Restaurant**, cheapest breakfast in town. **Boston Beach**, east of town. Jerk cooking, but sometimes with jerks cooking who let their island-wide success go to their head. Rude, crude and delectable pork, chicken, fish and lobster. Bottles of jerk sauce to go.

KINGSTON

Accommodation

LUXURY: **Jamaica Pegasus Hotel**, PO Box 333, 1- 809/926-3691. **Wyndham Kingston**, PO Box 112, 1-809/926-5430. *MODERATE*: **Morgan's Harbour**, 1-809/924-8464. Yachtie ambience on Palisadoes Rd. **Oceana Hotel**, PO Box 986, 1-809/922- 0920. **Terra Nova Hotel**, 17 Waterloo Road, Kingston 10, 1-809/926- 2211. Former home of Bob Marley's record producer. *BUDGET:* **Hotel Four Seasons**, 18 Ruthven Rd., Kingston 10, 1-809/929-7655. **Ivor Guest House**, Jack's Hill, Kingston 6, 1-809/927-1460. In the Blue Mountains at 2,000 feet. **Mayfair**, PO Box 163, Kingston 10, 1-809/926-1610.

Restaurants

LUXURY: **Blue Mountain Inn**, 1-809/927-1700. Formal. **El Dorado**, at Terra Nova Hotel, 1-809/926-2211. Fancy. **Ivor Guest House**, 1-809/927-1460. Reservations only. *MODERATE*: **Devon House**, 1-809/929-7046. **Minnie's Ethiopian Herbal Restaurant**, 176 Old Hope Rd., 1-809/927-9207. *BUDGET:* **Gino's**, open 24-hours. **Hot Pot**, near Jamaica Pegasus. Kingston office-workers eat here.

MANDEVILLE / SOUTH COAST

Accommodation & Restaurants

Hospitality and bargains, accommodations and dining are inexpensive. **Astra Hotel**, PO Box 60, Mandeville, 1-809/962- 3265. Country inn, restaurant food grown in the owner's garden. **Hotel Pontio**, PO Box 35, Black River, 1-809/965-2255. Jamaican- style, seafood. **Mandeville Hotel**, PO Box 78, Mandeville, 1- 809/962-2138. Same ownership as Astra. **Treasure Beach Hotel**, PO Box 5, Black River PO, 1-809/965-2305. A personal favorite, not fancy, rooms near the sea, solitude abounds. Restaurant usually has lobster available. **Milk River Spa & Hotel**. End-of-the-world hotel, restaurant and spa containing the most highly radioactive mineral water in the world. Jamaicans come for healing in the buoyant hot baths. Some drink the water, which is labled safe for short exposures.

NEGRIL

Accommodation

LUXURY: **Sandals Negril**, PO Box 12, 1-809/957- 4040. Romantic. **Grand Lido**, PO Box 88, 1-809/957-4010. Luxury, all-inclusive. **Hedonism II**, Box 25, 1-809/957-4200. All-inclusive adult play camp, nude volleyball, how-many naked-bodies-can-we- fit-in-a-hot-tub contests. **Swept Away Resorts**, PO Box 77. Newer all-inclusive. *MODERATE:* **Negril Beach Club**, PO Box 7, 1- 809/957-4220. Suites, kitchenettes. **Negril Gardens Hotel**, Box 58, 1-809/967-4408. **Negril Tree House**, PO Box 29, 1-809/957-4287. Cliff-side setting, no beach. *BUDGET:* **Bar-B-Barn**, Norman Manley Blvd., 1-809/957-4267. Beach cottages, kitchenettes. **Rock Cliff**, Box 67, 1-809/ 957-4331. On the cliffs. **Drumville Cove Resort**, PO Box 72, 1-809/957-4369. Cozy cottages on the cliffs.

Restaurants

Some dining in Negril is moderately priced, most is inexpensive. **Cosmo's**, 1-809/957-4330. Immortalized in the *New York Times*, so now a bit pricier, but still good fresh local food. **Miss Brown's**, hallucinogenic mushroom tea, which is legal in Jamaica. **Wharf Club**, a dive serving great conch chowder. **Evan's Restaurant**, handpick mushrooms for your tea. **Paradise Yard Café**, home of the original "Rasta Pasta".

CAYMAN ISLANDS

The Cayman Islands have been called the "Switzerland of the Caribbean", but not for its mountains. There are certainly more banks here than anywhere else in the Caribbean and Switzerland style banking laws are solidly in place. The islands enjoy a reputation for great political and social stability and one of the highest standards of living in all the Caribbean.

The trio of tiny coral islands lies about 288 km (180 mi) northwest of Jamaica and 768 km (480 mi) south of Miami. Columbus discovered them on his fourth voyage in May, 1503, when he was blown off course "in sight of two very small islands", as his son Fernando wrote in his diary, "full of tortoise, as was the sea about, in so much that they looked like little rocks". Actually, according to George S.S. Hirst's *Notes on the History of the Cayman Islands*, Columbus discovered the two smaller Cayman Islands, **Cayman Brac** and **Little Cayman**. Hirst wrote: "On the tenth day of May, 1503, Christopher Columbus returning from his fourth and last voyage from the Central America Coast discovered the Lesser Cayman Islands, which on account of the prodigious number of turtle seen both in the sea and on the shores, he called *Las Tortugas*." Columbus was followed in 1586 by Sir Francis Drake, who renamed them *Caymanas*, allegedly for crocodiles he encountered in the mangrove swamps. Many naturalists wonder if the reptiles were not actually large green iguanas. The year 1686 brought sanguinary Sir Henry Morgan fresh from his assault on Hispaniola.

Preceding pages: Replaying the past during Pirates' Weekend on Grand Cayman.

There are no documents to prove it, but island historians believe the first settlers were deserters from the English army who defected to Little Cayman and Cayman Brac around 1668 from their base in Jamaica. But from 1734, when the first recorded settlers arrived, until a century later, the Cayman Islands attracted a mixture of transplanted or shipwrecked (depending on who is telling the story) Welshmen, Scots, Irishmen and Englishmen whose customs are still visible in the contemporary Caymanian way of life.

Caymanians of today are a mixture of Scots, Welsh, Jamaicans, Africans and English. The islands never had the large, slave-operated plantations of nearby Jamaica. Emancipation of slaves took place in 1835 by proclamation of the Jamaican governor. Centuries of inter-marriage have produced a mixed population that takes great pride in the country's racial harmony. The early settlers created a quiet, peaceful and God-fearing society that remains today an oasis of tranquility at the western edge of the Caribbean. Crimes are relatively rare here and the penalty for criminal activity, such as drug use by Caymanians or visitors, is stiff.

Until very recently, most Cayman men took to seafaring. A family tradition of the sea and honesty and integrity from their forbears combined to make the Caymanians some of the most dependable seamen in the world. For years they could be found on ships in far-off ports of the world; their paychecks were sent home and built the neat, carefully tended homes that dot the Caymans. It was the long tradition of seafaring that is said to have contributed to the stability of these islands. Cayman men saw the world during their years as seamen and their experiences made them value the tidy little islands they call home. They also brought home a certain sophistication and worldliness that have helped them deal with the recent changes on the islands.

There has been very little agitation for independence here. Caymanians absolutely revel in their colonial status. Many of the first settlers were English and to this day, they are almost more English than the English in Great Britain. In fact, when a delegation from the United Nations arrived to investigate the islands and their colonial status the people of the Caymans politely, but firmly, told the U.N. delegates that they were very happy with the situation exactly as it was.

Keith Tibbetts, Cayman Brac's legislative representative at that time, said, "We made them understand in no uncertain terms that we had nothing against them individually, but we wanted them to understand they were not welcome as the United Nations."

Another Cayman resident asked the delegation, "Can you truthfully give us an example of any territory, especially among the smaller territories, that has moved to independence, and can claim success in independence?" The U.N. representatives sputtered that it was an unfair question.

Caymanians display an unusual maturity, an acceptance of their limitations as three tiny islands. They make a real distinction between political independence and economic independence. There is no arguing that the islands have economic independence, which many Caymanians believe could be upset by political independence. The people of the islands have accepted that there are some countries that are so small they may never be able to achieve the ingredients necessary for successful independence. They believe that their island home works – "If it ain't broke, don't fix it!"

One of the big attractions of the Caymans as far as bankers are concerned, is the absence of taxes. Legend has it that the tragic "Wreck of the Ten Sails" was responsible for this state of affairs. A convoy of Jamaican merchantmen bound for England was wrecked off Grand Cayman's East End in 1788. The *Cordelia*, lead ship in the convoy struck a reef. In a tragicomedy of errors, the *Cordelia* fired a signal to the others to keep away, but the signal was misunderstood and, one by one, the other nine vessels foundered on the same reef. The Caymanians proved their heroism by rescuing all of the passengers aboard the fleet of ten ships. As a reward, King George III decreed the islands' freedom from taxation.

The islands' reputation as a tax and banking haven dates back to the 1960s. In 1962, when Jamaica won independence, the Cayman Islands, which had been a dependency of Jamaica, were free to chart their own course. The islands voted to remain a British colony, a seeming contradiction considering the Caymanians' independent nature. The British colonial system required internal self-rule, something they had not had to contend with up to this point.

An important first-step in any government, is some kind of income. There

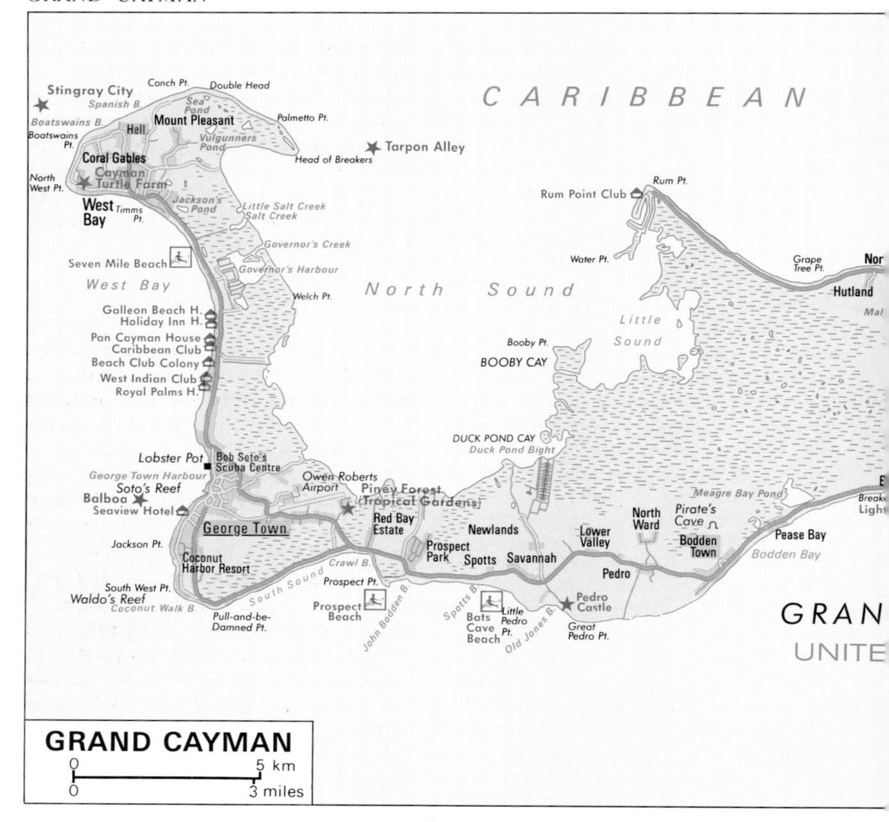

were no resources for exportation and just about everything had to be imported. In 1965, Vassel Johnson, a longtime civil servant was appointed financial secretary by the British governor. His first priority was to get rid of the mosquitoes, which made life difficult for everyone and did little to encourage tourism. Regular aerial spraying and canals to drain swampy areas gradually solved the problem, and thus the development of tourism began in earnest. The islands' evolution as a tourism center has been impressive and highly successful.

But something else was needed, something with more stability than tourism, and Johnson came up with the idea of turning the islands into a financial center. The Cayman people, like everyone else, basically hate taxes, and since they do not have to pay them to Britain, they carry on locally without paying income tax, land or property tax, death duty, inheritance tax, corporation tax, profits tax or capital gains tax. The only personal tax is an annual poll of $10 for every citizen between the ages of 18 and 60. Other minor taxes were abolished back in 1971 because no one wanted to collect them.

In late 1966, the Cayman legislature passed the first of a series of acts turning the Caymans into a financial center or tax haven, depending on your point of view. Within a few years the colony had its own currency, its own airline, an expanded airport and greatly upgraded communica-

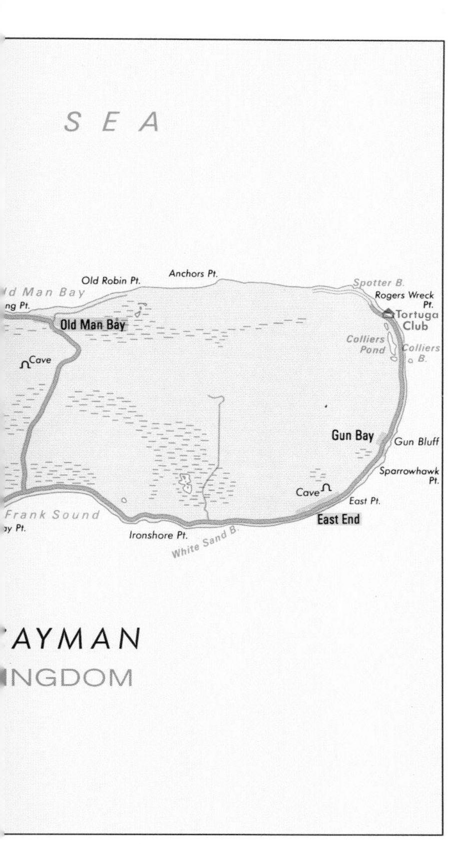

tions facilities. The Caymans offer banks, corporations and insurance companies secrecy and almost total freedom to operate as they please.

In return, the government receives annual licensing fees. The banking laws have also boosted tourism since people who travel to islands on business stay on to vacation. Today, Grand Cayman, the major island and capital, has more than 500 banks and 19,000 Caymanian corporations are engaged in international business.

The laws have brought success beyond anyone's dreams. Of course, the ironclad secrecy laws have had a down side as well. They have attracted drug smugglers and organized crime figures who found the island's location and stability perfect for money-laundering operations.

But for most tourists the lure is not the money or banks, but easy access to the U.S. mainland, top diving, miles of perfect beaches, fishing and congenial Caymanians, who are seemingly unchanged despite the major transformation of their islands in the past generation.

Grand Cayman

Most visitors land first in Grand Cayman, the largest and most developed of the trio. Visitors arriving by air land at the modern terminal building of the **Owen Roberts International Airport** – one of the most up-to-date in the Caribbean. The island has become an increasingly popular cruise stop and cruise ships generally anchor in **George Town** harbor. An average of three ships call each week year-round in this city, which has become one of the top ten cruise-ship destinations in the Caribbean in the past few years.

The island is 35 km (22 mi) long and measures 6-13 km (4-8 mi) in width. It is shaped somewhat like a fishhook in a horizontal position. The island has an estimated 22,000 inhabitants, approximately 90 percent of the country's entire population. The majority of the residents and businesses are at the western end of the island, stretching from George Town to **Seven Mile Beach**. George Town is the capital city, seat of government and commercial center for the entire colony.

Do not be surprised if you do not see many of the 500 or so banks in town. The majority of these banks are institutions engaged strictly in the offshore financial industry and are not the full-service banks that most people are more used to.

The entire town can be seen in an afternoon. It is small, clean and unpretentious. Sites to see include a clock monument to King George V; the **Legislative Assembly** on **Fort Street**; the **Courts Building**; the **Government Administra-**

tion Building, called the *Glass House* by locals; and the **General Post Office**. Building heights are limited to five stories. It is principally a place for restaurants, shops and, as mentioned above, banks. The **Cayman Maritime and Treasure Museum** on the waterfront in the heart of George Town offers a wide assortment of displays ranging from the exploration of the New World by Columbus to the most modern, sophisticated treasure recovery techniques. Genuine treasure and artifacts are available in the museum's gift shop. Also on **North Church Street** is **McKee's Museum**, which displays treasures discovered by the late Art McKee, a notorious treasure hunter. There are also authentic old coins for sale, brought up from 16th- and 17th-century wrecks.

The town is a popular shopping haunt for duty-free bargains. There are Swiss watches, English china and crystal, porcelain, French perfumes and jewelry, including black coral creations. A shop called **Black Coral** is among the special places to see. It specializes in black coral jewelry and features the works of sculptor Bernard Passman, whose talent in black coral has been recognized by royalty three times. Passman designed the official gifts presented on behalf of the Cayman Islands Government to Prince Charles and Princess Diana for the royal wedding, a gift presented to Queen Elizabeth and the Duke of Edinburgh to commemorate the first royal visit in 1983.

Above and right: Everyone seems to like lounging about.

Driving north from George Town along **West Bay Road** there are dozens of hotels and condominium apartments. Most are along the famed **Seven Mile Beach** which is actually only 8 km (5 1/2 mi) long. At **Northwest Point** there is the **Cayman Turtle Farm**. It is the only green sea turtle farm of its kind in the world and the most popular land-based tourist attraction in the islands. Although there were once a multitude of turtles in the waters surrounding the islands, they are now sadly few in number. The farm was established in 1968 by a private entrepreneur and is now owned by the Cayman government. The farm has a twofold purpose, to provide the local market with edible turtle meat and to replenish the waters with hatchlings and yearling turtles. The turtle steaks or turtle soup served in local restaurants come from here.

Turtles range in size from 170 g (6 oz) to 272 kg (600 lb). The first of the female turtles raised in the compound crawled up onto a beach in mid-1975 to lay her first batch of eggs. The following year, 29 turtles laid 186 eggs, and the hatch rate was recorded at over 88 percent. Today there are almost 60,000 turtles, most of which live in 40 tanks ranging between 9 and 21m (30-70 ft) in diameter. The water changes in the large tanks every 30 minutes and in the small tanks every five minutes. At one time items purchased

from the Cayman Turtle Farm were granted an exemption to the U.S. ban against the importation of turtle products. However, there is no longer an exemption and no turtle products, regardless of their origin, are allowed into the United States. A few minutes away is the village of **Hell**, where you can buy postcards and stamps at the tiny post office and have them postmarked *Hell, Grand Cayman.*

The large black rock outcroppings prompted a former commissioner to name the area after commenting, "This is what Hell must look like." A ramp leads to a photo vantage point above the limestone fields and a gift shop where visitors can buy memorabilia from Hell and refreshments.

Driving south from George Town are many of the remaining small Cayman-style cottages. A few miles out of town there's Grand Cayman's **Piney Forest** of towering Australian pines. The next stop is **Bodden Town**, the original capital of the Cayman Islands. It is a quaint village featuring the **Pirate's Caves**, a small underground cave system where 18th-century rogues are thought to have sought shelter. The north side is quiet and favored for its beautiful secluded beach areas. During the summer red-headed Cayman parrots can sometimes be seen in the brush along the roads. The road connects **Old Man Bay** with the island's least-developed district, the **East End**. Queen Elizabeth II cut the ribbon, officially opening this road in February, 1983, and a plaque proclaims it the **Queen's Highway**. Offshore lies what is left of the wreck of the **M.V. Ridgefield**, a 7,500-tonne ship that ran aground on the reef in 1962 during the Bay of Pigs invasion in nearby Cuba.

Many of Grand Cayman's sites are underwater. The residents of the islands have long been aware of the value of the undersea reefs and marine life. In 1978 the government instituted strict marine conservation laws. These regulations protect many local species. The most important regulation is the prohibition of taking any type of coral or sponge anywhere in

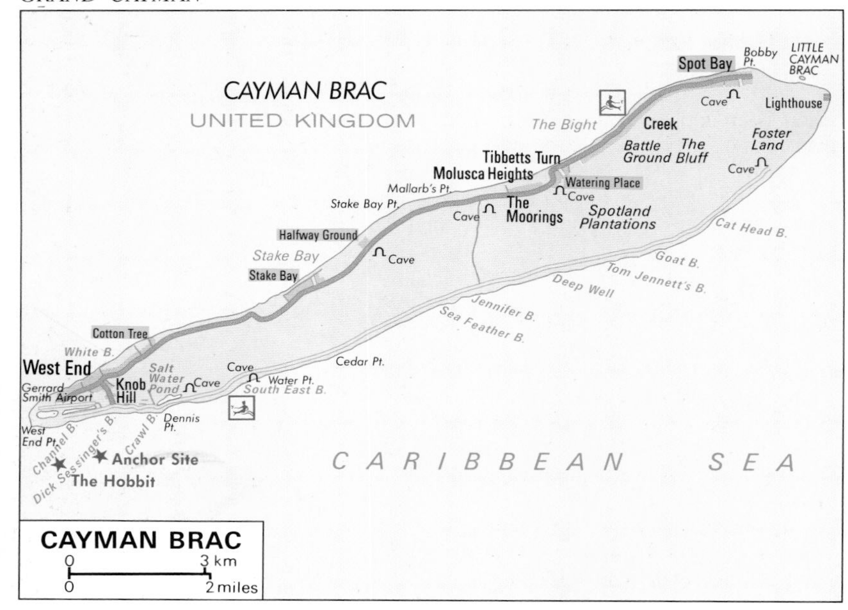

Cayman waters by anyone. Violation can result in a year in jail and a $5,000 fine.

The island offers the greatest variety of catalogued **diving sites** of any single island in the Caribbean. Literally hundreds have been discovered, charted and photographed during the island's 25 years of resort diving. However, visitors do not need to get wet to enjoy the underwater world of Grand Cayman. There are two submarines that regularly take passengers under the sea. The 28- passenger *Atlantis* travels at a depth of 12-18 m (40-60 ft) along the reefs. Another submarine, a two-passenger operation, takes dives down to 243 m (800 ft) along the island's wall. Since sport divers seldom dive below a depth of 38 m (125-ft), the submarine passengers will have a view of the underwater world that no scuba divers are ever likely to see.

Grand Cayman is best known for its dropoffs. A sheer vertical wall encircles the entire island. There are also several good **shipwrecks** that lie in shallow to medium depths and are loaded with fish and tiny creatures. Many commercial movies have been shot on these wrecks. There is some excellent diving just offshore, allowing divers or snorkelers to explore without having to hire a boat.

Right: Exotic abroad, but quite common in the Caribbean.

Cruise passengers who arrive in George Town harbor can just hop overboard and find themselves on some lovely reefs good for snorkelers or divers. **Soto's Reef** is just offshore from the **Lobster Pot** and **Bob Soto's Scuba Centre**. Coral heads are less than 1.8 m (6ft) below the surface, making it perfect for snorkelers. For divers there are many tunnels and coral chambers to explore. The remains of the 114-m (375-ft) **Balboa** are scattered over a wide area of the harbor's ocean bottom. It is only 182 m (200 yd) off the town pier and attracts thousands of divers. It is popular with novice divers, photographers and wreck divers. A popular shore diving site is **Waldo's Reef**, which is directly off **Co-**

conut Harbor Resort. It has been named for a resident 1.8-m (6 ft) green moray eel named Waldo. Another tame fish is a giant black grouper called *Bugsy,* and then there is *Snaggletooth,* a very curious barracuda.

Off **Seven Mile Beach** is one of the most popular Grand Cayman dives. It is the **Oro Verde**, which was deliberately sunk in 1980 by the Cayman government and dive operators. The 56-m (184-ft) ship lies on her starboard side and has become a refuge for a wide variety of marine life. A pair of friendly French angelfish can be found here. The wreck's most impressive resident is a 1,5- m (5-ft) long, 50 kg (110-IG) jewfish named *Sweetlips*. She is gentle and has no fear of divers.

Off the north shore are several exceptional diving sites. **Tarpon Alley** is an exciting spot where more than 100 giant tarpon swim together in a narrow canyon. Divers can swim through the canyon almost touching the tarpon as they slowly cruise back and forth. Underwater photographers can capture some spectacular shots here. Nearby is **Stingray City**, which is regarded as the most exciting-shallow dive in the Caribbean. Diving depths range from 3.6-5.5 m (12-18 ft). The site is a gathering place for twelve to twenty tame stingrays that can be handled by divemasters. The stingrays are totally fearless of divers or snorkelers. Generations of Cayman fishermen have used this spot for anchoring and cleaning their catch. The fish scraps have attracted the stingrays and presumably contributed to making these otherwise redoubtable fish tame.

Cayman Brac

The sister islands of Cayman Brac and Little Cayman lie 142 km (89 mi) and 118 km (74 mi) northeast of Grand Cayman respectively. The two are almost twins, similar in size and shape.

Cayman Brac is the larger of the two, 19 km (12 mi) long and 3 km (2 mi) wide. The west end is flat and almost at sea level, while the east end rises to a 43-m (140-ft) sheer cliff which plummets into the Caribbean.

Brac is Gaelic for bluff. The Brac is much like Grand Cayman used to be some twenty years ago. There are about 1,700 people on the entire island. They live along the coastline of the north shore in tiny settlements with descriptive names like **Stake Bay**, **Watering Place**, **Cotton Tree**, **Spot Bay** and **Halfway Ground**. The pace is slow and the Brackers are even more hospitable than their Grand Cayman cousins. The island has an old-fashioned Caribbean charm, with two of the finest and friendliest small hotels in the Caribbean and virgin reefs.

People come to the Brac for diving, birdwatching, exploring the caves, bonefishing, snorkeling or just relaxing. The island is a major flyway for migratory birds and is a refuge for a rich variety of rare species, including the elusive green,

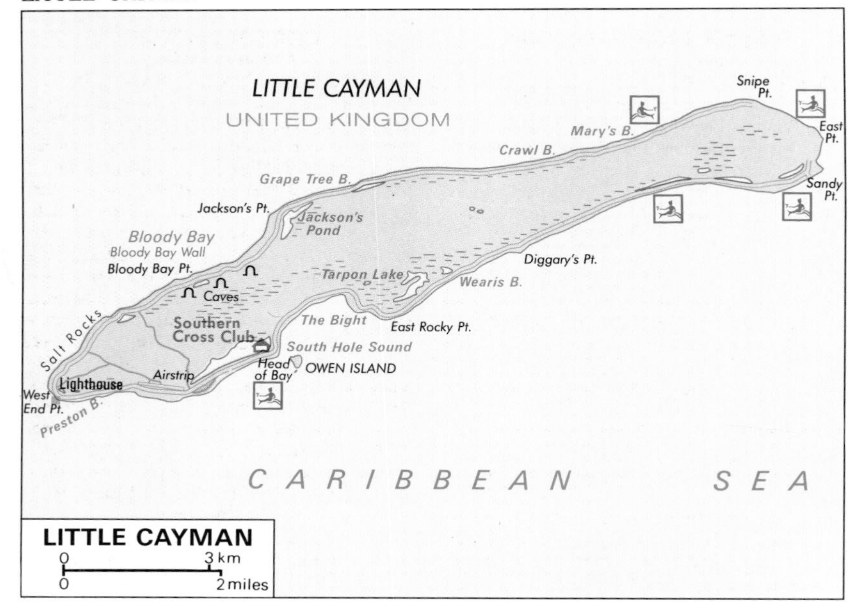

blue and red Caymanian parrot. The island is honeycombed with caves, many of which remain unexplored. Legend has it that there are fabulous pirate treasures buried in these cliffs. The island is not known for its beaches although it does possess a few sandy patches. There are, however, nearly 50 diving sites around the island and more are being discovered every year. One of the more popular sites on the south side is the **Hobbit**, named after the story written by J.R.R. Tolkien because of its fairyland appearance. It features a number of bizarre-looking sponges. There are several giant barrel sponges measuring 1.2 m (4 ft) in diameter. **Anchor Site** is a wall dive that begins at 20 m (65 ft) and drops vertically to at least 304 m (1,000 ft).

Little Cayman

Little Cayman is one of nature's last outposts in the Caribbean. More than 98 percent of the island remains uninhabited and undeveloped. It is 13 km (8 mi) long and less than 3 km (2 mi) wide. The resident population numbers about two dozen. The airport is a grass landing strip. Most of the roads are unpaved trails. The island has one of the largest rookeries in the Caribbean for boobies and frigate birds. A great salt pond is filled with a miniature version of tarpon. Little Cayman is one of the top bonefishing areas in the western hemisphere.

There are three small, self-contained hotels for divers and fishermen and the diving here is nothing short of legendary. The tiny island offers some of the most spectacular reef diving in all the Caribbean. At one place along **Bloody Bay Wall**, the drop-off begins at 5 m (18 ft) and plummets vertically to 365 m (1,200 ft). **Soto Trader** is the sunken wreck of a 36-m (120-ft) long steel-hulled cargo vessel. She caught fire and sank in April 1975 and now rests upright in 15 m (50 ft) of water. The hull is totally intact and there are even two jeeps in the cargo hold. The wreck has become a haven for fish life.

Access & Local Transportation

Cayman Airways, American, Pan American and Northwest serve Grand Cayman from Miami. Cayman Airways flies from New York, Houston, Tampa, Atlanta and Kingston, Jamaica. Cayman Airways flies twice weekly between Miami and Cayman Brac. Cayman Airways flies from Grand Cayman to Little Cayman and Cayman Brac. There are special three- island fares or day-long excursions. On Grand Cayman taxis meet arriving flights, rates fixed. A bus runs hourly from George Town and West Bay along Seven Mile Beach, stopping at hotels. Car rentals from Budget, Hertz, National, Coconut. Driving permit: $3. Caribbean Motors, Cayman Cycle Rentals, Soto's Scooters rent motor-cycles, mopeds, scooters. The submarine *Atlantis* carries passerngers to depths of 150 feet, day or night dives. Research Submersibles has two 2-passenger craft diving to 3,000 feet. Surfside Watersports, Bob Soto's Diving and Aqua Delights have glass-bottom boat trips.

Formalities & Currency

For stays to six months, visitors from the U.S. and Canada need proof of citizenship such as passport, birth certificate or voter's registrations card and a return or ongoing ticket. Visitors from other countries need a valid passport.

One Cayman dollar equals US $1.25 Stores and restaurants accept U.S. dollars. Most shops and hotels also accept credit cards. Travelers checks can be cashed at banks, hotels, restaurants, shops. Departure tax is $7.50.

Special Events

The biggest annual events are *Batabanbo*, an April carnival with parades, exhibits and dances, the Queen's Birthday celebration in June and the country's national festival, *Pirate's Week*, a week-long celebration with costumes, parades and special events in late October. Activities include underwater photography contests and treasure hunts, golf and swimming tournaments. Cayman Brac celebrates *Brachanal* the last Saturday in April, a carnival-style festival. Easter is celebrated with a traditional weekend of water-sports with various classes of sailing, windsurfing and powerboat racing. June is called the Million Dollar Month, a month-long international saltwater fishing tournament with cash prizes for record catches of marlin, tuna, wahoo, dolphin.

Tourist information

Cayman Islands Dept. of Tourism, 420 Lexington Ave., Suite 2733, New York, NY 10170, 212/682-5582; Frankfurt, Hans Regh Associates, Postfach 930247, Elbinger Str. 1, D-6000 Frankfurt/Main 90, Germany, 69-70 40 13/15.

GRAND CAYMAN

Accommodation

Casa Caribe, pool, tennis, $350-$500. **The Colonial Club**, kitchens, tennis, pool, beach, $350-$420. **Grand Pavilion**, continental plush, Louis XV-style furniture, canopy beds. Wedgewood, crystal, sterling in **Le Diplomat** dining room, $200- $1,500. **Hyatt Regency Grand Cayman**, pools, tennis, restaurants, beach club, golf, conference facilities, condos, townhouses, $250-$625. **Holiday Inn Grand Cayman**, tennis, pool, nightclub, $180-$300. **London House**, kitchens, pool, beach, $225-$260. **Radisson Grand Cayman**, beach, pool, health club, water-sports. $225-$300. **Ramada's Treasure Island**, pools, tennis, nightclub, top-rated dining, $200-$235. **Villas of the Galleon**, kitchens, $240-$400. **Retreat at Rum Point**, beach solitude, pool, tennis, sauna, gym, water-sports, diving, $220-$400. **Sunset House**, for divers, thatch-roofed **My Bar** is a gathering place for anglers, divers, pilots and local politicians, $100-$165.

Restaurants

Dining on Little Cayman and Cayman Brac is limited to the hotels. Expensive, $45 and up, moderate, $25 to $44, inexpensive, under $25.
LUXURY: **Chef Tell's Grand Old House**, run by TV chef Tell Erhardt, reservations. **Lobster Pot,** seafood. **Periwinkle**, conch, turtle steak, lobster. **Pappagallo**, elegant tropical, northern Italian menu, seafood. *MODERATE:* **Almond Tree**, good value. **Cracked Conch**, conch and seafood. *BUDGET:* **West Bay Polo Club**, locals' gathering place. **Crow's Nest**, family- style Caymanian food. **Liberty's West End Bay**, curried goat, codfish and ackee.

CAYMAN BRAC

Accomodation

Divi Tiara Beach, beach, diving, fishing, tennis, pool, apartments, conferences, $140-$200. **Brac Reef Beach Resort**, pool, beach, diving, relaxing environs, $110.

LITTLE CAYMAN

Accomodation

Fishing, diving, bird watching and a get- away-from- it-all feeling on an island with only two dozen residents. **Sam McCoy's Diving and Fishing Lodge**, ten rooms, $120 per person includes meals. **Southern Cross Club**, fly fishing, diving, ten rooms, $125 per person with meals. **Pirate's Point Resort**, six rooms, bonefishing, deep-sea fishing, $180 per person includes meals and 2 dives.

TRABAJO
FUSIL
UJC

CUBA

The *habaneras,* melancoly laments once sung by Spanish soldiers having to leave their beloved in order to fight wars in distant lands, describe Cuba's beautiful women, the beaches and bays of that verdurant island with its palm trees and coffee, which seemed a veritable paradise to the simple fellows from Spain's barren regions. Cuba's reputation as a pearl in the Caribbean persists to this very day.

When Columbus discovered America in the year 1492, he first landed on one of the Bahamas Islands and then on Cuba. It became one of the first colonies in the 16th century, and its cities were built to resemble towns in the Spanish mother country and were given the same names. The inhabitants of the island, Indians, succumbed quickly to brutal treatment and to the diseases imported by the colonial rulers. Hardly any traces of them have survived. Black slaves were brought in from Africa to replace the Indians, and their descendents, mixed with the Spanish colonialists into a panoply of skin colors, form the approximately 11 million Cubans living on the island today.

The resident descendants of the first colonial generation grew increasingly recalcitrant with the local rulers chosen by the central government in Spain, which led to repeated instances of armed independence struggles during the 19th century. Toward the end of the century, the national hero José Martí founded a revolutionary party and intensified the resistance against the colonial powers-that-be. Using the excuse of an attack on the warship *USS Maine,* the USA intervened in the conflict as an alleged liberator. The treaty of 1898 between the USA and Spain gave Cuba its independence, but at the same time created an economic dependence on the USA.

Years of political ups and downs, interspersed with periods of economic growth and depression, followed; in 1940, Cuba was ruled by Juan Batista, a puppet of Washington. Most Cubans lived in total poverty, without proper education, unemployed, some found seasonal work in the sugar-cane industry, prostitution was rampant; Cuba earned a reputation as an *El Dorado* for American businessmen who for a handful of dollars could fly in a half-hour to the island, leaving their priggish society behind to revel in countless establishments, in bars, nightclubs and gambling joints of Havana.

Guerilla fighters under Fidel Castro tried to overthrow the regime for the first time in 1953. They attacked the Moncada

Preceding pages: The old Presidential Palace in Havana, Cuba, is a museum to the revolution. Left: Anyone for a cigar?

barracks in Santiago, but were defeated. After his release in 1955, Castro consolidated his forces in Mexico. Che Guevara joined the guerillas at this point. In 1956 Castro began a new offensive using the ship *Granma*. By January 8, 1959, they had won the war and the US-supported rulers and a great many Cubans opposed to Castro had taken off to the more friendly climes of Florida. In 1961 a group of US-backed Cuban exiles attempted a landing at the Bay of Pigs in the southern part of the island, but it failed miserably.

Since then the revolutionary government has attempted to create a modern Latin American nation with its own political aims. The first tasks were to alphabetize the people, to offer them health care, to distribute milk to every child and senior citizen in the country, full employment, to offer culture for everyone, build roads, establish a public transportation system and finally to properly supply the provinces.

Recent global developments, as the world-wide collapse of the price of sugar, the dwindling economic support of the Soviet Union, the dissolution of the entire East Bloc, the continued trade embargo by the USA, effectively strangulated the initial rise in the standard of living. Since the 1980s, Cuba has been opening up to western tourism in an attempt to earn the hard currency necessary to purchase medical supplies and technological

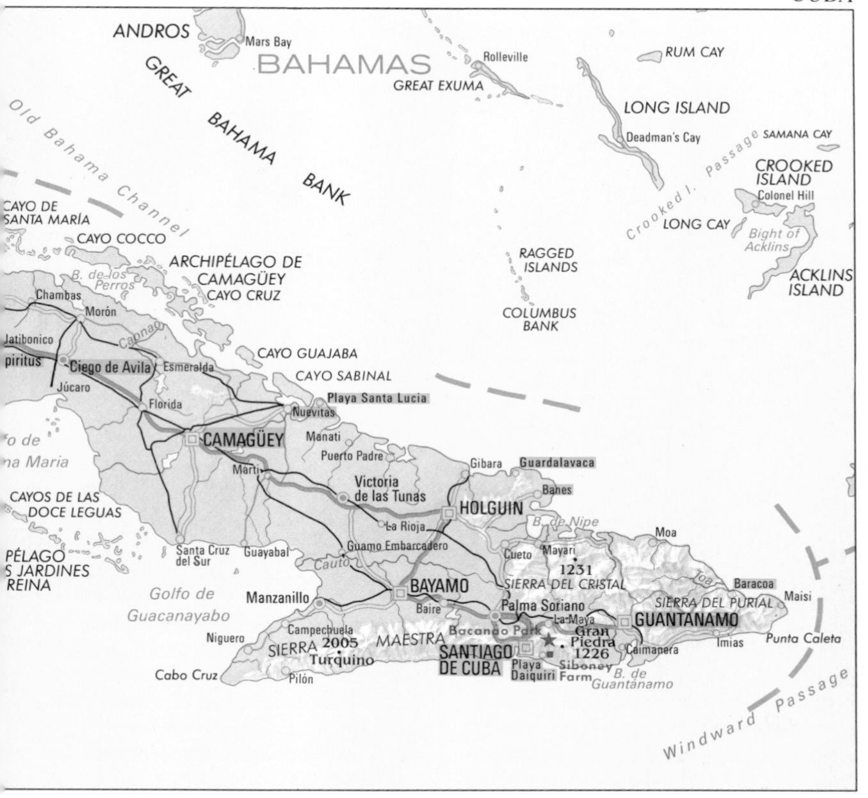

wares. The collateral problems are clear for all to see: Tourists expect the kind of attention and quality with regards to hotels, restaurants and overall infrastructure that the goverment cannot begin to offer its own people.

Its length of 1250 km makes Cuba the largest of the Antilles. Strategically, its geographical situation is optimal: It lies arched before the Bay of Mexico and offers a wide sampling of Caribbean climates and landscapes. Mountain ranges cover the western and southern parts of the island, whereas the central section consists by and large of flatlands. Coffee and cacao grow in the warm and damp mountainous areas in the southeastern region, and tabacco and cattle have a home to the west of Havana, in the province of **Pinar del Rio**, with its fertile valleys which are sprawled between strangely-shaped mountains. The entire central part of the island is occupied by the sugarcane monoculture.

All three parts of the island provide for beautiful beaches, remote and solitary coves and a great deal of virgin nature. The offshore sand banks and the coral reefs are paradisical spots for divers. The elongated sandy promontory of **Varadero** and the **Island of Youth** have both been turned into vacation centers. The main attraction of the island besides the beaches lies in the friendliness of its inhabitants. It is the kind one finds in school children who show their knowl-

edge of foreign languages off to visitors – by questioning them relentlessly about their own country.

If in search of the place where the great Havana cigars grow, head to the western section of the island, the site of the largest tobacco plantations. If you come from Havana you will first of all reach the **Sierra del Rosario**. The luxury resort of **Soroa**, with its orchid gardens, parks and waterfalls and a splendid view of the **Mountain of Venus**, lies in this series of approximately 600 m high hills. The **Güira National Park** is located in the mountains further to the west. The woods conceal a pleasant vacation resort offering accomodations in the kind of pile dwellings once used by the Indians of the mountains.

The **Sierra de los Organos** sprawls to the north of Pinar del Rio. Typical of the landscape of this area are the so-called *mogotes*, peculiar limestone cones that stick out of the otherwise perfectly flat topography. This fertile stretch of land is used for the cultivation of tobacco, corn or yucca, according to the season. The little huts dotting the plain serve as drying houses for the tobacco. There is no denying the fascinating aspects of the landscape. One local oddity is the **Mural de la Prehistoria**, a mural created by modern artists on a cliff side depicting the evolution of man from a single cell to an upright, full-fledged biped.

The Island of Youth, **Isla de la Juventud**, the erstwhile *Isla de Pinos*, served once upon a time as a penal island where Fidel Castro himself did time after his first attempted revolution. Today it is the site of a training school, a lemon plantation and of a modern tourist resort with the Hotel Colony at its center. Deep sea diving in coral reefs is possible at the **Cabo Frances**. Further diving and swimming opportunities exist on the **Cayo Largo**, offshore from the Zapata peninsula.

Above: The cathedral in the early light. Right: In the Bodequita del Medio where Hemingway once hung out.

La Habana

Havana is without the slightest doubt Cuba's most interesting city. Its population of 2 million is spread out over innumerable city districts, every one of which can be easily investigated on foot, whereas one is better off using a taxi or the extensive bus network to get from one district to the next. The **old town**, that still recalls the early colonial days, is deployed around the cathedral and contains the most important historical sights. To the west, beyond the area of long streets and four-storied buildings developed in the hey-day of capitalism, lies the district where North American influence is most felt, even to this day. **Vendado**, an area marked by modern stores, office buildings and hotels, and with a checkerboard street pattern, expands on both sides of 23rd Street, known as **La Rampa**. The wealthy part of town, where villas house government offices and embassies, is the **Miramar district**. The western beaches of the city begin here. Residential quarters consisting mostly of low houses unfold to the south in a generous arch around the city's natural harbor. Its end is dominated by the mighty fort **Castillo del Morro**, the site of an elegant restaurant. To the east, right on the edge of town is the little fishing village of **Cojimar**, which is famous for having guested Ernest Hemingway. At this point begin the two most popular beaches **Santa María del Mar** and **Boca Ciega**.

The center of Old Havana, **La Habana Vieja** in Spanish, is **Cathedral Square**. The 18th century cathedral, the old palaces and the public buildings around the square have all been restored. They are open to visitors, as is the **Colonial Museum** and the bars and restaurants.

The **Castillo de la Real Fuerza**, a redoubtable fortified construction, extends behind the square. Several blocks of houses in the old town have already been subjected to exemplary restoration measures. But even the **Plaza Vieja**, the Old Square, which is still in need of renovations, is pretty. It often serves as a backdrop to open-air theatrical performances. Otherwise the old town has been densely built up, and putting it entirely back into shape will cost both a lot of money and effort. Those who have settled there in the meantime have to frequently put up with substandard living conditions in dark and damp houses. Just meandering through the streets of the district gives an idea of how stately the buildings were once upon a time.

A fortified wall originally girded the outer periphery of the old town, later providing a vast surface area for the **Av. Agramonte** and the representative buildings of the **Prado**. The model for the **Capitol** is not difficult to guess. Today it hosts the **Museum of Natural Sciences**. Other buildings on this peripheral strip are the old city hotels, the Partagás cigar factory, the **Museum of Art**, the **Pavilion** where the ship *Granma* has been put on display, and right beside it, in the erstwhile presidential palace, the **Museum of the Revolution**. The fortified complex of **San Salvador de la Punta** marks the end of the Prado; it guards the entrance of the harbor, together with the Castillo del Morro that stands on the opposite side. The row of houses that has welcomed seafarers for centuries begins right here: the **Malecón** with its intimidating jetty-wall and its buildings supported by piles.

Behind this façade lies the old town quarter of central Havana, a mainly residential area that does boast the isolated movie house or shop. It is not unusual to see one of the great American gas hounds left over from the pre-revolutionary days standing out in front of people's houses. Spare parts have a very high price, and if need be, are made from scratch. The **Av. Simón Bolívar**, that later turns into the **Av. Salvador Allende**, runs straight through the old town, linking it to Vedado. It ends at **Revolution Square**, the great parade ground with Party buildings, monuments and the national theater. It borders on the university, the hospital

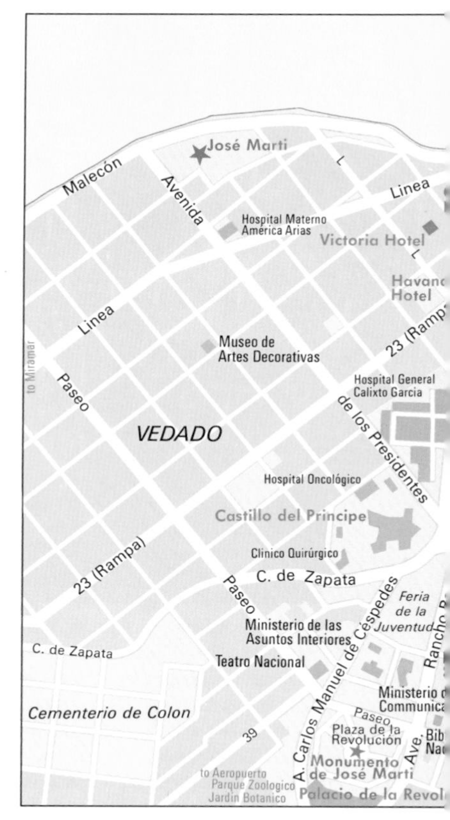

quarter and the modern Vedado quarter, whose streets are either numbered or lettered. The famous hotel **Habana Libre** stands on the corner of 23rd Street (La Rampa) and L Street. Most hotels, cinemas, restaurants, book stores and other shops have conglomerated on La Rampa. The interesting cemetery of **Colón**, the **botanical garden** and the **zoo** are all located to the south in **Nuevo Vedado**. And further out, beyond the river, you will find the open-air premises of the **Tropicana Cabaret.** Even if you are immune to long-legged beauties in glittering apparel, it is worth visiting the place for its great atmosphere. Equally far from the city center is the popular **Lenin Park**, offering many recreational activities.

The Southern Coast

In 1961, the US-backed counterrevolutionaries landed in the Bay of Pigs, the **Bahía de Cochinos**, and in the **Zapata Marshes**. Those events are vividly recalled in a special museum and on oversized billboards. Several holiday resorts have sprung up in the immediate neighborhood, on beaches in the midst of beautiful vegetation: the bungalo villages of **Playa Girón** and **Playa Larga**. The lacustrian pile village of **Guamé**, patterned after an authentic Indian village and accessible only by boat, lies in the middle of a swamp and also functions as a holiday resort. Just next to it is a crocodile farm.

Cienfuegos lies cradled in a natural harbor basin. In spite of its 100.000 inhabitants the town has a definitely provincial air about it. It nevertheless boasts modern docking facilities, factories and an atomic power plant. **Parque Martí**, home of the municipal museum, the old-fashioned **Terry Theater** and several public establishments, constitute the center of the checkerboard street plan. You will find the **Museo Historico Navál** on one of the points of land, and all the way at the end of 37th street, on the **Punta Gorda** peninsula, are a number of good restaurants. One pretty excursion is in a passenger boat across the Bay of Cienfuegos to the 18th-century fortress towering over the town of **Jagua**.

The town of **Trinidad** lies on the coast to the south, concealed by the mountains of the **Sierra de Escambray**. The prosperous colonial overlords had great palaces built here at the beginning of the 19th century when the area bustled with economic activity spawned by sugarcane, tobacco, gold and silver. The workers of the plantation could be watched from the **Torre de Iznaga**, a tower at the western edge of town. The rebellions of the 1830s that brought about the end of slavery also brought over 50 sugar mills to a standstill, and Trinidad turned into a ghost town. Because of its remote location, it remained forgotten even in the 20th century; its colonial architecture survived almost untouched by modern developments. The entire town has been placed under conservation in order to protect its unique stylistic uniformity. In the past decades efforts have been made to restore the buildings. The town exudes a sleepy atmosphere, like some open-air museum documenting the colonial architecture that one finds more clearly explained in the **Museo de la Architectura Trinitaria**. Further museums are located in the palaces and the church around the Plaza Mayor: the **Museo Romántico** with furnishings from old villas; the **Museo Municipal**, housed in the former palace of a sugar manufacturer; the **Museum of Nature Studies**, and the **Archeological Museum**.

Above: Young pioneers in Trinidad. Right: Left-over Americana still baring its teeth.

The Northern Coast and the Center

Package tours from the west usually head straight to Varadero. The 19-km-long land strip of Hicacos is dotted with innumerable large hotels, restaurants, discotheques and nightclubs, in the idyllic surroundings of palm trees and beaches. Numerous recreational opportunities, beach bars and the climatic guarantee of lots of good weather almost guarantee a restful vacation. One discotheque has nested in the **Cueva del**

Pirata, a cave formed by the sea, once used as a hiding place by pirates. The large hotels offer excursions to Matanzas and Havana, to the coral reefs, the islands and to the **Bellamar Cave**.

Matanzas is one of the most important centers for the export of sugar cane, nevertheless its two rivers and pretty harbor give it enough appeal to warrant a visit. Buses and taxis to and from Varadero all stop at the train station. The road to the old town, which lies between the Río San Juan and the Río Yumurí, crosses the **Pueblo Nuevo district**. Hotels, the theater, the cathedral, the restaurants and public establishments have gathered around the main square.

A number of mid-size and relatively widely-spaced towns occupy the central part of the island, serving as supply, administrative and industrial centers to the largely agricultural area surrounding them: **Santa Clara**, **Sancti Spiritus**, **Ciego de Avila** and **Camagüey**, one of Cuba's oldest and largest cities, where the famous poet Nicolás Guillén was born. Numerous beautiful beach resorts have sprung up on land spits and sand banks in the mid-section of the region as well as northwest of Camagüey, in the town of **Nuevitas**, near whose cove you will find the **Cayo Sabinal** and **Santa Lucia** beaches.

Southeast Cuba

The superb beaches and the vacation resort of **Guardalavaca** are on the northern coast, not far from the little provincial town of **Holguin**. The **Museo Arqueológico** in the town of **Banes** has an exhibition of finds from the original Indian people of Cuba. To the extreme south, west of Santiago the **Sierra Maestra** mountains – where guerilla fighters hid out for years – follow the coastline. Their steep peaks rise up to 2000 m only to plunge in spectacular fashion down to the coast, where one often finds pretty but stony coves.

Santiago de Cuba served as Cuba's capital in the 16th century and is the is-

land's second largest city today. It has always played an important role in Cuba's tumultuous history: It is where slaves were bought and sold, where the Spanish surrendered, and where the Moncada barracks were stormed. The city's houses, built low because of earthquakes, spread over several hills that enclose the bay. The old colonial style has survived in the old town, around **Cespedes Park**, with the wonderfully old-fashioned Hotel Granada. The **Casa de Velázquez**, where the island's first governor once lived, has been turned into the fascinating **Colonial Museum**. The nearby **Casa de la Trova** was the birth place of the *Nova Trova*, the Cuban songwriters' movement of the 1960s and '70s. On Saturday evenings **Heredia Street** comes alive with the sound of music. The fluorescent signs of the shops on this strip suggest its economic importance in the 1950s.

The center of town seems a little provincial, considering its 350.000 inhabitants, but life here is buoyant and colorful. Long streets lead from the harbor into simple residential neighborhoods with old wooden houses, carrying with them the rays of the setting sun and casting the entire town in gold. The harbor, site of a rum factory, is the main economic pole. From here one can take trips through the bay to the beautiful **Granma Island**. Another fort named **Morro** stands guard at the entrance of the harbor.

Santiago is perhaps the most ideal place on Cuba to simply spend a little idle time. The best time to go is during Carnival, whose tradition is as long as that of Rio, and though it is far more limited in size, it nevertheless drags the whole town in its wake. Because of the sugar cane harvest in February, however, it was moved to summer. One site to see is **Siboney Farm** southwest of Santiago, where Castro and his rebels hid before storming the Moncada barracks. It adjoins the **Bacanao Park** excursion area, where you can enjoy nice beaches, such as the **Daiquiri**, and several hotels and bungalows with genuine Caribbean atmosphere. But the landscape towards Guantánamo quickly becomes barren and remote.

Guantánamo is not only the name of an unwelcome US military base, but also the home town of the girl in the world-famous song *Guantanámera* who sings of her native town and laments the tragic fate of those who live there. It sits in a dry area, in the midst of saltworks somewhat off the main routes of Cuba. It is bypassed by the road that leads into the mountains where coffee and cacao grow in the shade of trees. Beyond the mountains the air becomes increasingly damp and the vegetation luxuriant. Colorful straw-roofed houses, the so-called *bohío* of peasants, dot the plantations. The road winds its way through jungle-like banana and cacao plantations, all the way to the bay of **Baracoa**, which is famous for its black sand beaches.

Above: A quiet family portrait in the shade.

HAVANA

Accommodation

LUXURY: **Havana Libre** (Vedado); Capri (Vedado); Nacional (Vedado).
MODERATE: **Inglaterra; Sevilla; Plaza; Colina** (Vedado).
BUDGET: Budget hotels, such as the (noisy) Bruzón, are not on the official list of tourist hotels and can only be "booked" by arriving there and checking in!

Restaurants

All larger hotels offer good food, especially the **Hotel Sevilla**; also try the **Bodeguite del Medio** of Hemingway fame and the **El Patio** (Cathedral Square); **La Casa de los Vinos**; **El Floridita; Los Andes; El Cochinito; La Carreta; El Conejito; La Tasca Española.**

Museums / Sightseeing

Hemingway Museum; Museo de la Ciudad, Town Museum; Afro-Cuban Museum; Museo de la Revolución, Revolution Museum; Museo de Arte Colonial; Museo de Artes Decorativas; Museo de Bellas Artes; Acuario; Parque Zoologico; Jardín Botanico; Castillo del Morro.

Entertainment

Cabaret Tropicana (outside of town), book a table through your hotel; **Café Cantante**; Casa de la Trova; **Teatro Mella**; **Teatro Karl Marx; Teatro Nacional; Teatro Musical.**

Tourist Hotels (other Towns)

MATANZAS: **Hotel Velsco** (old-fashioned flair).
SANTIAGO: **Hotel Casa Granda** (old-fashioned, central); **Balcón del Caribe** (modern, outside of town at the harbor entrance).
CIEGO DE AVILA: **Hotel Ciego de Avila** (modern).
SANCTI SPIRITUS: **Los Laureles** (modern).
TRINIDAD: **Costasur** (a fair distance out of town, modern seafront hotel); **Las Cuevas** (outskirts), **Las Cuevas** (Motel at the fringe of town, mountain with caves).
GUAMÁ: **Villa Guama** (Indian-style log-and-pile- cabins).
SANTA CLARA: **Hotel Santa Clara Libre**.
CIENFUEGOS: **Rancho Luna**, **Pasacaballos** (outside of town on the beach).
CAMAGÜEY: **Gran Hotel** (Center).
PARQUE GUIRA: **Cabañas Los Pinos** (pile-foundation log cabins in the wood).
VIÑALESTAL: **Ermita**; **Los Jazmines** (both hotels in rural surroundings, lovely views).
BARACOA: **Castillo** (fringe of town, view across the bay).
SOROA: Villa Turística Soroa.

Beach Hotels

ISLA DE LA JUVENTUD: **Colony Hotel.**
CAY LARGO: **Hotel Isla del Sur**.
SANTA LUCIA BEACH: **Hotel Mayanabo.**
PLAYA GIRÓN: **Villa Playa Larga** (bungalow village); **Playa Girón.**
VARADERO: *LUXURY:* **Los Palmeras, Paradiso** (ultra-new); *MODERATE:* **Internacional, Siboney, Oasis**; *BUNGALOWS:* **Villa Solimar, Villa Los Delfines, Villa Caribe**

Food and Drink in Cuba

Although the supply-situation is far from satisfactory, all hotels try their best to serve good international cuisine. Local dishes are mostly simple, a base of rice or beans served with chicken, pork or beef. The drinks, on the other hand, offer something for every taste: most hotels serve fresh fruit juices; try the invigorating, slightly sour tamarind juice or *guarapo*, sugarcane juice. The local beer is surprisingly good and cool; enjoy rum-based cocktails like Cuba Libre, Daiquiri or Mojito at any time of day or night. The delicious desserts are fairly sweet, and every town has its **Coppelia Icecream Parlor** with a wide variety of ice cream.

Car Rental

All larger towns or settlements have car rental agencies, usually in larger tourist hotels. Although the network of public buses is efficient, you'll need time and patience to get to your destination.
HAVANA: **Cubatur**: Corner Calle 21/ O, Vedado; **Havanautos**: Hotel Capri, Calle 21, between N and E. Calle 36, Nr. 505, corner 5ª Av.; Airport José Martí.
VARADERO: 1ª Av. / Calle 55, Nr. 5502.
CIENFUEGOS: in the Hotel Rancho Luna.
You will have no problem getting an (inexpensive) **taxi** in any town.
Overland Buses: Although the good network of buses gets you anywhere in Cuba, you should buy your ticket one or two days prior to departure. The queues at the ticket-counters are hair-raising.
Collective Taxis: The collective taxis (for six or eight people) waiting around the bus terminals profit from racked nerves and lost patience: they usually arrive in the next town before you have reached the end of the queue. Collective taxis are more expensive than buses, but prices are still reasonable.
Inland Flights: All towns and tourist centers on the island have their own airport, and inland flights are relatively inexpensive. Reservations and tickets through the CUBANA agency: Habana: Calle 23, 156, Vedado.

SAILING

Sailing in Puerto Rico, the Dominican Republic, Haiti, Jamaica and the Cayman Islands is still the reserve of a few cruising sailboats which venture off the beaten track or use them merely as stopover points. Lacking infrastructure and wide expanses of open water, none of the large sailboat charter companies have considered them for a base yet. Day-sailing out of one of the island resorts or a privately arranged charter are possible.

The same is true for Bermuda, venue of the biannual Bermuda race from Newport, Rhode Island, and training ground for America Cup teams, but too far, too small and too dangerous an area for commercial sailboat charter operations.

The Bahamas are another story. Generations of Floridans and other North American sailors have cruised this 1,120-km (700-mi) long archipelago of crystal clear water, pink and white beaches, and 3,077 islands and cays. The latitudes, between 20.56 and 27.25 degrees north, make for almost perennially fine weather. The trade winds are stronger in the winter months and there may be an occasional cold front. In the summer, barring the afternoon thunderstorm build-up, Nassau Radio monotonously broadcasts "light winds over the waters". Some of the island chains in the Bahamas, Abacos, Exumas and Eleuthera are ideal for short-term charters with facilities to match.

Chartering out of Miami, Fort Lauderdale or Palm Beach in Florida is a possibility, but the Gulf Stream's width of about 80 km (50 mi) makes for a long haul and not always a pleasant one, even to the nearest islands of Bimini or Grand Bahama. From there it takes another day to reach the most popular cruising grounds of the Abacos, or two days to the Exumas or Eleuthera. The choice is between bareboat and crewed charters. For

Preceding pages: The show goes on. Junkanoo on Cuba. Above: Striking out into the great blue. Right: A dream from the past.

the novice, a crewed charter is the obvious way to go. Even an experienced sailor may want to have a captain aboard until he or she becomes familiar with the Bahamian way of mooring with two anchors and "eyeball" navigation, the art of letting water color, as it reflects the depth, be the navigational aid.

After a flight from Nassau or Florida, *Sunsail's* 9-16-m (30-52 ft) shallow draft cruising boats can be boarded in Marsh Harbour and Abaco. From there, given enough time, the protected shallow waters of the Abacos, between Walker's Cay to the north and Little Harbour to the south, can be explored. Most short-term charters delight in the relatively small area of the Hub of Abaco, which includes the beautiful settlement of Hopetown with its much photographed and painted candy-striped lighthouse, the former boat-building center of Man-o-War, and Green Turtle Cay at the northern end.

Eleuthera-Bahamas-Charters, in Hatchet Bay, Eleuthera, makes Eleuthera and the Exuma Cays accessible. The west and north side of Eleuthera, from Spanish Wells and Harbour Island in the north and Governor's Harbour and Rock Sound in the south, offer great sailing, diving and even spelunking. Hatchet Bay, too, is a good starting point for a trip along the 144-km (90-mi) long chain of the Exuma Cays – 395 of them according to local lore – and beautiful passages between them. The wonders of Warderick Wells, the Pipe Creek Archipelago north of Staniel Cay, where the James Bond movie *Thunderball* was filmed in a nearby cave, make for great sailing and gunkholing. If time permits, the cruise can be extended to Elizabeth Harbour, and the protected anchorages near Stocking Island would be perfect destinations, across the water from George Town, the largest town on Great Exuma Island. Essentially undiscovered, it is sleepy and quiet most of the year except for the regatta at the end of April when every cruising sailboat in the area converges on the island to witness the spirited race between Bahamian work boats.

CRUISES

In 1492, Christopher Columbus sailed into the Bahamas, touching down on Cuba and Hispaniola in what sometimes is facetiously referred to as the first small boat cruise in the world. Of Hispaniola (though also claimed by Jamaica), he wrote in his log, "This is the most beautiful land that human eyes have ever seen." Despite the suffering he and his successors wrought, the islands of the Caribbean are still beautiful to behold and are being visited by more and more cruise ships every year. On any given Saturday and Sunday, six or seven superliners steam out of Miami, Fort Lauderdale and Port Canaveral to head for the Bahamas, San Juan, Puerto Rico, the islands of the Lesser Antilles, and to the Western Caribbean which includes the islands of the Greater Antilles.

Above: Sturdy dock worker in Nassau. Right: Safety exercises even on the biggest liners.

The Bahamas: With their proximity to Florida, the Bahamas are the ideal market for three- and four-day cruises. Carnival Cruise Lines' *Fantasy* and Royal Caribbean Cruise Line's *Nordic Empress*, mega-ships that carry well over 1,500 passengers, as well as the other mid-size ships with 600-1,000 passenger capacity of the Carnival, Norwegian and Royal Caribbean Cruise Lines, sail the Nassau-Freeport route. They offer one day in each port plus one day at sea or on the beach at one of their private islands, with all the traditional beach activities like snorkeling, barbecues and island music.

To see the Bahamian family islands by cruise ship, there are only two possibilities. Premier Cruise Lines sails out of Port Canaveral on three- or four-day cruises to the Abacos, an island chain settled by British loyalists after the American Revolution. Before docking at quaint villages like New Plymouth and Man-o'- War Cay, launch excursions give an impression of what the cruising sailor is likely to see: green and turquoise bank waters and white sand beaches.

American Canadian Caribbean Line calls on San Salvador and Nassau and the most beautiful cruising ground in between: the Exumas, Aklins, Crooked and Long Island, Rum Cay and Ascencion Island. Unfortunately, there are only a few twelve-day sailings each year, namely in March and April.

Bermuda: The best and only time to go by ship is in the summer. After crossing from New York the ship serves as a floating hotel on the typical seven-day cruise: either tied up in Hamilton, the Dockyard, or St. George's. Passengers return each night to the ship to eat and sleep. Bermuda is quite proper and prosperous. The island government has never succumbed to mass tourism, so arrivals are limited by the number of hotel rooms and cruise ship callings are kept to a minimum too, which at present are regularly used by Royal Caribbean Cruise Line,

Royal Viking Line (definitely upscale and refined) and Chandris Celebrity Cruises. The visitor can enjoy colonial architecture, perfect pink beaches and the many golf courses. With no rental cars for tourists, you get about by taxi or, what is more fun, by moped. Hamilton is one place where there are some excellent bargains, at least for the U.S. visitor, for British goods like cashmere sweaters and Wedgewood china.

Western Caribbean: With Haiti, the Dominican Republic and Cuba off limits for political or economic reasons, the number of ports visited by cruise ships is limited. The so-called Western Caribbean itineraries typically sail from Miami or Fort Lauderdale for stops in Cozumel or Playa del Carmen, Mexico, with an option to visit the Mayan ruins of Tulum or Chichen Itza, then Grand Cayman in the Cayman Islands and Ocho Rios or Montego Bay in Jamaica. San Juan, Puerto Rico, is usually part of the Lesser Antilles cruise circuit or is visited on combination eastern/western Caribbean cruises. Only American Canadian Caribbean Line visits small ports and secluded coves around Puerto Rico on spring sailings from St. Thomas, Virgin Islands, to Ponce.

Gone are the days when cruising was reserved for the privileged few. Newer and bigger ships, built at an almost feverish rate, enter the Caribbean cruise circuit every year. Ships fly flags of convenience and carry an international crew. But most spring out of the American, Norwegian, British, Italian and Greek seafaring traditions, which set the general tone and ambience, while keeping the demands of today's younger, active passenger in mind. They run the gamut from small, intimate ships for 70 passengers to floating mega-resorts for 2,500. Most popular and numerous are those carrying 600-1,100 passengers. With the exception of a few small vessels that focus on island destinations, all other modern cruise ships have adopted the ship-as-destination concept with several variations: upscale, plush, refined; casual, friendly, fun-loving; brash and action

filled. As a general rule, the shorter the cruise, the more action-packed the pace is likely to be. The range of ships is impressive in size, number of passengers, variations of life style and programs offered.

American Canadian Caribbean Line's small, 72-passenger vessels are decidedly informal, basic and inexpensive – probably the cheapest way to go as far as cruise lines are concerned. No gambling, no night clubs, but the most interesting winter and spring itineraries to Puerto Rico, to the Bahamas and to Belize in the far western Caribbean.

Carnival Cruise Lines is the company that changed the image of cruising. Young, brash, sassy, with continuous action and entertainment – they are known as the *FUN-ships*, and include exercise classes to work off the eight meals served, weightrooms, shuffleboard, ping pong and skeets, swimming pools and jacuzzis, bars, casinos, futuristic decor of neon and multi-story central atriums around which the action revolves. Carnival's ships are foremost in the affordable Bahamas short cruise market, with the superliner *Fantasy* built especially for that market at reasonable prices and sailing to the western Caribbean out of the port of Miami.

Above: Roasting away the hours on a cruise. Right: Nightly Broadway-shows on the S. S. Norway.

Chandris Fantasy Cruises aim at the budget-minded passenger, sailing year round from Miami to Key West and Cozumel/Playa del Carmen.

Costa Cruises sails out of Fort Lauderdale for the western Caribbean. Comparable in price to Carnival and Norwegian Cruise Line ships, but with a definite Italian flare that is friendly and exuberant.

Cunard Line's British touch is also evident on the 589-passenger *Sagafjord* and 736-passenger *Vistafjord*, which sail the eastern Caribbean in the winter months.

Both hold ultra-deluxe ratings from the World Ocean and Cruise Liner Society and are luxury cruising at its best with gourmet meals, an excellent fitness program, and supper club-type entertainment.

Holland America Line is now a subsidiary of Carnival Cruise Lines, but has maintained its elegant charm, reflected in the art and antique collections aboard their 34,000-tonne ships that carry about 1,100 passengers on voyages from Tampa, Florida, to the western Caribbean and Key West. No tipping on this reasonably priced traditional line, which is favored by more mature passengers as well as families.

Norwegian Cruise Line ships, under the same ownership as the Royal Viking Line, sail the popular western Caribbean route and make short Bahamas runs at equally popular prices. Their sports program is legend, as is the Broadway-style entertainment which is considered the best in the industry.

Premier Cruise Line, Disney World's official cruise line, is for the family-fun vacation if one has a weakness for comic-strip figures! Disney characters enliven each three- or four-day cruise to Nassau and Freeport. Another itinerary goes to the Abaco chain, offering traditional cruise ship entertainment in addition to visiting the relatively isolated Bahamian settlements of Green Turtle Cay and Man-o-War.

Princess Cruises provided the original "Love Boat" of television fame. Good snorkeling and scuba programs and special theme cruises mark their affordable seven- or ten-day cruises from Fort Lauderdale to highlights of the eastern and western Caribbean.

Royal Caribbean Cruise Line has been the leader in introducing specially designed ships for Caribbean cruising and has maintained that by building a 74,000-ton cruise mega-ship for 2,600 passengers, the *Sovereign of the Seas*, and the even larger *Monarch of the Seas*, which will commence sailing out of Miami in 1991. These ships are true floating resorts, with consistent good quality in the mid-price range. RCCL perfected the concept of the private island, like Coco Cay in the Bahamas and Labadee on the north shore of Haiti, a little tropical oasis, a true fantasy island that bears no resemblance to the reality that is Haiti.

Royal Viking Line's mid-sized 710-passenger ships are similar in ambience to Cunard's Vistafjord line. Single seating, guest lectures, sedate entertainment, interesting theme cruises are what to look for in the winter Fort Lauderdale to Barbados sailings.

Cost: The Caribbean cruises are generally a bargain, especially in the summer and so-called shoulder season months. Christmas, Easter and the months in between are usually higher-priced, but still affordable if you book well in advance. (Six months' advance is not unreasonable.) Travel agents with frequent cruise bookings usually obtain sizable discounts, and discounts are also offered as the sailing date draws near and cabins go unsold. Those are usually advertised

in larger metropolitan papers such as the *New York Times* Sunday edition in the United States. Cabin type is obviously a determining factor. Some of the small cruise ships have all outside cabins, but the vast majority of ships like to entomb a third of its passengers in the inside cabin. Unless you plan to party day and night – and many people do, especially on the short cruises – and only use the cabin to wash, change and sleep, then avoid it at all cost. All things being equal, it is still steerage! The same goes for a cabin above the engine room and kitchen. A cruise vacation is usually labeled as being all inclusive, but with the exception of a few ships, there are expenses you must count on. Tips average about $8-$12 a day per person on a mid-market cruise. Multiplied by four for a small family, this will add quite a bit to the cost. Holland America Line is a notable exception to

Above: Keeping fit is one of the aims of cruisers. Right: Exploring the underwater magic of the Caribbean.

the tipping game. Wine and other alcoholic beverages, for which some cruise lines charge unconscionably high prices considering they can buy duty-free, are extra. Shore excursions are usually priced between $15-$75 per person. Scuba diving and golf are expensive. If you go snorkeling on the tour, inquire first whether you may bring your own gear at a reduced tour cost. Then be sure to carry along one of those small inflatable vests because, for insurance reasons, you will not be allowed in the water without one. Then there is gambling on the ship and shopping ashore or aboard – few can resist the temptations. As a matter of fact, many passengers spend a good deal of their shore time shopping.

Cruise directors on the low to mid-market cruises actually give shopping tips (as well as tipping guidelines that may make you feel your tip is anything but optional) about particular bargains that can be obtained in each port of call. Prices aboard ship are usually quite competitive and it is a fact that many of the great bargains do not exist anymore. A warning here on shore excursions: Cruise lines must contract with land-based tour operators and although they try their best to make quality tours available, the fact is that they range from excellent to truly awful. Best of all are those where your on-board lecturer accompanies a small group, but that service is not available on large low- and mid-market ships. You seldom go wrong on scuba or snorkeling trips or if you decide to spend the day ashore playing golf.

Beware of tours that try to cover too much ground, especially if they include shopping stops in addition to sightseeing. In cities like Nassau, Ocho Rios or Montego Bay, it is preferable to walk the towns after a perusal of the guide book and shore talks by the cruise staff. In the Cayman Islands the snorkeling, diving and submarine sightseeing tours are generally excellent.

DIVING, HIKING AND CAMPING

The Caribbean has acquired such a powerful image of a destination for lovers of sun, sand, golf and good living that people tend to forget its outstanding qualities as an active outdoor paradise too. The Caribbean Sea is an aquatic basin filled with improbably blue water. Arranged in an arc, like a 2400-km (1500-mi) long string of precious jewels, are the West Indies. This splendid archipelago consists of hundreds of islands from Cuba, below the southern tip of Florida, to Trinidad, Aruba, Curaçao and others floating just above South America's northern coast. The western end of Cuba divides the Caribbean from the Gulf of Mexico and lies south of Alabama. The Windward Islands – the French West Indies, St. Lucia and Barbados – lie between the Caribbean and the Atlantic and are as far east as Newfoundland.

Some of the islands are volcanic, others are coral reefs, still others are tiny outcroppings that appear only on maritime charts. Nevertheless, that amounts to hundreds of miles of coastline. Around each island – from Cuba, the largest but still not even ten times the size of Connecticut, to those unnamed map dots – fabulous undersea rock formations, brilliant marine life and shipwrecks await exploration by scuba divers and snorkelers. Marine ecology is increasing awareness of the fragility of the environment beneath the sea, and to protect delicate coral and assure the continuation of other species, underwater parks are proliferating in the Caribbean.

If the Caribbean were drained, it would look like a huge crater whose most prominent feature would be a curving mountain range. Even with the water in place, many mountains thrust impressively and aggressively from sea level to the clouds. Pico Duarte, in the Dominican Republic's Cordillera Central, the highest peak in the Caribbean, tops the 3,000 m (10,000 ft) mark, which is higher than anything in North America east of the Rocky Moun-

tains. Hiking to Pico Duarte or in some of the region's other major mountains is an unforgettable adventure, but even a horizontal meander on a low-lying country lane or a beach-combing stroll gives the non-athlete a pedestrian's impression of the island of choice. Since private ownership of automobiles is out of the reach of many people who live in the Caribbean, walking is a universal common denominator and recommended for visitors.

Camping is forbidden on most beaches and totally prohibited on some islands, but where it is possible, roughing it offers a special Caribbean experience because the sounds, the smells and the feel of the tropics surround you like a cocoon.

Snorkeling and Scuba Diving

To glimpse the magical world underwater, you only need a well-fitting face mask, snorkel, fins and minimal swimming skills, for wonderful sights are found in the shallow waters all over the Caribbean. Most resorts lend or rent the gear and can point you to good snorkeling right offshore, and there is not an island that lacks snorkeling.

Above and right: Exciting underwater encounters of a different kind – octopus and a French angel fish.

Exploring the marine environment and even scouting out a wreck takes more sophisticated paraphenalia and more skill.Equipment can be your own, rented or a combination, and must include snorkeling gear plus a wet suit, a tank for compressed air, a regulator, a buoyancy control device and a weight belt. These items, plus a certification card from PADI, NAUI or another recognized organization, constitute a passport to a magical underwater world. Here are the top spots.

Bahamas: Nassau, Cable Beach and Paradise Island have several dive shops, and popular sites include places where underwater sequences in James Bond films and *20,000 Leagues Under the Sea* were filmed. A barrier reef, at 160 km

(100 mi) one of the world's longest, runs east of Andros and is known as a top wreck and wall diving site. One wrecked freighter is in just 7 m (25 ft) of water 183 m (600 ft) off Guana Cay, near Long Island.

Other notable diving sites are **Pelican Cay National Park**, off Abaco; **Bond Cay**, in the Berry Islands; **Exuma Cay Land and Sea Park**; and **Pinder's Point**, on Rum Cay.

Bermuda: A long barrier reef, its coral nurtured by the Gulf Stream, provides the excellent diving, both for fish and for wrecks. Large hotels can arrange excursions with nearby operators.

Cayman Islands: These islands are to scuba divers what Mecca is to Muslims. You will find dozens of well-staffed, well-equipped diving supply shops and Cayman-based live-aboard boat resorts specializing in dive packages. Fish and turtles abound in the coral forests which have grown in the Caymans' pristine waters, and 300 wrecks, including the *Balboa* which is a mere 18 m (59 ft) from the **George Town dock**, combine to provide a wealth of underwater displays. In 1986, the islands began a marine parks system, with permanent moorings for dive boats at top sites.

Dominican Republic: Compared to other destinations, this part of Hispaniola has fewer dive operators and fewer sites suitable for spoiled divers. In the Dominican Republic, larger hotels are the best bets for arranging trips. **Isla Saona**, **Isla Catalina, La Caleta Submarine National Park, Punta Cona, Las Terrenas and El Portillo** are among the more popular sites.

Haiti: What is true for the Dominican Republic is even truer for its neighbor, Haiti. With its exrutiatingly poor sanitation, Haiti's close-in waters, especially in the vicinity of Port-au-Prince and other cities, are polluted. Snorkeling is not recommended except at such isolated offshore spots as **Labadie**. The **Kaliko Beach Club** is recommended for arranging dives.

Jamaica: The large hotels in Montego Bay, Negril and Ocho Rios all have associated dive operations. The quality of the diving itself is fair.

Puerto Rico: Coastal waters are tops for snorkeling, but scuba is usually best from a dive boat. Dive shops and hotels can arrange trips.

Turks & Caicos: The **Turks Island Passage**, a worth-seeing 2133-m (7,000-ft) drop-off, is one of the Caribbean's renowned diving sites. It has spawned numerous operators on the islands, and dive packages are common in resorts. The islands are so protective of their marine life that spear guns are illegal. The **Turks & Caicos Underwater National Park**, on Pine Cay, is a big draw, as is the barrier reef along Providenciales' north coast. North and South Caicos are also considered tops for diving. Hawksbill turtles sun themselves and swim so close to the surface that even snorkelers often see them.

Hiking

If you want to explore an island's heart and observe the birds and the beasts, a hike on foot will offer a new perspective on the tropics. Soaring mountains with zones that range from tropical jungle to cool temperate peaks make hiking an adventure. Sturdy boots and rain gear are advised for rougher spots, but in other secluded places in the tropics hikers have been spotted in the nude, wearing only sneakers and carrying an umbrella. There is little climbing as such, but hiking possibilities – with and without guides – abound. Here are some top hikes.

Cayman Islands: While not technically a hike due to the generally flat topography, many people consider an excursion into **Grand Cayman's Bat Caves** worthwhile sportive experience, for it requires scrambling down a small cliff and of crawling on hands and knees.

Above: Jamaica, among others, offers some spectacular hiking trails.

Cuba: Cuba has six national parks, three in **Pinar el Rio**, west of Havana. The topography includes mountains, swamps and forests. Ancient trees appear to be left only in the mountains of the southeast and the mangroves of the **Zapata Peninsula**.

Dominican Republic: There are eleven national parks, which protect the country's remaining old forests. The **Isla Cabritos National Park**, dipping to 39 m (130 ft) below sea level, is the lowest. The highest are the parks of the **Cordillera Central**. This inland range, crowned by **Pico Duarte**, is a tropical trekker's delight lush but tough. A guide is recommended, and many hikers take a jeep or a mule to the trailhead. Even in the tropics, it can be cool at 3,000 m (10,000 ft). **Los Tres Ojos de Agua**, three caverns near Santo Domingo, are a sightseeing attraction that requires some steep climbing (now via stairs).

Haiti: Poverty has taken its toll on the forests and their inhabitants. The best hiking of a poor selection is found at very high elevations, preferably with the services of a guide.

Jamaica: Jamaica is a nature lover's paradise and also one of the better hiking islands. It has a number of outfitters who can organize hikes, and with luck you will be assigned a guide who is knowledgeable about the island's 3000 species of flowering plants, 500 types of fern and other flora and fauna.

The **Blue Mountains** in eastern Jamaica peak at 2256 m (7402 ft), and you can count on a 11-km (7-mi) hike from Whitfield Hall. This is also where Jamaican Blue Mountain coffee is grown. Considered by some to be the best coffee in the world, you can buy it directly from growers in these hills. And you can hike for days on end, visiting tiny villages, camping out or staying overnight at government-owned hostels or rural guest houses. Additional hiking areas include the southcoast headlands, a sparsely inhabited area little developed for tourism, or along the **Montego River**, just a few miles outside the country's largest tourist destination. Less intrepid hikers can climb the 183 m (600 ft) to the top of **Dunn's River Falls**, for a view usually encumbered by other tourists.

Puerto Rico: El Yunque offers many hikes along marked trails through this 11.336-ha (28.000-acres) rain forest and up 1064-m (3493-ft) **El Yunque Mountain**. The **El Toro Trail** to the summit is tricky. The terrain ranges from mild to rugged. It is America's only tropical national forest, receiving 609 cm (240 in) of rain annually and boasting 240 species of native trees and 50 types of birds. Learn about them at the interpretive center before you set off. Of the other protected forests, mangroves and sanctuaries, hikers enjoy 40 km (25 mi) of marked trails through the **Pinones Forest** and **El Toro Negro Forest**, which features hikes and climbs to **Ferro Punta**, at 1338 m (4390-ft), the island's highest mountain.

Turks & Caicos: Spelunking enthusiasts among others, will get their money's worth in the large and interesting caves on Middle Caicos, and there are nature reserves at **Big Pond** on that island and at **Three Mary Cay**, on North Caicos.

Camping

Cuba: With the growth of the tourist industry official campgrounds are becoming more common on this island.

Dominican Republic: Camping is permitted in natural areas, but facilities are rare and provisioning is spotty, so it is wise to take everything you will need for your stay.

Haiti: There are no camping facilities, and you will need to bring all supplies with you. Haiti's rugged landscape and difficult political and economic situation make roughing it a hobby for the resilient. The country is so densely settled that isolation and privacy are rare.

Jamaica: Do-it-yourself camping is permitted, but the Forest Department maintains hostels and campsites in the Blue Mountains and other park locations. Reservations are required from the office in Kingston. In addition there are numerous private camping areas, many offering tent rentals, as well as spartan accommodation in tiny *cabanas* that cost little more than the campground fee.

Puerto Rico: Public and private campgrounds are relatively abundant, and the Puerto Rico Department of Tourism maintains a list and the Department of Natural Resources issues permits for camping on public lands. Camping in the El Yunque rain forest, which is part of the U.S. National Forest system, requires a permit (free), **Flamenco Beach**, on Culebra, and **Sun Bay**, on Vieques, two offshore islands, are also popular.

Turks & Caicos: Camping is relatively common on private land with the owner's permission. Providenciales' north coast has some attractive spots.

CARIBBEAN CUISINE

Think of Caribbean cuisine as a huge cauldron filled with tropical ingredients, of fruits, vegetables and spices, seafood and a few imported foodstuffs drawn on by an equally diverse and interesting mix of peoples.

After the extinction of the original Amerindians, the scores of Africans, unwilling participants in the nefarious slave trade, and the East Indians who later came as indentured servants, formed the basic cultural ingredient, governed by the distant colonial powers and their immediate representatives on the islands: the British, French, Spanish, and Dutch colonials, *mestizos* and *creoles*. Since emancipation and, for many, independence, the power structure has changed but the cultural inheritance as expressed in the cuisine has not. Overpopulation on some islands, especially Haiti, as well as over-reliance on the monoculture of sugar, continue to threaten some islands, yet the Caribbean is a wondrously diverse food basket with a year round growing season and an astounding variety.

Above: Fresh ingredients are the root of Caribbean cuisine. Right: Oursins – as the French call them – or sea urchins.

Driving around the islands is a good introduction: By now, the breadfruit trees introduced by the British through the good offices of Captain Bligh tower magnificently over the lowliest cottage. Coconut, mango, and avocado trees are part of many rural gardens. There are pigeon peas (beans), from the common African heritage, bananas and plantains that do not need a plantation to grow. Goats are tethered precariously close to road traffic and the occasional cow might decide to stroll along the beach.

To experience the flavor of the islands in concentrated form, there is no better way than to join the islanders on market day, usually on Friday or Saturday morning for the best offerings. In Nassau, sloops arrive from the family islands, laden with produce. In Montego Bay and Ocho Rios, in Jamaica, and in Santo Domingo, farmers arrive from the outlying areas, and higglers, as the vendors are known, set up their produce in neat little bundles and heaps – a veritable visual feast: hands of bananas, plantains for cooking and frying, breadfruit, tamarind, christophene, mangoes and grapefruit, bundled cinnamon, bowls of nutmeg, and a bewildering array of peppers – notably the Scotch bonnet pepper, hotter than any *jalapeno* ever tasted. The bundles of fresh callaloo and green onion, ackee fruit, an essential ingredient in Jamaica's national dish, pyramids of tomatoes, papaya (paw-paw) and soursop for the making of ice cream, the rich brown tubers of cassava and bags of pigeon peas. Hot sauces to spice up the most humdrum meal and barrels of salt pork and salt cod, introduced in the days before ice and refrigeration as a cheap di-

etary supplement for the plantation workers. They are still relatively inexpensive and people are nostalgically attached to them. Down by the fish market in the proper season, unopened conch shells are kept alive in a little sea water together with crawfish, the Caribbean clawless lobster. The array of fish is bewildering: grouper, snapper, jacks, tuna, flying fish and crab.

Chefs from the islands' hotels and restaurants may have their direct suppliers for the more expensive items on the tourist menu, but the best ones will shop at the native market for the freshest ingredients, for Caribbean native dishes are finally finding their way to the visitor's table after years of standard continental food and token native cuisine in the form of conch fritters and rum punches. Here and there, small island restaurants are opening up. In the past, with the exception of the French West Indian islands, the average islander did not eat out much – as much a matter of tradition as of economics. Altered economies, at least in the towns and near resort centers, are changing that and the visitor can only profit, for the menus are as varied and unusual as the visit to the market suggests. Different islands mean different interpretations of the same basic ingredients, making each visit a culinary discovery.

Bahamas: Once pineapple was grown commercially in the Bahamas and small truck farms still exist on the larger islands of Eleuthera and Great Exuma, but the bounty lies in the sea that surrounds the 3,000 plus islands and cays. Peas and rice, cooked with pigeon peas and "Johnny Cake" are the staples, the rest comes from the sea. Conch (always pronounced "konk") appears on the menu in every possible way: in fritters, chowders, and steaks, creamed as blue-eye virgin conch, or cracked, pounded and deep fried and served in conch salad. Grouper comes on fingers and crawfish is baked, stuffed or just plain boiled.

Bermuda: Well north in the Atlantic but warmed by Gulf Stream waters, Bermuda has strong colonial ties to the

Caribbean and its predominantly black population shares in the African experience. A traditional Sunday breakfast is still salt cod and bananas. Cassava flour, once the main ingredient for bread, is now mainly used only at Christmas time to bake the traditional cassava pie. *Hoppin' John* is their version of peas and rice, the predominant life-sustaining food throughout the Caribbean. Fall and winter, admittedly not the warmest time to visit the island, are when fresh guinea chicks are on the menu – the Bermudan spiny lobster. For the rest of the year, it is protected. Conch steaks, fritters or chowders make a good substitute.

Cayman Islands: The Cayman Islands have long experimented with turtle farms where green turtle are bred for commercial purposes, making them the only islands where you might possibly consider eating turtle, an endangered species in the whole Caribbean basin. Many restaurants feature everything from turtle schnitzel to turtle soup and other generally West Indian specialties like curried goat, salt cod and ackee, or many conch and crawfish dishes.

Cuba: The best Cuban food can probably be sampled in Miami, Florida. In the days of shortages on the island and limited tourist travel, Calle Ocho, the quintessential Cuban street in southwest Miami, serves up the traditional Cuban dishes in great style. *Cuba Libre,* for starters, the potent mix of rum and coke with a twist of lime, black bean soup or *moros y cristianos* (black beans and white rice), *picadillo*, a ground beef hash with raisins, olives, capers, tomatoes and hot chili peppers, and topped off with *flan*, a baked custard with a thimble-full of extra strong Cuban coffee would be a good initiation into Cuban cuisine.

Dominican Republic: Spiced rice and beans on this western side of Hispaniola are called *moro de habichuelas*. Served with the many pork combinations so beloved in the Hispanic islands, like *chicharrones* (fried pork rinds) or *mondongo* (pork tripe stew), topped with *cocoyuca flan*, makes it a typical meal for the Dominican Republic.

Haiti: Haiti's cuisine can be a fortuitous blend of African, Creole and French elements in the few rich enclaves of hotels and restaurants that shut out the reality of a devastated country. *Homard* and *langouste*, both of the crawfish family, are served in delicious Creole creations of ragouts or grilled with Creole sauce. *Riz et pois rouges collés* uses red kidney beans in this local rice and beans dish. Conch is known as *lambi* in many imaginative Creole combinations.

Jamaica: Peas and rice here means rice and red kidney beans enriched with coconut cream. Other menu items are pumpkin soup, the national dish – codfish and ackee, an African fruit that looks like and even tastes like scrambled eggs; *pickapeppa* sauce, to spice up any dish; spicy beef patties, a local fast-food; and, most famous, jerk pork. Before cooking, the meat is *jerked*, that is holes are punched into it which are then stuffed with pounded bird peppers, tiny but hot peppers, and, according to the particular chef, any number of ground spices. A slow, smoky wood fire does the rest.

Puerto Rico: Puerto Rico follows the Spanish heritage with its own special version of peas and rice, made with red kidney beans. *Sofrito,* a salsa type sauce, is widely used to flavor many Puerto Rican dishes like pilafs, stews, even rice and beans. *Chicharrones* and *bacalaitos* (salt cod fritters) can be bought from street vendors and in the markets. In restaurants, you will find food similar to those of other Hispanic Caribbean island but in a Puerto Rican adaptation: *morcillas* (blood sausages), *tostones* (fried plantains), and *asapao* (chicken or seafood with rice).

Right: A betting office at the race tracks in Caymanas Park (Kingston).

GAMBLING

A number of Caribbean countries are popular for more than beaches and sunshine. In fact, for those so inclined, it is possible to leave out the beaches and sun entirely, and spend all or most of one's time in the islands ensconced in mammoth gambling casinos. These are uniformly large glitter palaces, usually attached to some equally ostentatious resort hotel.

Most popular with the more compulsive gamblers are junkets providing bargain airfares and steep hotel discounts in exchange for a stated minimum purchase of gaming chips. Otherwise, in the typical holiday mode, vacationers simply stop in for a few hours of fun at the tables that offer blackjack, craps or roulette, or the ubiquitous slot machines. In addition, numerous baccarat tables are available to the high rollers.

Among the countries covered in this volume, casino gambling is found only in the Bahamas, Dominican Republic, Haiti and Puerto Rico. Jamaica has rejected casino gambling several times, although horse racing, in season, is popular at **Caymanas Park**, in Kingston. If playing the ponies is your game, you can also satiate yourself at the **Hipodromo Perla Antillana**, in Santo Domingo, or at **El Comandante Race Tracks**, outside San Juan. And although most countries do not allow their residents to gamble in their casinos, visitors are most welcome, and frequently indulged with free drinks and other inducements such as free tickets to shows.

The legal gambling age in the countries covered here is eighteen. The minimum bet is sometimes as low as $1 in Haitian casinos. Although the action does not go on round-the-clock, as in Las Vegas casinos, there is still plenty of time to indulge yourself. Bring money, but leave your expectations at the door. As in all casino gambling, the odds are stacked against you.

The following is a rundown of casino gambling operations in the islands of the

Greater Antilles and the Bahamas, but not for Bermuda, where there quite simply are no gambling halls.

The Bahamas: The Bahamas are undoubtedly the largest gaming center of all the Caribbean, with casino gambling accounting for a large proportion of the gross national product. Bahamians are not allowed to gamble, but foreigners are most welcome. The country's proximity to the United States makes this a prime destination for gambling junkets and there are a number of flights from the south Florida area specifically earmarked for gamblers only. Some of these trips do not even include overnight stays; gamblers hop on board in the early evening flights leaving from Miami or Fort Lauderdale, alight in the Bahamas less than an hour later, spend a few hours testing their luck on the tables and return home late that same night, or early the next morning, as the case may be. Bahamian casinos are open from 1 p.m. to 4 a.m., and during those hours, but particularly late at night, the halls hum with action.

Above: Gambling for smaller stakes. Right: Local handicrafts for sale in Jamaica.

The by far biggest and glitziest of the Bahamian casinos is probably the **Carnival Crystal Palace**, located on Cable Beach, in Nassau, which is now known as the **Bahamian Riviera.** This is the largest resort in the Bahamas and even includes the most expensive hotel room in the world, a $25,000-a-night suite that comes equipped with a lucite grand piano and a robot that is programmed to call guests by name and serve drinks, something, perhaps, to aspire to if one hits the jackpot downstairs in the casino. The other casino in Nassau has its own grandeur, the **Paradise Island Casino**, which includes the additional allure of backgammon to the usual roster of casino activities. Two other Bahamian casinos operate on Grand Bahama Island, in Freeport, the **Princess** and **Lucayan**.

Dominican Republic: The sports-oriented Dominican Republic has even more casinos than the Bahamas, with the greatest concentration of gaming in Santo Domingo. All casinos are open from 4 p.m. to 6 a.m., which means that instead of coming home with a casino pallor, gamblers may even find time to step outside into sunlight. But do leave your nickels and dimes at home. There are the usual gaming tables, but no slot machines.

Haiti: Haitian casinos offer free drinks and are open from 8 p.m. to 4 a.m. These are located in Port-au-Prince at the **International** and at the **Royal Haitian**. There is a casino in Pétionville, at **El Rancho**.

Puerto Rico: Last, but by no means least of the islands in this book offering casino gambling is Puerto Rico. More formal than most, drinking is not allowed at these tables, and men are required to wear jackets after 8 p.m. For those without jackets, most casinos are open by 1 p.m.

SHOPPING

While the duty-free shopping in the Caribbean is not the great and wondrous bargain that it was at one time, there are nonetheless numerous opportunities to purchase a wide variety of goods ranging from liquor, jewelry, watches, chinaware, perfumes, cameras and electronics, to typical and unusual island crafts, as well as inexpensive souvenirs – in other words, whatever your budget and tastes may dictate. In all cases, unless money is no object, be sure to compare prices before you buy. Rates for the same goods may vary widely, and in the case of purchases made at the street markets or vendors and stalls you will encounter throughout the islands, haggling is quite acceptable. The first price you are quoted for a Haitian painting or Jamaican black coral jewelry may be many times more than the seller will ultimately accept. In such cases, haggling is expected and is considered part of the game. But be forewarned about street vendors who may become quite emotional if you bargain hard and long and fail to buy. This is their livelihood and the competition is fierce, so carry compassion along with cash.

For imported goods visit the tourist strips near cruise ports and major resort hotels. For folk arts and crafts, you may choose from a wide variety of local markets, small shops and vendors selling batik fabrics, straw goods, pottery, woven hammocks, leather goods, wooden carvings which vary from execrable to excellent, or paintings, which also vary widely in quality and are prevalent in Haiti, and, to a lesser extent, in Jamaica. Jewelry abounds throughout the islands, from gold and precious stones sold in the best shops, to tortoise-shell jewelry which is not allowed into the United States, as Caribbean tortoises are considered an endangered species.

Different kinds of rum products are ubiquitous through out the islands, and a number of islands produce prized cigars, best purchased at the in-bond stores in airports or cruise ship ports.

The following is a brief description of what you may expect to find in the various islands detailed in this book.

Bahamas: The prices in the Bahamas can be outrageously high, but many people nevertheless come here to purchase cameras, crystal and china, perfumes and imported clothing. Better deals can be found on handicrafts such as straw goods, hats, baskets, place mats and the like, especially in Nassau's **Straw Market**, located at Rawson Square, within sight of the cruise ship docks. Here hundreds of vendors sell the same things, usually mass produced lookalikes, so if you do not like the price at one stall simply move along. There is also an **international bazaar** located in Freeport, featuring an array of imported goods from all around the world.

Bermuda: In-bond purchases of liquor are the best buys here, but must be ordered 24 to 48 hours before departure. Imported British linen and wool clothing can also be purchased at some savings, and there are those who rave about shopping here for other imported British goods, including china and jewelry.

Caymans: Georgetown shops offer the best buys on imported goods, which are available at duty-free prices. Among items on which savings may be realized are liquor, perfumes and clothing, but the best buys are found on locally produced jewelry and straw goods. Unfortunately, the tortoise-shell jewelry at which local artisans excel is made from an endangered species and thus not allowed into the United States.

Cuba: Cuban cigars are probably the number one shopping treasure here. Americans are restricted to 100 stogies every six months, but such restrictions generally do not apply to travelers from other countries. Check with local customs before you buy. Cuban rum is also quite popular and there are buys to be had in pottery and paintings, as well.

Right: The famous Rastafarian dreadlocks indicating nobility.

Dominican Republic: A duty-free shopping area is located in the **Centro de la Heroes**, in Santo Domingo, for imported goods, or try the **Mercado Modelo** for locally produced amber or *larimar* jewelry, straw goods, embroidered fabrics and wooden or bone carvings.

Haiti: The **Iron Market** in Port-au-Prince is the place for the widest selection of primitive paintings in bright and vibrant Caribbean colors, although art work is also available elsewhere throughout the island. Wooden carvings, straw goods and locally produced clothing may also be good buys.

Jamaica: The locally produced goods are far better bargains than imports. Jamaican rum products are superior, and Blue Mountain coffee is a connoisseur's delight. Coffee prices are regulated by the government, though, so if you want a bargain head for the hills and contact a local grower for the freshest beans as well as the best prices. All the tourist areas have shops selling imports at not particularly good prices, and there are numerous local markets offering the best buys on wooden carvings, paintings, shell jewelry and the like, with the best prices available at market areas outside the main tourist haunts. Reggae records and tapes are available, with some offerings not available outside the country.

Puerto Rico: Although not regarded as a bargain shopper's paradise, there are nevertheless certain goods available here that you can find nowhere else. *Santos* are the wooden religious objects carved locally, and there are other contemporary and traditional paintings and carvings.

Old San Juan contains many shops, as does the Condado area, but there is no shortage of shopping venues in other parts of the island. Puerto Rico is the world's largest producer of rum, and some who cannot visit Cuba have developed a taste for Puerto Rican cigars.

REGGAE, RASTAFARI, STEEL BANDS

It is something every visitor to the Caribbean expects. That lilting sound from the steel drums, the hypnotic rhythms of reggae. You hear it everywhere you go. Such generic performances are not particularly authentic; they are the result of the superstardom of calypso singer Harry Belafonte and the ensuing boom of calypso bands throughout the Caribbean to entertain tourists weaned on his music. In reality, the music of the Caribbean is much more local, varying between islands, and more complex: the percussion and vocal styles that came to the region from West Africa blend with harmonies and melodies derived from European music and rhythms from Indian music. The notes of New Orleans rhythm and blues, soul and jazz also figure, as a result of radio stations from the U.S. sending this music to the islands in the 1950s and 1960s. To most visitors, though, Caribbean music is and will always be steel bands and reggae. They have become such an integral part of the Caribbean experience that it is almost Pavlovian in scope. Listen to a few strains of any of that music and you begin to feel warm breezes blowing, as well as the urge to have a rum punch. Perhaps more than that of any other culture, these shimmering sounds and haunting rhythms translate musically the feelings of the place.

If you are talking steel bands, that place is Trinidad. These shimmering sounds were born there in extraordinarily humble conditions: Discarded 55-gallon oil drums were the basis for the musical drums. They became the people's drums, called pans, and brought forth the people's rhythm; not surprisingly, because of that they did not go down too well with the more affluent members of society. Just before World War II, this disapproving upper crust succeeded in having steel drums banned. After the war, a crafty bunch of teachers found a way to draw the humble drum back into the cul-

tural limelight. They figured out a plan to use them as a teaching aid. They were used to instruct students in the art of classical music, which could hardly offend the ruling class anymore. This guise effectively elevated and vindicated the steel drum, making them safe throughout the Caribbean for tourists today.

Reggae, that syncopated, sensual rhythm from Jamaica also comes from the streets, but these streets are meaner, with more symbolism involved. To truly understand how these rhythms developed, you have to go back to the breeding ground, a sect of the Rastafarian movement, and the movement of Marcus Garvey that predated it. The Jamaican-born Garvey developed the notion of self-reliance among native Africans, wherever they happened to live, and named it the Universal Negro Improvement Association. His ideas caught on in Jamaica in the first quarter of this century, and in such a big way that he expanded his movement to Central America and then to the U.S. where it truly soared. By the 1930s, though, Garvey's "Back to Africa" movement was waning; others inspired by it were taking shape. Chief among them was a movement advanced by three mystics, built around the notion that the Emperor of Abyssinia was the true Messiah known as *Ras Tafari* and crowned by the name Haile Selassie. It seems an enormous leap of faith to skeptical outsiders, but to Jamaicans these mystics made sense.

Above: From an oil drum to a steel drum. Right: Bob Marley 's sculpture in effigio.

In this movement, the concentration on one's African roots was paramount; in contrast, Garvey's "Back to Africa" was merely a hint. Followers of Ras Tafari regard themselves as children of the *Negus*, a title of Ethiopian kings descended from King Solomon and the Queen of Sheba. Implicit in this is that all followers should return from their exile to their homeland, Ethiopia. In the meantime, they engage in a deep spiritualism helped, no doubt, by the ritual smoking of *ganja* – marijuana in layman's terms. Not all Rastafarians smoke; it is, in fact, a controversial practice, but those who partake make a ceremony out of it, preparing a chalice, mixing the weed and lighting it accompanied by prayers and benedictions.

With or without *ganja,* though, Rastafarians meditate and contemplate, activities helped by drumming, chanting and intensive reading of the Bible. Their desires are minimal; they want no luxuries, merely the necessities of life, and fear nothing except the loss of their Bibles or beards. The beards are evidence of their agreement with God, the Bible is their source of knowledge. Paramount is the belief in the superiority of Ras Tafari and, as children of God, of themselves.

Rastafarians are fairly easy to discern, at the very least, because of their hair. Dreadlocks, the long, braided shoots of hair pouring forth from their heads are distinctive, and, according to followers, noble in origin. They compare it to a lion's mane – their revered Selassie's title was Lion of Judah – and trace similar hairstyles to the Masai and Galla tribesmen of Africa. Despite their shared beliefs, their pride in their heritage, their deep spirituality, their concentration on the virtues and not the sins of human behavior, there are schisms in the Rasta community. The Ethiopian Coptic Church, for example, has more of a mercantile bent, and has been known to get involved in the *ganja* trade, landing some members in jail. The younger, angrier, political Rastas have been drawn to a group known as the Twelve Tribes. In this group are many of the reggae founding fathers.

To give a brief recap of the Jamaican music scene pre-reggae: *Mento*, Jamaica's first native pop music – syncopated rhythms descended from the drumming of African slaves brought to the island – was popular all through the 1940s and 1950s. It faded under the weight of American rhythm and blues being beamed to the island's radios. But then it reemerged, in a new form mixing in the American sounds. By 1959, recording studios started to churn out this new Jamaican blend of pop. Soon it had a name, *ska*, after the sounds made by tapping a key on the piano, and a group, the Skatalites, whose lively sound was dominated by horns and guitar. By 1966, *ska* faded, however, and the whole tempo of Jamaican music changed. It has been suggested that the tempo reflected the mood of the people, that after winning independence in 1962, no one knew what to expect. The faster rhythms of the post-independence jubilation gave way to this slower, pensive syncopation.

As the inequities in society began to emerge, the lyrics in the songs took on an angrier tone. Reggae took shape in the ghettoes in the 1960s, giving expression to the poor whose situation just kept getting worse and underscoring a tense

political time as two warring political factions tried to solve the brewing crisis.

Some of the early leaders of the form had been around during *ska*, but while their instrumental abilities were emphasized in the earlier style, now their voices and lyrics took center stage. Among the first voices to be heard was that of Toots Hibbert, of the band Toots and the Maytals, who named the movement *reggae* after the "regular" people and their poverty and suffering.

More famous was Jimmy Cliff, a Montego Bay-born singer who had nominal success in his native land before relocating to England in the mid 1960s. While in England, he recorded a melancholy ballad of his hard times back home called *Many Rivers to Cross*. It made him a star and led to him being cast in the film *The Harder They Come*, the story of a doomed singer in the underside of Jamaica. It became an international cult hit and brought reggae to the attention of the world. On another front, Cliff brought a talented, young reggae singer to the at-

tention of a record producer; that singer, Bob Marley, a more politically involved Rastafarian, became the most famous reggae star of all.

Marley had started in the tough Trench Town section of Kingston with two other musicians, Peter Tosh and Bunny Wailer, comprising the group *The Wailers*. Originally, they called themselves the *Wailing Rude Boys* with tough music to echo the name; these were songs to accompany the looting and gunfire erupting in the streets in the poverty-infested cities. Marley's lyrics were inimitable; so was the music. *The Wailers* perfected the chaka-chaka-chaka rhythm that the world now knows as the reggae beat, with a heavy emphasis on bass and drums. More important, he brought all of the elements together: his Rastafarian faith, the spiritual but reality-based lyrics and those hypnotic rhythms. As often happens in musical groups, one person emerges and eclipses the others. Bob Marley was the focus of the *Wailers*, a fact that did not sit too well with the other members of the group. Eventually, they went their separate ways with Marley becoming an international superstar on his own – and not just in musical circles. His political influence was such that he was invited to perform at the independence day celebrations in Zimbabwe in 1980 and was granted Jamaica's highest award, the Order of Merit. Marley's time at the top was brief, however. He died in 1981, at the age of 36, of brain cancer. He was given a state funeral with the prime minister and other government officials in attendance. As proof of his significance, the funeral procession extended approximately 88 km (55 mi).

Above: Toking in Jamaica. Right: The other side of the tracks.

After Marley the whole reggae scene splintered. His wife Rita took over his studio and captured some of his success on the music charts. Four of his children formed a band called *The Melody Makers*, and his son Ziggy, while still in his teens, has had some success. Other reggae stars have emerged or reappeared, such as *Toots and the Maytals*, the *Mighty Diamonds* and *Third World*.

Some of the more successful practitioners of reggae have nothing to do with Jamaica, however. As often happens with a fresh, indigenous form, outsiders come in and borrow. British rock idol Eric Clapton had a hit with Marley's *I Shot the Sheriff*. The Rolling Stones' Mick Jagger recorded a song with an original Wailer, the late reggae star Peter Tosh. Their listeners may know nothing about Rastafarianism, about the poverty boiling over in the Kingston streets. They just know that when this music starts, bodies involuntarily sway to the beat. As a result, a Jamaican event held annually in the summer is now a big draw to music lovers from all over the world. *Reggae Sunsplash*, held in Montego Bay, seems to get bigger every year, with 150.000 in recent attendance.

POVERTY AND PLENTY

It is hard to make generalizations about the economic and political conditions in the 3200-km (2000 mi) stretch of islands that make up the Caribbean. Some are still attached to their colonial patriarchs, such as Bermuda and Turks and Caicos, others are self-governing and independent democracies, such as the Bahamas, Jamaica and the Dominican Republic, others such as Haiti and Cuba may be independent but are far from democracies. Other islands seem to follow the form of whichever group can get the upper hand at any given time.

More of an agreement seems possible in the economic sector, but it is not an optimal situation. While some seem to be flourishing – Puerto Rico, for one, has one of the highest per capita incomes in the Latin world, a situation no doubt fostered by its U.S. territory status and resulting agricultural and manufacturing development – many others are grappling with crushing debts, high unemployment and a paucity of marketable exports. Sugar sales, a mainstay for nations such as the Dominican Republic, dropped in the 1980s due to increased world competition, causing economic chaos. Others rely on crops like these, or on mineral exports no longer in demand such as bauxite. They have had to look for other means of support. A transition like that invariably takes time and creates economic strain.

What many countries are relying on, not surprisingly, is tourism – an industry that can provide for jobs in the service sector. Tourism also has an historic base: Going back to the beginning, the Caribbean's beauty was its basic draw – the first European explorers sailed by in the 1400s in search of gold and other valuable minerals, but what they found was spectacular physical beauty. In the words of the man who was, in effect, the first travel writer to cover the area, Nicolo Syllacio, who tagged along with Columbus in 1493: "The beauty of its mountains and the amenity of its verdure must be seen to be believed."

Now, economies rely on other visitors feeling the same way. But, as some visitors have noticed, that can have a down side in the simmering resentment of island residents who feel they owe their futures to the rich foreigners they have to wait on. As officials insist, however, that attitude is on the way out. It did exist in the 1960s, when tourism began to rise in the area, but the pragmatic residents have discovered that it is better to work in tourism and feed one's children than to have no work at all. And, in reality, there have been few episodes in recent years to disprove what they say.

Whether tourists will continue to patronize an island, though, depends on that place maintaining its appeal. Any negative changes in the landscape can be economically disastrous. Haiti, for example, is a washout for tourists now, at a time when the economy needs it most.

Thirty years ago, at the beginning of the brutal Duvalier regime, the island was beset by poverty; tourists saw it, but the natural beauty was so overwhelming as to overshadow it. After decades of tyranny and looting by the Duvaliers and the political instability and the brutality that surrounded them, the poverty and misery of the people engender tremendous sympathy on the part of outsiders. But they do not exactly want to go there and see it. Given the political situation, they also do not want to take the chance of being caught in a coup.

Jamaica is another case of an island hurt by an economic and political downturn. The economy was stagnant in the 1970s and declined in the 1980s while the population grew. In the past, when hard times hit, armed Jamaican thugs often took to the streets and the police were not always able to restore order. Warring political factions also sparked episodes of violence. As a result, tourists, naturally, stayed away; when things quieted down, they were actively wooed back. Now, the country seems to be stable but there is always a feeling that anything could happen again.

Above: Agriculture means a lot of work and little reward. Right: Something is in the air.

On the other hand, the economic power and political stability of islands such as the Caymans, the Bahamas and Bermuda bring in additional tourism and help boost their economies even more. In Bermuda particularly, the standard of living is so high and the scenery is so perfect that tourists come back again and again. The seeming lack of slums, unlike the other, even prosperous islands, the perfectly painted houses and ultra-clean streets combine to form a feeling that one is in Disneyland.

Unfortunately, even in areas thought to be politically stable and economically solid, unexpected elements can appear to endanger the tourism-derived economy. One of the chief elements is nature. Hurricanes can do swift damage and destroy all of the tourism facilities on an island.

HURRICANES

Because of the devastation that a hurricane can cause, there is tremendous emphasis on and fear of these storms in the Caribbean during hurricane season, June through October. There is even a jingle popular in Jamaica: "June, too soon, July, stand by, August, prepare you must, September, remember, October all over." And there is ample evidence to justify concern.

Going back only to 1979, Hurricane Frederic caused $753 million worth of damage to the Bahamas, a mere two weeks after Hurricane David had slammed into the Dominican Republic, killing 1,200 people. In 1988 Hurricane Gilbert pounded Jamaica, damaging or destroying four fifths of the island's homes and leaving 500.000 people homeless. It might have been worse if island residents had not taken precautions; 37 years earlier another hurricane had completely flattened the island. In 1989, another murderous hurricane, Hugo, battered Puerto Rico and St. Croix. Officials in the area downplay the hurricane threat, explaining that it only seems to be so sinister because of the double punch of Gilbert and Hugo a year apart. The threat exists every single year, they say, but the storms actually hit land much more rarely than people think. The storms develop in the Caribbean and gain their force here over all that water, but they often pack their fiercest punch on the coastline of the United States.

Still, as the evidence suggests and with the decreased resources to cope with a natural disaster, those statements are hardly comfort to islanders faced with an oncoming storm. To this end, officials are updating hurricane procedures, although the specifics seem a bit vague. All of the islands are working on this. There will be a manual, they say, that should be completed before hurricane season begins in 1991. In the meantime, though, officials insist that their early warning procedures have improved; they now have signals three days ahead that a hurricane is approaching. Of course, these storms take unexpected turns and no one, until the very last moments, can really predict where a storm will hit.

No one who winds up in the middle of a storm like this can ever forget how it feels – the drenching rain, ripping winds, the sense of powerlessness as the forces of nature tear buildings apart. But, as the residents of one island learned, the aftermath of a hurricane can be as treacherous as the winds themselves. After Hurricane Hugo destroyed the buildings on St. Croix, looting on a grand scale erupted. The U.S. sent troops to quell the disturbances and stationed them for weeks, keeping the peace in paradise. But, as captured on news video, the pictures of the island's citizens looting its stores and of decent, respectable store owners parking themselves outside their shops with shotguns probably did more damage to the island than the hurricane itself.

TOURISM

Anyone who first went to the Caribbean several decades ago invariably has a similar response upon returning today – "It sure does not look like it used to." Indeed, it does not. In those days, the mid-1950s, when tourism began in the region due to World War II veterans who had been stationed in this paradise, the islands were a completely different place than they are today. No one went there, they were isolated, inexpensive, quiet. Now, tourists remembering isolated beaches with not so much as a cottage upon them return to discover vast multi-service resorts with thousands of people. It seems that every decent beach is being developed, every remote little pocket of quiet is being explored. Some feel the Caribbean is not the Caribbean anymore. Some who feel that way live there. If visitors feel proprietary about their stretches of paradise, imagine how those who have been raised there feel. Sometimes visitors get a sense of it, a feeling of resentment on the part of the residents – a barely suppressed facial expression, a somewhat harsh tone of voice. But that has been on the decline in recent years, most likely due to economic necessity. The same development that chews up those desolate spots also provides jobs for citizens who desperately need them – an estimated 300.000 of them. The only thing they truly resent, they will tell you, is when people come to their island and misbehave. Invariably, some tourists do.

Above: Waiting for customers. Right: The easy life of tourists.

Islanders have to put up with it, though, because these countries rely increasingly on tourism to pick up the slack in their economies; an estimated $6 billion is turned over annually in the Caribbean nations through tourism. And residents do benefit in other ways from their patronage. To support the massive complexes going up in these under-developed nations, services are being upgraded for all. Water, electricity, telephone lines – one can not argue about improvements of those services. Still, there is a negative side to development, as even the most revenue-hungry government functionary would admit. The environment is suffering from the increased population – at the very least, the increase of garbage dumping, litter and pollution of the water. Sometimes the infrastructure can not support the projects – the sewer systems just are not comprehensive enough, the electricity is not sufficiently upgraded.

In order to guarantee these services, hotels have to make enormous investments, and usually they are not alone in pouring out cash. The government in each island is an investor in these projects, which they may, given their precarious economies, not be in the best position to fund. They also have no guarantee that once completed, these projects will return their investments. If they do not, the islanders benefit from the

aforementioned improvements, meant for the hotel guests and now left for the citizens. But the budget gaps remain for the government. If projects do succeed and bring in more visitors, another disadvantage emerges – the social problems that come along with the outsiders. The incidence of divorce has gone up in the Bahamas since the influx of tourists, one piece of evidence that the social traditions of islanders are being changed by their visitors.

Many islands did not have hard drug problems either, until visitors from other countries brought them in; now governments unfamiliar with them are grappling for solutions. Similarly, violent crimes are on the rise in some islands unaccustomed to facing them. Even a bona fide paradise like Bermuda has had to call a referendum on the death penalty recently to come to terms with the problem there.

Apart from these drawbacks, though, is the one that most fear from development, the point that the return visitor to a favorite island notes. If you overdevelop a beautiful spot, you destroy what made it beautiful in the first place. It is a lesson the governments of certain islands – Puerto Rico and the Bahamas among them – should have learned. People come to see scenery, they do not come to see buildings, or, in the case of those still heavily involved in developing, a landscape of cranes. In some cases, governments are learning their lesson and are curtailing future large-scale development. Jamaica and Puerto Rico seem to be drawing the line to show they have had enough. Bermuda has no major plans, having filled every available scenic space. Other islands, though, are the new scenes of attack. The Dominican Republic has increased its number of hotel rooms six-fold in the last several years – certainly a daunting number and, skeptics argue, an unnecessary one. But, as usually happens in a popular destination, the option always remains to drive a distance and get away from the fray. The true Caribbean will always exist – in spots.

Nelles Maps ...the maps, that get you going.

Nelles Map Series

- Afghanistan
- Australia
- Burma
- Caribbean Islands 1/ Bermuda, Bahamas, Greater Antilles
- Caribbean Islands 2/ Lesser Antilles
- China 1/ North-Eastern China
- China 2/ Northern China
- China 3/ Central China
- China 4/ Southern China
- Crete
- Hawaiian Islands
- Hawaiian Islands 1/Kauai
- Hawaiian Islands 2/ Honolulu, Oahu
- Hawaiian Islands 3/ Maui, Molokai, Lanai
- Hawaiian Islands 4/Hawaii
- Himalaya
- Hong Kong
- Indian Subcontinent
- India 1/Northern India
- India 2/Western India
- India 3/Eastern India
- India 4/Southern India
- India 5/North-Eastern India
- Indonesia
- Indonesia 1/Sumatra
- Indonesia 2/ Java + Nusa Tenggara
- Indonesia 3/Bali
- Indonesia 4/Kalimantan
- Indonesia 5/Java + Bali
- Indonesia 6/Sulawesi
- Indonesia 7/ Irian Jaya + Maluku
- Jakarta
- Japan
- Kenya
- Korea
- Malaysia
- West Malaysia
- Nepal
- New Zealand
- Pakistan
- Philippines
- Singapore
- South East Asia
- Sri Lanka
- Taiwan
- Thailand
- Vietnam, Laos Kampuchea

GREATER ANTILLES, BERMUDA, BAHAMAS
First Edition 1991
©Nelles Verlag GmbH, München 45
All rights reserved
ISBN 3-88618-379-3

Co-Publisher for U.K.:
Robertson McCarta, London
ISBN 1-85365-256-3 (for U.K.)

Publisher: Günter Nelles
Chief Editor: Dr. Heinz Vestner
Project Editor: Steve Cohen
Editor: Marton Radkai
Cartography: Nelles Verlag GmbH

DTP-Exposure: Printshop Schimann, Pfaffenhofen
Color Separation: Priegnitz, München
Printed by: Gorenjski Tisk, Kranj, Yugoslavia

No part of this book, not even excerpts, may be reproduced without prior permission of Nelles Verlag
- 01 -

TABLE OF CONTENTS

PREPARATION

Climate

More than beautiful beaches, friendly people or all-inclusive resorts, the main reason people visit the Caribbean is for the balmy climate. Save for Bermuda, which has a sub-tropical maritime climate, warm, with a noticeably cooler winter, combined with sometimes strong winds, the Caribbean islands of this book are graced with virtually perpetual sunshine buffered by year-round trade winds.

Surrounded by warm tropical seas, the Caribbean exhibits a mostly predictable and stable climate, hottest in summer, but still quite warm in winter, combined with high humidity at all times. Air temperatures generally stay within a range of 20-30° C (68-86° F). These temperatures are more or less guaranteed by limits set by the surface water and a location near enough to the equator to make variations between summer and winter slight, although certain high mountainous areas in Jamaica, the Dominican Republic or Cuba may see temperatures dip lower for short times.

Throughout the Caribbean, length of daylight, placement of the sun at noon, as well as average temperatures vary only marginally between summer and winter. Low-lying islands or areas tend to be driest, while higher ones attract rain from constant winds. Summer is usually the rainiest time of year, often including daily rain showers, rather than day-long or multi-day rains, except during hurricane season, which can combine drenching rains with cyclonic winds, occurring with a fair degree of regularity in late summer through early fall.

Even after a hurricane the sun generally can be counted on to pop right back out in the Caribbean, and it can be fierce. Carry sunscreen, and forget about even a light sweater, unless you plan to climb Jamaica's 2255-m (7400 ft) Blue Mountain Peak in the middle of the night. In mid-winter you will probably need a sweatshirt. Some people prefer to make that particular hike in the nude, wearing tennis shoes and perhaps carrying an umbrella in case of rain, which is far more likely than a cold snap.

Count on high temperatures and seasonal rains, along with high humidity year round, throughout the Caribbean. Despite tourist office claims that summer is not different from winter, increased summertime humidity can make a big difference in how you feel. No matter if you came to spend most of your time in a casino, but it could make a difference if tennis or golf is your game. The sea is warm and inviting year-round.

Arriving in the Caribbean

Someone checks your identification before you are allowed entry into any of the countries in this book. Depending on the country you are trying to enter and the one you are coming from, the process can be more or less of a hassle. Visitors from North America are, for example, not required to produce vaccination certificates, while people from other countries may be so required. The one constant is variety.

Jamaica has, for example, recently streamlined procedures, requiring only proof of citizenship and photo I.D. for Americans and Canadians, along with a ticket for onward destination. People from Belgium, Austria, British Commonwealth, Denmark, France, Greece, Iceland, Irish Republic, Israel, Italy, Japan, Luxembourg, Netherlands, Norway, Portugal, Spain, Sweden, Switzerland, Turkey, Germany, Argentina, Brazil, Chile, Costa Rica, Ecuador, Mexico, Uruguay, Venezuela, Portugal, Spain need a passport. People from other countries need a passport and visa. Simple, right?

Each Caribbean country has a different bureaucracy, but all require, at the very least, some proof of citizenship. Acceptable documents are an original birth certificate, passport or voter registration card. Some will allow you to use a recently expired passport or a certified copy of a birth certificate.

It is a good idea to carry your driver's license if you plan to rent a car or moped, although you may be required to purchase a temporary local license in certain countries. Although not generally required of North Americans, certain countries require visas or tourist cards for tourists from Europe or other countries, and many of the immigration officials you encounter will ask for proof of onward passage in the form of an ongoing or return plane ticket. Some will ask for proof of sufficient funds for your stay. Check with tourist authorities in each country and at home if you have any questions.

Cuba is a little different: Providing you're non-American, you won't have any problems getting a tourist-visa for a stay up to 4 weeks from the Cuban Embassy. Group or package tour travelers will have to produce their booking-confirmation at the embassy; individual travelers need to show a hotel reservation for the first three days at least.

Departure

Allow at least two hours for departure formalities such as ticketing, seat assignment and security checks, which can be elaborate. Most countries charge a departure tax payable at the airport, in local funds. And there is usually an opportunity to spend the balance of any local funds at in-bond airport stores, or to reconvert funds at an airport exchange bureau, provided you saved a purchase receipt from the original transaction. Always re-confirm flights 24 to 48 hours before your scheduled departure. Consult your carrier for any additional departure requirements or fees that may be required.

Currency and Exchange

Currency and exchange facilities are different in each country, with details included in the guidepost section after each travel chapter. In general, it is best to carry travelers checks issued in U.S. funds, as opposed to cash or credit cards, in the Caribbean, and there is frequently a small benefit in the exchange rate for checks over cash, depending of course on where the exchange is made. Banks typically provide slightly better rates than hotels, and using U.S. dollars instead of local currency for smaller transactions, while widely acceptable, may exact a higher charge.

U.S. dollars are the official currency in some of the islands. On others the local currency is on par with U.S. dollars. Official currencies and approximate rate of exchange for U.S. dollars are as follows: Bahamian dollar, on par with U.S. dollar. Bermudian dollar, on par with U.S. dollar. Cayman dollar, 1 to U.S. $1.30. Cuban peso, 1 1/4 to U.S. $1. Dominican Republic peso, 6 1/2 to U.S. $1. Haitian gourde, 6 to U.S. $1. Jamaican dollar, 7 to U.S. $1.

1 Cuban Peso is officially on par with a dollar, but 10 to 1 on the black market which is illegal, of course. Puerto Rico officially uses U.S. currency, as do the Turks and Caicos. Rates fluctuate daily, and are usually posted at banks or hotel exchange facilities.

Banking hours vary according to local practices. Hotel and airport exchange facilities are generally available round-the-clock, or as needed, although in an out-of-the-way hotel that might be out of cash at 3 a.m., you could be out of luck So it will be necessary to inquire just where you are..

International credit cards, such as Visa, Mastercard, American Express, Carte Blanche and Diner's Club, may or may not be accepted in certain establishments, but can be used for cash advances from most banks.

AIRLINES

This section provides additional and detailed information about traveling throughout this region. It is up-to-date as of publication, but in travel and tourism things change, and sometimes quite dramatically in the Caribbean, which is so frequently raked by the shifting winds of economics and politics, not to mention hurricanes. For further questions consult heading sections for the name, address and phone number of specialized sources for the most currently reliable rate and service information.

An increasing number of airlines are signing international agreements for Caribbean routes all the time, while some are always dropping out of this high stakes game. Many of the islands have national carriers, which tend to dominate those markets in frequency of flights, if not service. And there are hundreds of charters and small airlines flying local routes. It is somewhat confusing, and made all the more bewildering by schedules clocked in on "Caribbean time", which can be flexible, to say the least. And then there is the matter of air fares, which can vary from the last minute full fare that will make you feel faint, to tempting low season bargains. Other variables that enter into air fares are your particular route, with extra savings often realized on heavy routes between the U.S. northeast and the Bahamas, Jamaica or Puerto Rico, special promotions sponsored by the airline or hotels, or package deals that may include hefty savings on airfare from certain cities.

Depending on what is going on, such as "post-hurricane super savings", which may or may not be a bargain, or "Haitian election-eve special", which probably would not be fun without a bullet-proof vest, there always seem to be fantastic Caribbean deals year-round in the Sunday travel sections of the newspapers in major Caribbean gateway cities, such as

New York, Miami, or Toronto, as well as Washington DC, Boston, Baltimore and so forth. Check for current rates and offerings. Or if you prefer to work directly with airlines, the following are currently offering Caribbean service.

Bahamas: Air Canada, Bahamasair, Delta, Eastern, Midway, PanAm, TWA and USAir serve Nassau or Freeport, with commuter lines serving the out islands. Among these are American Eagle, Comair, Delta Connection, USAir Express. Additional service is provided by Aero Coach, Chalk's International, which flies romantic small seaplanes, or Paradise Island Airlines. A number of charter firms and package tours operate in the Bahamas, as well.

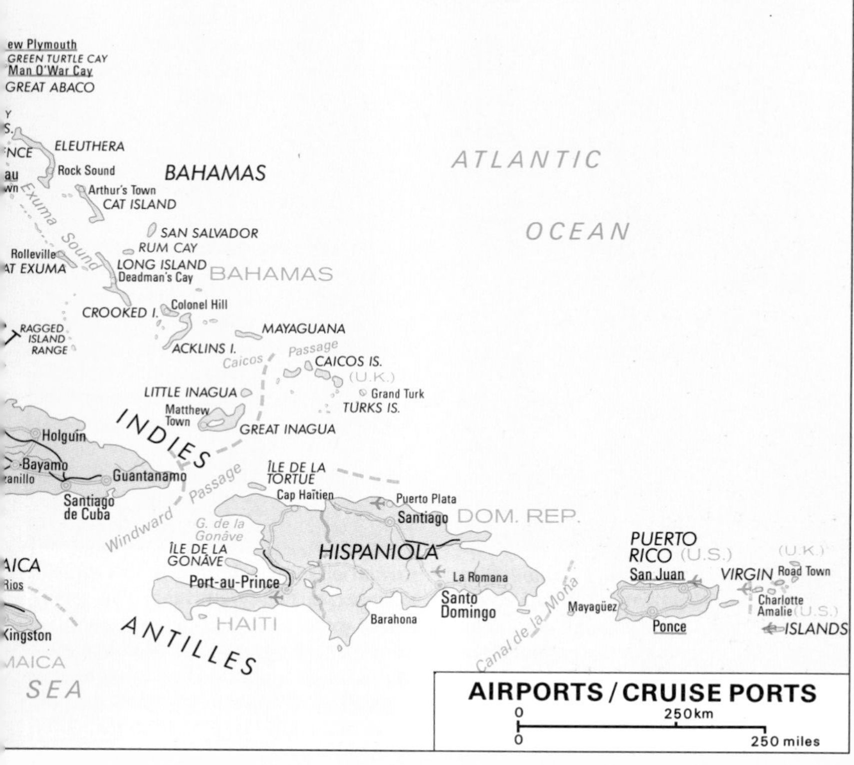

Bermuda: Air Canada, American, British Airways, Continental, Delta, Pan American, USAir.

Caymans: American, Cayman Airways, Northwest, Pan American. With charters operating in high season from the U.S. northeast.

Cuba: Cubana Aviacion, or charters arranged through approved tour operators. Air Canada Touram operates package tours, including airfare, from Toronto or Montreal. Currently two U.S. companies are operating charter flights from the United States, with round-trip seats available from around U.S. $250 at presstime, from Miami. These are ABC Charters and Southern Tours.

Dominican Republic: Air Canada, American, Continental, Dominicana, Pan American. Many charters are available. And there is inter-island service, as well as connections to other Caribbean cities via American Eagle, ALM, VIASA and Air BVI, as well as charters.

Haiti: Air Canada, Air France, Air Jamaica, ALM, American, Haiti Trans Air, Pan American.

Jamaica: Air Canada, Air Jamaica, Aeroflot, ALM, American, British Airways, BWIA, Cayman Airways, Continental, COPA, Jamaica Shuttle, Northwest, TWA. There are numerous charters available. Scheduled domestic air travel is handled by Trans-Jamaica Air. Airways International, Ltd., offers domestic charters.

Puerto Rico: Air BVI, ALM, American, BWIA, Delta, Dominicana, Eastern, LIAT, Pan American, TWA, USAir, Wardair. Commuter lines and flights connecting to other Caribbean destinations include American Eagle, Eastern Express, Virgin Islands Seaplane Shuttle and Vieques Air-Link.

Turks & Caicos: Pan American currently offers the only service to North America, with inter-island connections to Turks & Caicos National Airways.

PRACTICAL TIPS

Accommodation

Accommodations throughout the islands of the Greater Antilles, the Bahamas and Bermuda truly covers the entire range in cost and amenities. At the top end there is the most expensive hotel room in the world, a $25,000 nightly suite at the Carnival Crystal Palace Resort on Cable Beach in Nassau. It comes with a robot/ maid who pours drinks and calls guests by name. On the other hand, there have been nights I could barely remember my own name, in a sleeping bag on a Jamaican mountainside, stars twinkling, mango trees swaying in a breeze, swapping tales with local people.

In between there are the merely state-of-the-art resort hotels, including some of the best-managed properties in the world, at least according to the likes and dislikes of royalty, rock stars and diplomats, or more democratic all-inclusives, a concept pioneered in Jamaica, but now spread throughout the Caribbean. At an all-inclusive, guests who cannot afford to emulate royalty a la carte are granted the fantasy of access to everything the resort offers for a fixed price, including food, drinks and even cigarettes, as well as swimming, sailing, disco and so forth.

There are high-rise hotels, with complete sports and entertainment facilities, as well as modest cottage hotels. Apartment, condo and villa rentals, ranging from the spartan to the fully-staffed are an option. Small local hotels and guest houses are sometimes stronger on local color than upkeep or service.

Of special note are the country inns or small hotels that seem to proliferate throughout the Caribbean. Uniformly small in size, but large on charm and character, these properties offer the unique personalities of their diverse ownership, frequently the same person who greets you, drives and cooks your breakfast in this sort of multi-talented establishment. Under 50 rooms is the only common element these lodgings share, and indeed they span a great range from ultra-exclusive to more traditional bed & breakfasts. Despite the presence of more and more big chain mega-hotels, it comes as no real surprise that more than 65% of the members of the Caribbean Hotel Association qualify as small properties. They come from a strong tradition of family ownership and management. The people who run these places make it their business to know the islands and their people, all part of providing personalized service that makes a visit feel, at the best of times, like a stop at someone's home.

The *paradores* of Puerto Rico are a classic example of inns offering the opportunity to explore beyond the big coastal resorts to discover the pulse of a country. They are scattered throughout the island in places that appeal to different special interests, but at prices that appeal to everyone.

Or take Jamaica's Hotel Astra, in Mandeville. Far from the seaside glitter of busier resorts, in fact hours from the sea, Jamaica's McIntyre family operates the cozy Astra, where the fruits and vegetables served in the breezy, fan-cooled, mountainside dining room are grown in the family's garden.

Other small Caribbean properties boast villas with private pool and tennis courts, maid service, VCR libraries and satellite dishes. While some have historic links to the past, having been converted from sugar mills, plantation houses or colonial government buildings, others are famous for having historic figures pass through them. Haiti's Hotel Olofson was the inspiration for *The Comedians,* by Graham Greene, and has hosted the likes of Truman Capote, Robert Kennedy and Mick Jagger.

A thorough travel agent is a valuable helper in sifting through the variety of choices in accommodation, as well as in planning all trip details with regard to airline flights or steamship bookings, rental cars or other local transportation. Most Caribbean accommodations will have swimming pools, but then you are not likely ever to be far from a superlative swimming beach, river or mountain waterfall. Amenities such as air conditioning, although standard in some lodgings, are unnecessary in others thanks to congenial winds, or ceiling fans, but then do not be surprised to find a mosquito coil along with soap and shampoo in such places, or mosquito screens over bedding. Television is not yet all that common in the Caribbean, although satellite dishes are becoming more so, and phones can be somewhat primitive in more out of the way locales.

The only real problem, in all categories, is the choice of accommodation. You can find any sort of lodgings you might require, and at any price. Selecting one place to stay can be a problem. If it helps to make up your mind, most rates are adjusted seasonally, with high season running from December 15th through April 15th. Rates tend to be lower at other times of the year, with the lowest prices traditionally available during the summer months June, July and August, when the weather is a bit hotter, maybe rainier, too, but the savings are substantial and the sands far less crowded with other tourists. A lot of people prefer summers for this reason, and if you want to enjoy the best of both worlds, skip the mid-summer, which can be incredibly hot and humid, but head for the Caribbean in May or November. Those months are almost exact duplicates of the high season weather- wise, but with fewer travelers and the same big savings you would realize in the summer. Very little changes in Jamaica on April 16th except your wallet gets heavier. All sorts of package deals are available through tour wholesalers, hotels or airlines, as well as special- interest groups for divers, gamblers, shoppers and so forth.

Accommodation Information

Some Caribbean hotels and resorts are linked through marketing networks that can supply you with information and details at no cost through a toll-free phone number from the United States or Canada. Increasingly, Caribbean properties are marketing to Europe, as well, with a number of islands maintaining tourism offices in England or Germany, among others. Check local listings for numbers in your area, or consult the following hotels groups.

Americana Hotels, 405 Lexington Ave, New York, NY 10174, 1- 800/228-3278. **Best Western**, Box 10203, Phoenix, AZ 85064, 1- 800/334-7234. **Conrad International**, 301 Park Avenue, New York, NY 10022, 1-800/445- 8667. **Club Meditarranée**, PO Box 4460, Scottsdale, AZ 85261, 1-800/528-3100. **Concorde Hotels**, 551 Fifth Avenue, Suite 2530, New York, NY, 1-800/228-9290. **Cayman Reservation Service**, 10 S. Franklin Turnpike, Ramsey, NJ 07446, 1-800/526-9059. **Divi Hotels**, 54 Gunderman Road, Ithaca, NY 14850, 1-800/367-3484. **Dominican Republic Hotel Representatives**, 7204 N.W. 79th Terrace, Miami, FL 33126, 1-800/327-9826. **Elegant Resorts of Jamaica**, 1320 S. Dixie highway #1100, Coral Gables, FL 33146, 1-800/666-0447. **Hilton Reservation Service**, Waldorf Astoria Hotel, New York, NY 10021, 1-800/445-8667. **Holiday Inn Reserva-**

tions, 757 Lexington Ave., New York, NY 10022, 1-800/238-8000. **Hyatt Resorts Caribbean**, 341 Madison Ave., New York, NY 10017, 1-800/233-1234. **Jamaica Reservations**, 1320 S. Dixie Highway, Coral Gables, FL **33146, 1-800/666-0447**. **Jack Tar Resorts**, 1314 Wood St., Dallas, TX 75202, 1-800/527-9299. **Leading Hotels**, 747 Third Ave., New York, NY 10017, 1-800/223-6800. Loews Reservation International, One Park Ave., New York, NY 10016, 1-800/223-0888. **Marriott**, 420 Lexington Ave., New York, NY 10170, 1-800/228-9290. **Ramada Inns**, 7720 Crown Point Ave., Omaha, NE 68134, 1-800/272-6232. **Radisson Hotels**, 2223 North 91 Plaza, Omaha, NE 68134, 1-800/228-9822. **Sheraton Hotels**, 1700 Broadway, New York, NY, 1-800/334-8484.

Business Hours

Actual hours of operation vary widely throughout the Caribbean but roughly you can count on stores open from 8 a.m. to 6 p.m. Monday to Friday, till noon, at least, on Saturday; banks open from 9 a.m. to noon, Monday to Friday with afternoon hours on certain days only. Museums and tourist attractions are generally open 9 a.m. to 5 p.m. Tourist craft markets are open daily, while local food and produce markets are generally on Friday and Saturday. Roadside entrepreneurs and other small business people put in longer working hours, often well-into the night.

Clothing

It is ironic that clothing is a major consideration for Caribbean travelers who want to be sure to have the latest in resort-wear fashions. Rarely does one need to be attired in more than a pair of shorts and a T-shirt. Of course, there are the clothes-conscious resorts where this will not always work. In fact, in certain circles dressing ostentatiously tends to mark one as fair game to be charged higher prices according to one's relative affluence.

Just like on the cruise lines, which still have individual dress codes, some Caribbean resorts, hotels, restaurants and night spots require guests to be more formally dressed for evenings, which may mean a jacket without a tie for men, pants or dress for women. Only the rarest few properties will require more formality.

Cool, loose-fitting clothing works best, in light-weight natural fibers, shorts, T-shirts, sandals or sneakers. Swimwear, perhaps with a cover-up, is acceptable attire in most places during the day, less so away from the beach or at night. At many resorts and beach areas throughout the Caribbean, swimwear is not even required on the beach. Inquire locally about nude beaches.

If your visit is going to include any time on the mountains or upland areas, a light rain-proof jacket is recommended, and those who chill easily in air-conditioning may want to pack a sweater. Caps, straw or sun hats are recommended. Sunscreen should be part of your outdoor attire at all times. Also carry insect repellent.

Dress codes tend to be more formal in the Spanish islands, where men still wear ties to work and tourist fashions are not much seen on city streets in San Juan or Santo Domingo. There are elements of formality lingering in Bermuda, as well, and with cooler winters, visitors at that time need to bring warmer clothes, too.

It is highly recommended, when traveling by plane in the Caribbean, to pack a day or so of clothing, toiletries and other necessities in a carry-on bag, just in case there may be a delay with your luggage.

Crime

Unfortunately crime is becoming more and more of a Caribbean reality. Do not leave your $2000 camera unattended on a public beach. Larger hotels and resorts have room safes, or check valuables with the desk. Carry travelers checks, not cash. Keep your rental car locked, and your wits about you.

Cruise Directory

The cruise industry had its biggest growth year ever in 1990, with sixteen new or refurbished ships sailing into service. Many of these ships will cruise the excellent harbors and year-round calm seas of the Caribbean, making these islands the top cruise destination in the world. The Caribbean's pre-eminence in cruising is expected to continue through the 1990s, with increasing capacity opening more ports to shorter and more reasonably-priced cruises, designed to appeal to modern travel patterns.

The biggest cruising news of late has been the inauguration of the mega-ships offering full-scale health spas, two-deck show-rooms, multi-story atriums, large cabins, numerous restaurants and so forth. The biggest so far is Carnival Cruise Line's 2,600 passenger *Fantasy*, offering three- and four-night sailing between Miami and the Bahamas.

Other recent cruise news includes: Royal Caribbean cruise line's 1,610 passenger *Nordic Empress*, sailing in the Bahamas; *Club Med I*, a sail-assisted ship offering seven-night Caribbean cruise itineraries; Princess Cruises' 1,596 passenger *Crown Princess*, offering seven-day Caribbean itineraries out of Fort Lauderdale; Chandris Celebrity Cruises' *New Horizon* will carry 1,354 passengers sailing out of San Juan on seven-day cruises in the Lesser Antilles; the *Crown Monarch,* Crown Cruise Line's latest entry into the Caribbean market is scheduled to carry 550 passengers on seven-day itineraries out of Palm Beach, Florida.

Royal Viking Line's refurbished *Royal Viking Star* is offering ten- and eleven-day cruises from Fort Lauderdale to seventeen Caribbean ports from November through March. The rest of the year it covers week-long itineraries between New York and Bermuda. Carnival Cruise Line's *Tropicale* sails out of San Juan for ports in the Lesser Antilles. Carnival's *Carnivale* sails from Port Canaveral on three- or four-day Bahamas cruises run in conjunction with group packages including visits to Disneyworld. Chandris Cruises' *Amerikanis* sails only in the Caribbean, out of San Juan, year-round. B.S.L. Cruises, Inc., has renovated the *Queen of Bermuda* and the *Bermuda Star* for service from New York to Bermuda or San Juan. The numerous options available to cruise passengers only serves to point out one of the biggest changes in recent years, which is the number of cruise ship ports and departure points to choose from among New York, Miami, Fort Lauderdale, Port Everglades, Port Canaveral, St. Petersburg, New Orleans, San Juan, St. Thomas or Montego Bay.

Among cruise lines sailing Caribbean waters are the following: Admiral Cruises, 1220 Biscayne Blvd., Miami, FL 33132, 1-305/373- 7501; Bermuda Star Line, 1086 Teaneck Road, Teaneck, NJ 07666, 1- 201/837-0400, fax 201/837-0915; Canberra Cruise, offers 22 day sailings on the Canberra from Southampton, England, to numerous Caribbean ports; Carnival Cruise Lines, 5225 NW 87th Ave., Miami, FL 33178, 1-305/599-2200; Chandris Celebrity Cruises/Chandris Fantasy Cruises, 4770 Biscayne, Blvd., Miami, FL, 1-305/573-3140, fax 305/576-9520; Club Mediteranee, 40 West 57th St., New York, NY 10019, 1-212/977-2100; Commodore Cruise Line, 1007 N. America Way, Miami, FL 33132, 1-305/358-2622, fax 305/371-9980; Costa Cruises, World Trade Center, 80 S.W. 8th St., Miami, FL 33130-3097, 1-305/358-7325, fax 305/375-0676; Crown Cruise Line, PO Box 3000, 2790 N. Federal Highway, Boca Raton, FL 33431, 1-407/394-7450; Cunard Line, 555 Fifth Ave., New York, NY 10017, 1-212/880-7500; Dolphin Cruise Line, 1007 N. America Way, 3rd Floor, Miami, FL

33132, 1-305/358-2111, fax 305/358-4807; Holland America Line, 300 Elliot Ave., Seattle, WA 98119, 1- 206/281-3535, fax 206/281-7110; Norwegian Cruise Line, 95 Merrick Way, Coral Gables, FL 33134, 1-305/445-0866; Ocean Cruise Lines, 1510 S.E. 17th St., Fort Lauderdale, FL 33316, 1-305/764-3500, departs from Barbados; Ocean Quest International, 1-504/586-8686, or 1-800/338-3483, departs from St. Petersburg on Caribbean diving itineraries; Pacquet French Lines, 240 South Country Road, Palm Beach, FL 33480, 1-800-999-0555; Paquet's Mermoz, sails from San Juan or Pointe-a-Pitrie; Premier Cruise Lines, 400 Challenger Road, Cape Canaveral, FL 32920, 1-407/783-5061; Princess Cruises, 10100 Santa Monica Blvd., Los Angeles, CA 90067, 1-213/553-1666, fax 1-213/277-6175; Regency Cruises, 260 Madison Ave., New York, NY 10016, 1-800/457-5566, fax 1-212/687- 2290; Royal Caribbean Cruise Line, 903 S. America Way, Miami, FL 33132, 1-305/379-2601; Royal Cruise Line, 1 Maritime Plaza, Suite 1400, San Francisco, CA 94111, 1-800/227-0925; Royal's Golden Odyssey sails from San Juan or Curaçao; Royal Viking Line, 95 Merrick Way, Coral Gables, FL 33134, 1-305/447-9660; Seabourn Cruise Line, 550 Francisco St., San Francisco, CA 94133, 1- 415/391-7444.

Trans-Panama Canal itineraries, including stops in Caribbean ports, are offered by Bermuda Star Line; Costa Cruises; Crystal Cruises; Cunard Line; Holland America Line; International Cruise Center, offering a seventeen-day cruise from Ensenada to Puerto Plata, via Acapulco, Puerto Qetzal, San José, Balboa, Cristobal, Kingston, Santiago de Cuba and Nassau; Princess Cruises; Regency Cruises; Royal Viking Line.

Customs

Duty-free allowances were recently increased for U.S. residents returning from certain Caribbean countries. The duty-free allowance was increased from $400 to $600 for travelers returning from the Bahamas, Dominican Republic, Haiti and Jamaica, among other places. A number of restrictions apply as to what can and cannot become a souvenir, and these vary according to country of residence. In general, fresh fruits, meats, or flowers, or anything alive, would be disqualified by customs, and there are limitations as to how much liquor and tobacco one may bring home duty-free. After reaching the duty-free allotments, a flat duty rate is imposed according to a local formula, although some craft items are duty-free regardless of their cost.

Driving in the Caribbean

Some driving is on the left, British-style, some on the right, American-style. Happily, there is consistency in this regard on each island, so, for example, you will not ordinarily find people driving on the right and left in Jamaica, but only on the left. Likewise, Puerto Ricans, Hatians and Dominican Republicans will all drive American-style, on the right. The important thing for you to remember is where you are at the moment and which way traffic is flowing, not always the easiest thing to do in these intoxicating islands. Some main roads are pretty good in some parts of the Caribbean, but most roads are not super-highways. They are rather narrow and winding. Frequently cars must share the middle of the road with people walking, cattle, stray pigs, dogs, goats and so forth, and frequently one of these obstacles will greet you as you wheel around a blind curve on a narrow dark road, with a bus coming at you the other way.

Most foreign travelers are allowed to operate a motor vehicle in most Caribbean countries provided they are holding a valid license issued at home. Residents of certain countries may have to produce an International Driver's permit issued at home. And in certain Caribbean countries, drivers will have to buy a temporary local permit issued at the time they pick up a rental car. Tourism authorities should be able to give you all the details for your specific situation.

Electricity

The countries covered in this book all operate at the same electric current as the United States, 110 volts, 60 cycles, alternating current, most of the time. There could be local variations. At the very least, European appliances will require adapters. Inquire in advance regarding any special power requirements.

Emergencies

Some travelers experience health problems in the Caribbean due to changes in climate, drinking water or food, or from too much sun, insects or rum. Larger resorts and hotels will have a nurse or doctor on call. The farther out you go the less likely you are to be within easy reach of medical help. If you are involved in an accident or medical emergency the following numbers will put you through to emergency services. In Cuba health services are free, and pharmacists can be relied upon to help for lesser emergencies. The Bahamas, 322-2221 for ambulance, 322-4444 for police. Bermuda, 911. Caymans, 98600 for ambulance, 94222 for police. Cuba, 0. Dominican Republic, 711. Haiti, 50281. Jamaica, 110. Puerto Rico, 343-2222 for ambulance, 343-2550 for police. Turks & Caicos, 0.

Etiquette

Remember that the local people you encounter live here. Unlike yourself, they are not on vacation. The variety of ethnic, social, religious and economic conditions mixed together and steaming in the Caribbean cauldron causes tensions you may not recognize, others you may see all too clearly. Some local people may be helpful and gung-ho for tourism, while others may consider tourism an extension of colonialism. At all times consider yourself a guest in a place where rules of behavior vary from Western standards. Punctuality, for example, is a general concept in the Caribbean. Things happen slowly, appointments are delayed and so forth. Hurried and harried visitors may be patronized with cynical humor if not ignored. At the very least, those who are most rushed will inevitably face the longest delays. The Caribbean operates at its own pace. This is one of the reasons you came, right? Slow down. Take time to be polite about taking photographs. If someone says no, do not push.

Festivals and Holidays

Festivals and holidays are an important part of the social fabric of Caribbean life, as well as nifty for hanging marketing hooks to attract more and more tourists. Individual tourist offices can provide festival and holiday calendars.

The following are some of the more notable annual events in Bermuda, the Bahamas and the Greater Antilles in 1990, with dates subject to change yearly.

January: 1; New Year's Day is celebrated on all the islands. 1-2; Haiti, Independence Day-Forefathers' Day, two-day blow out, parades, fireworks. 5; Maroon Festival, Jamaica, dates to 1700s in honor of escaped slaves. 8; Grand Bahama Grand Prix, vintage cars race. 10; Supreme Court opens, Bahamas, with robed judges and police band. 18; San Sebastian Festival, musical parade in Old San Juan, P.R. 21; Windsurfing regatta, Bahamas, mid-January through early February; Carnival, Varadero, Cuba, street dances, parades.

February: All month carnivals in Puerto Rico's villages. 4; San Blas Marathon, Puerto Rico. 6; Miami-Montego Bay Yacht Race finishes in MoBay. 15; Sanchez Carnival, Puerto Rico, includes parade, queen and burial of the sardine. 16; Coffee Harvest Festival,

Puerto Rico. 19; Tour of Americas, world-class cycling, Puerto Rico. 22; Ponce Carnival, Puerto Rico, parades, floats, street parties. 24; Grand Bahama 5000, road race through Freeport, Grand Bahama. 27; Independence Day, Dominican Republic, carnival.

March: 3; Feria Dulce Sueno, *paso fino* horse competition in Quayama, Puerto Rico. 16; Fish Festival, Cabo Rojo, Puerto Rico. Sugar Cane Festival, Vega Alta, Puerto Rico. University Singers Concert, Jamaica. 18; Hemingway Championship Fishing Tournament, Bahamas. 22; Regional Crafts Fair, Ponce, Puerto Rico. 23; Copa Velasco Regatta, features 100 yachts on the first leg of the Caribbean Ocean Racing Triangle, Puerto Rico. 30; Western Hemisphere Spring Championship Yacht Race, Bahamas.

April: 1; Championship Billfish Tournament, Bahamas. 4; Supreme Court opening, Bahamas. 6; Grand Turk Tennis Tournament, Turks & Caicos. 8; Palm Sunday, Puerto Rico. 12; MoBay Yacht Club Easter Regatta, harbor races, Jamaica. 13; Carnival Week, reggae street dances, bands, jump-up, dwarf-tossing, Jamaica. 14; Rugby Festival, Freeport, Grand Bahama. 15; National Dance Theatre Easter Sunrise Concert, Jamaica. 16; St. Elizabeth Horticultural Show, Jamaica. 21; Cricket matches, Bahamas. 27; Batabano, Caymans, street dances, steel bands, costume competition. 28; Horticultural Society Show, Jamaica. The largest flower show in the Caribbean. 30; Brachanal, Cayman Brac.

May: 18; International Hot Air Balloon Festival, Jamaica. 19; Negril Carnival, road race, costumed parade, reggae concert, water sports, Jamaica. 20; Treasure Cay Championship Fishing Challenge, Bahamas. 21; Virgin de Pozo Marathon, Sabana Grande, Puerto Rico. 23-26; Negril Carnival, Jamaica. floats, mento, police band, Junkanoo dancing. 24; Bermuda Day, Bermuda. parades, races. 25; South Caicos Regatta, Turks & Caicos. 25; Weaving Festival, Isabella, Puerto Rico. Pineapple Festival, Lajas, Puerto Rico.

June: All month Junkanoo Festival, Bahamas, street dances, limbo, races. 7; Bomba y Plena Festival, Ponce, Puerto Rico, African music and dance heritage. 9; Casals Festival, Puerto Rico, symphonies. 11; Queen's Birthday, Caymans. Bands, parades. Cat Cay Fishing Tourney, Bahamas. 15; Queen's Birthday, Turks & Caicos. 23; Aibonito Flower Festival, Puerto Rico. 24; San Juan Bautista Day, Puerto Rico. Patron Saint Day includes a walk into the sea backwards for good luck. 25; All-Jamaica Open Tennis Tournament.

July: 1; Billfish tournament, Turks & Caicos. 5; Commonwealth Trade Fair, Bahamas. 8-16; Manchester Golf Week, Jamaica. Movements Dance Company, Jamaica. 10; Independence Day, Bahamas, week-long festivities, parades. 15; Barranquitas Artisans Fair, Puerto Rico. 16-21; Reggae Sunsplash, Jamaica, world class event, people's fair and state-of-the-art reggae. 20- Aug 19; National Dance Theatre Company, Jamaica, world renowned. 20; Festival de Loiza Aldea, religious festival, Puerto Rico. Vieques Folk Festival, Puerto Rico, costumes, floats. 26; National Rebellion Day, Cuba. Late July; Merengue Week, Dominican Republic.

August: 4-6; Royal Jamaican Yacht Club Regatta, Jamaica. 6; Independence Day Festival, Jamaica, street parties, stadium events. 14; Fox Hill Day, Bahamas, emancipation celebration. 31; Billfish Tournament, Puerto Rico.

September: 17-21; Montego Bay Marlin Tournament, Jamaica. 27; Inter-American Festival of the Arts, Puerto Rico.

October: 1-6; Ocho Rios Marlin Tournament, Jamaica. 12; Columbus Day celebrations, Puerto Rico. 15-20; Port Antonio Marlin Tournament, Jamaica. 27; Pirate Week, Caymans. 27-28;

Woman 90, trade fair and conference, Jamaica. 28; Crystal Springs Jazz Festival, Jamaica.

November: 1; All Saints Day, Haiti. 10; Kelly Cup Regatta, Puerto Rico. 17; Jayuya Indian Festival, Taino Indian heritage crafts, dances, Puerto Rico.

December: 1; Old San Juan's White Christmas Festival, Puerto Rico. 1-2; Women's International Polo Tournament, Jamaica. 2; Bacardi Arts Festival, Puerto Rico. Granma Festival, Cuba, celebrates Fidel's return to Cuba in the late 1950s. 14; New York Life Champions, Senior Pro Golfers Association Tour, Dorado, Puerto Rico. 15; Navidades, island-wide Christmas festivities, nativity scenes, children's programs, symphonies, Puerto Rico. 24; Christmas Eve. 25; Christmas. Hatillo Mask Festival, Puerto Rico. 26; Boxing Day, junkanoo parade, Bahamas. 28-29; Superjam Reggae, Jamaica, top artists. 30; Annual Criollisimo, national folkloric ballet, Puerto Rico.

Guides

Multi-lingual guides are probably best set up through package tours. Local guides, however, tend to be quite plentiful, usually youthful free lances or cab drivers who wait for flights at the airport or outside tourist sites. Many of these guides will be overly enthusiastic, although good connections can be made on the spot if one develops a quick rapport. Always negotiate a fee in advance.

A good way to find where you are going in the Jamaican country- side, for example, is to give someone a ride. Jamaicans waving on the road for you to stop are hitch-hiking. They do not stick out their thumb. Offer a ride to someone if you are lost or looking for some local insight. Local tourist offices can sometimes secure the services of a multi-lingual guide. For guided tours organized under a variety of special interests and itineraries, contact tourist offices for a listing of approved operators.

Photography

Still photography and video recording are popular with Caribbean tourists. Although film, video tapes and batteries may be available in certain areas, they will be expensive. It is always advisable to bring everything you need from home especially in Cuba. In the latter country it is prohibited to photograph military installations.

Postal Services

Postal services and fees vary according to each country. Mail moves slowly in the Caribbean. Always use air mail, not surface. It will still take a long time.

Telephone Service

Telephone service is getting better throughout the Caribbean all the time, although at times there are still glitches. Service is by no means standardized, and you will need to check locally for idiosyncracies such as three-, five- or seven-digit dialing. The Caribbean area code is 809 for the countries included in this book, except for Haiti and Cuba. To call Haiti, dial the international code 011 - country code 509 - city code - local number. There is no direct dialing from the United States to Cuba, although it is possible to dial direct from other Caribbean countries, Canada and Europe. Consult the international operator for details, and always check with a local operator about calls.

Tipping

Tipping is expected everywhere, except Cuba, where it is not allowed. Many times a service charge will be added to your hotel or restaurant bill. If it is not, count on tipping airport porters, bellhops and doormen $1 per bag; cab drivers 15%-20% of taxi fare; hotel maids $1-$2 daily; food servers, barbers or hairdressers 15%-20% of total bill. Cruise lines offer their own guidelines for tipping.

Tourist Information

In addition to the numerous information sources listed throughout this book, the following sources can provide you with current information on rates, schedules, facilities and services.

Bermuda Department of Tourism: 310 Madison Ave., Suite 201, New York, NY 10017, 1-212/818-9800; 1200 Bay St., Suite 1004, Toronto, Ont. M5R 2A5 Canada 1-416/923-9600. U.S. offices also in Atlanta, 1-404/524-1541; Boston, 1-617/742-0405; Chicago 1- 312/782-5486.

The Bahamas Tourist Office: 30 Rockefeller Plaza, New York, NY 10112, 1-212/757-1611; 1255 Phillips Square, Montreal, Quebec H3B 3G1, 1-514/861-6797. Offices also in Atlanta, 1-404/633-1793; Boston, 1-617/426-3144; Charlotte, 1-704/532-1290; Dallas, 1-214/742-1886; Detroit, 1-313/357-2940; Houston, 1-713/626-1566; Los Angeles, 1-213/385-0033; Miami, 1-305/442-4860; Philadelphia, 1-215/925-0871; St.Louis, 1-314/569-7777; San Francisco, 1- 415/398-5502; Toronto, 1-416/968-2999; Washington, DC. 1-202/659- 9135.

Cayman Island Tourist Board: 420 Lexington Ave., Suite 2733, New York, NY 10170, 1-212/682-5582; 234 Eglington Ave. East, Suite 306, Toronto, Ontario M4P 1K5 Canada, 1-416/485-1550; Trevor House, 100 Brompton Rd., London SW3 1EX, 071/581-9960. U.S. offices also in Chicago, 1-312/944-5602; Dallas, 1-214/823-3838; Houston, 1-1713/461-1317; Los Angeles, 1-213/738-1968; Coral Gables, 1-305/444-6551.

Cuba: The Cuban Interests Section, 2639, 16th St. NW, Washington, DC 20009, 1-202/797-8609; Cuba Tourist Board, 55 Queen St. E. Suite 705, Toronto, Ont. M5C 1R5 Canada, 1-416/362-0700.

Dominican Republic Tourist Office: 485 Madison Ave., New York, NY 10022, 1-212/826-0750; 29 Bellair St., Toronto, Ont. M5R 2C8 Canada, 1-416/928-9188. Also in Miami, 1-305/444-4592.

Haitian National Office of Tourism: 18 E. 41st St., New York, NY 10017, 1-212/779-7177; 50 Boulevard Cremazie Quest, Suite 617, Box 344, Montreal, Quebec H2P 2T3 Canada, 1-514/389-3577.

Jamaica Tourist Board: 866 2nd Ave., New York, NY 10017, 1- 212/688-7650; 1 Eglington Ave. E., Toronto, Ont. M4P 3A1 Canada,1-416/482-7850; Jamaica House, 63 St. James' St., London SW1A 1LY, 011/44-1-493-3647. In addition, tourist board offices are located in Atlanta, 1-404/250-9971; Boston, 1-617/367-2438; Chicago, 1-312/346-1546; Coral Gables, 1-305/665-0557; Dallas, 1- 214/361-8778; Los Angeles, 1-213/384-1123. Outside the United States, JTB offices are located in Mexico City, phone 660-4433 ext 2663; Montreal, 1-514/849-6386; Frankfurt, 011/49-69-5975- 675; Paris, 01-45-61-9058; Rome, 039-656-9112; Tokyo, 03-289- 5767.

Puerto Rico Tourism Company: 575 Fifth Ave., New York, NY 10017, 1-212/599-6262; 11 Yorkville Ave., Suite 1003, Toronto, Ont. M4W 1L3 Canada, 1-416/925-5587. Offices also located in Chicago, 1- 312/ 861-0049; Dallas, 1-214/262-2903; Los Angeles, 1-213/ 874-5991; Miami, 1-305/381-8915.

Turks & Caicos: 48 Albemarle St., London W1X 4AR, 071/629--6353.

Caribbean Tourism Organization represents a number of countries, including the Bahamas, Caymans, Haiti, Jamaica, Puerto Rico and Turks & Caicos, as well as islands in the Lesser Antilles.

For information about events, attractions and activities, as well as further resources, contact CTO, 20 East 46th St., New York, NY 10017, 1-212/682-0435.

For information on U.S. Customs call 1-212/466-5550. Information on U.S. State Department Travel Advisories are available by phoning 1-202/647-5225.

AUTHORS

Steve Cohen, project editor of this book, is a writer and photographer specializing in travel and world-wide adventure. His work appears regularly in major North American newspapers as well as more than 150 publications around the world. He is the author of *The Adventure Guide to Jamaica,* and was project editor for the *Nelles Guide Florida.*

Janet Groene has traveled in the Caribbean by cruise ships and scheduled airlines, as well as her own boats and planes for twenty years. Her books, along with her husband, photographer Gordon Groene, include *How To Live Aboard a Boat* and *Dressing Ship*, published by Hearst/Morrow. Florida-based, she also contributed to the *Nelles Guide Florida.*

Laurie Werner is a New York-based writer and member of the Society of American Travel Writers. Her work appears in major North American newspapers and magazines including *Ladies Home Journal*, *Vis-a-Vis* and *USA Weekend*.

Ute Vladimir is a German-born writer who has lived in Florida for thirty years during which time she has sailed and traveled extensively in the Caribbean. She writes a travel column for Florida's *Palm Beach Post* along with her husband Andrew Vladimir.

Deborah Williams is a former newspaper reporter and editor. She has traveled in the Caribbean for more than twenty years and her work has appeared in a wide variety of books, magazines and newspapers in the United States and Canada.

Claire Walter is an award-winning ski and travel writer. Her books include the *Best Ski Resorts in America*, and *The Berlitz Handbook to Skiing the Alps*. She is Western Editor of *Skiing Magazine*.

PHOTOGRAPHERS

(All photographs courtesy of Viesti Associates, New York, with exception of Robert Batschari, Roland F. Karl, Gerd Krammer.)

Barba, Dan 66, 105
Batschari, Robert 24
Bauer, Geri 38
Cohen, Steve 212, 218
Downey, Mark 130, 211
Dunn, Jeffrey 50, 230
Hartl, Helene 35, 92, 213, 214, backcover
Hinze, Peter 1, 8/9, 29, 46, 54/55, 102, 110/111, 125
Hoa Quin, Valentin 221, cover
Janicke, Volkmar 23, 32, 41, 84, 151, 156
Kanzler, Thomas 10/11, 28, 39, 44, 47, 71, 72, 106, 143, 163
Karl, Roland F. 124, 146/147, 154, 155, 168, 220
Knoll, Franz 53, 201
Krammer, Gerd 141, 144
Lovell, Craig 215
Morse, Randy 91, 187, 216, 217
Nikas, Greg 14, 40, 223, 225
Purchia, Peter 17, 27, 48, 107
Radke, Volker W. 18, 19, 25, 30, 31, 33, 36, 49, 51, 123, 126, 127, 131, 132, 136, 142, 158/159, 160, 162,167, 169, 170, 171, 174, 175, 190/191, 192, 196, 197, 200, 202, 204/205, 208, 227, 229, 232, 235
Rosenstein, Carl 43, 74/75, 87, 93, 210, 231
Ross, Ken 2, 56/57, 58, 60, 62, 63, 67
Skupy, Hans-Horst 12/13, 21, 42, 45, 61, 70, 81, 86, 89, 90, 98, 100, 101, 118, 122, 128, 129, 172, 184, 209, 233
Skupy-Pesek, Jitka 234
Viesti, Joe 16, 20, 22, 24, 26, 95, 104, 112, 116, 117, 119, 134/135, 140, 150, 178/179, 185, 206/207, 224, 228